D1522500

Rethinking Coaching

Also by Angélique du Toit

CORPORATE STRATEGY: A Feminist Perspective

Also by Stuart Sim

BEYOND AESTHETICS: Confrontations with Poststructuralism and Postmodernism

BUNYAN AND AUTHORITY: The Rhetoric of Dissent and the Legitimation Crisis in Seventeenth-Century England (*with David Walker*)

THE CARBON FOOTPRINT WARS: What Might Happen If We Retreat From Globalization?

DERRIDA AND THE END OF HISTORY

THE DISCOURSE OF SOVEREIGNTY, HOBBES TO FIELDING: The State of Nature and the Nature of the State (*with David Walker*)

THE EIGHTEENTH-CENTURY NOVEL AND CONTEMPORARY SOCIAL ISSUES

EMPIRES OF BELIEF: Why We Need More Scepticism and Doubt in the Twenty-First Century

THE END OF MODERNITY: What the Financial and Environmental Crisis is Really Telling Us

FUNDAMENTALIST WORLD: The New Dark Age of Dogma

INTRODUCING CRITICAL THEORY (*with Borin Van Loon*)

CONTEMPORARY CONTINENTAL PHILOSOPHY: The New Scepticism

IRONY AND CRISIS: A Critical History of Postmodern Culture

JEAN-FRANÇOIS LYOTARD (Modern Cultural Theorists)

GEORG LUKÁCS (Modern Cultural Theorists)

LYOTARD AND THE INHUMAN

MANIFESTO FOR SILENCE: Confronting the Politics and Culture of Noise

POST-MARXISM: An Intellectual History

Rethinking Coaching

Critical Theory and the Economic Crisis

Angélique du Toit
Lead Academic in Coaching, University of Sunderland

Stuart Sim
Visiting Professor in Critical Theory, Northumbria University

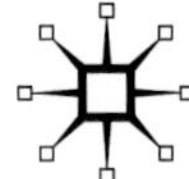

First published 2010 by
PALGRAVE MACMILLAN

Palgrave Macmillan in the UK is an imprint of Macmillan Publishers Limited, registered in England, company number 785998, of Houndmills, Basingstoke, Hampshire RG21 6XS.

Palgrave Macmillan in the US is a division of St Martin's Press LLC, 175 Fifth Avenue, New York, NY 10010.

Palgrave Macmillan is the global academic imprint of the above companies and has companies and representatives throughout the world.

Palgrave® and Macmillan® are registered trademarks in the United States, the United Kingdom, Europe and other countries.

ISBN 978–0–230–24054–4 hardback

This book is printed on paper suitable for recycling and made from fully managed and sustained forest sources. Logging, pulping and manufacturing processes are expected to conform to the environmental regulations of the country of origin.

A catalogue record for this book is available from the British Library.

A catalog record for this book is available from the Library of Congress.

10 9 8 7 6 5 4 3 2 1
19 18 17 16 15 14 13 12 11 10

Printed and bound in Great Britain by
CPI Antony Rowe, Chippenham and Eastbourne

Contents

Acknowledgements

We would like to thank our respective partners, Laurence Davies and Helene Brandon, for their continued support and encouragement in our efforts to produce this text. Thanks also go to Virginia Thorp and Paul Milner at Palgrave, and to our project manager, David Joseph.

Part I

Introduction

1
Rethinking Coaching

This book deliberately sets out to challenge the paradigms and mindsets that have dominated organizations in general and the banking sector in particular in the modern era. We seek to understand and offer some explanation for the recent, and still largely unresolved, crisis in the industry brought on by the spectacular credit bubble that had been allowed to accumulate, with grave consequences for the economies of all the world's countries, whether developed or not. We do so by drawing on the history of a critical theoretical perspective that has given rise to scepticism; scepticism of the metanarratives that control the running of organizations, often without any concern as to how these might impact on the public weal. Organizations, as we shall go on to argue, can be very 'petulant' in this respect, thinking of the welfare of no one but themselves – and of late we have all suffered from the effects of that petulance as displayed by the financial industry. Hardly a day passes without some new revelation as to the depth and breadth of the rot that has permeated the banking sector and the realization that icons of the industry are found wanting. The vehicle we propose as best suited to challenge and question these ideologies is that of coaching, and we shall set out a new, more radical approach to the activity based heavily on scepticism – particularly as it has been developed from the later twentieth century onwards by key postmodern thinkers such as Jean-François Lyotard, with his deep distrust of the motives of metanarratives in general (as outlined most notably in his highly influential book, *The Postmodern Condition*[1]).

The appetite for coaching over the last 10 years has seen an exponential growth as have the different styles and approaches to coaching as a professional practice. Numerous organizations, and the public sector in particular, have of late focused on creating their own internal capacity for coaching. There is a strong impetus in these organizations towards establishing a vibrant coaching culture, the objective being to develop a successful and productive coaching style for management and leadership. Irrespective of the approach, the unifying theme appears to be the development of the individual coachee, whether the focus of development is for personal or professional reasons or both. Whichever brand of coaching the coach subscribes to, it is apparent that the coaching relationship is unique and special. The coaching relationship is built on trust and support and provides a confidential space in which the coachee is able to be both challenged and supported by the coach. Across the various approaches there is abundant evidence to demonstrate that coaching provides significant value to both the individual and the organization, and that it should be an integral part of organizational life, an area that it would be a false economy to stint on in any substantially sized organization. An example of an organization which appears to be wholeheartedly committed to the integration of coaching at all levels of operation is the UK's National Health Service (NHS), which, as we shall go on to discuss in Chapter 3, is committing both the time and finances in making this happen.

We will explore and challenge the intricacies and complexities of the markets and unpick the doctrines of the belief system behind the financial failures throughout. It is apparent to us that the banking crisis is not attributable to any one cause, but that numerous factors can be perceived as having played a part and we will select and discuss the main causes identified. However, what has been apparent from our research is that at the core of the layers upon layers of financial jargon and explanations lies the human aspect of all these activities; it is ultimately down to human fallibility – perhaps even gullibility. Decisions have been made that were not in the public interest; activities allowed to go unchecked when they cried out for principled monitoring; excess encouraged when restraint should have been applied instead. The whole crisis stems from individuals and organizations overstretching their capabilities, risking more and more until the whole pack of cards catastrophically came tumbling down, leaving all the main players in a state of total confusion as to what to do next. This is where we need to begin in order to rebuild the future of the financial markets and the eventual return of trust in the abilities of those running them: abilities which at the moment are not inspiring a great deal of confidence amongst the general public, who had been led to believe by most politicians, financiers, and economists that major boom-and-bust episodes were a thing of the past. We propose that scepticism and sceptically oriented coaching should be partners on this journey as they will act as the conscience of those charged with the rebuilding of the sector, providing a constant source of challenge to the mindset that has led to the debacle in the first place. Without the fostering of such conscience we leave ourselves in the position where future crises will almost undoubtedly occur, and that plainly will be to no one's benefit.

Rethinking coaching

A fundamental assumption of economics for more than a century has been the reliance on the concept of investment decisions based on rationality. The assumed rationality of organizational leaders continues to permeate the ideology of organizations and organizational theories, bearing out our contention that there is a need to rethink coaching such that the *status quo* is challenged and the underlying reality to organizational life revealed. We are now in a position where everyone should be taking stock of past beliefs and practices since it seems abundantly apparent that investment decisions can often be very far from rational (the dotcom bubble of the 1990s alone should have alerted us to this). From a critical perspective, it is debateable whether coaching in its current form, and internal coaching provision in particular, is powerful and challenging enough on its own to stave off a future disaster such as we have experienced with the banking crisis and the many questionable practices and decisions it brought to light. The underlying philosophy of coaching is rooted in the humanistic school of psychology which in essence seeks to realize the potential of the individual. In principle this is a laudable and worthwhile goal to pursue, but if coaching is to provide the mirror of conscience to individual leaders and organizations, it needs to develop a sharper and more critical edge through which to confront the practices and assumptions of individuals and organizations. We believe that the theories of scepticism as discussed in the following chapters are best placed in achieving this. These theories will strengthen one of the key expectations of coaching, namely that individuals are responsible for the choices they make and the consequences that ensue.

The credit crisis has shaken public belief not just in the financial sector, but in the business world in general. Coming on the back of various scandals in that area in recent years the crisis has revealed that the market paradigm is internally deeply flawed and in desperate need of reassessment. Enron in many ways set the stage for what was to follow in the credit crunch, revealing a culture of corruption and unethical conduct in the upper echelons of the American business community that was quite breathtaking in its scope; a case of bankruptcy, 'Texas-style', as one commentator put it, 'in the biggest and gaudiest way possible – with superlatives aplenty'.[2] It was at the time the biggest recorded bankruptcy in American history, but the crunch was soon to outdo it in terms of superlatives, all but wiping out the banking sector and in the process bringing the entire global economy to the verge of collapse. The picture that emerged of business practices in the banking sector was to say the least unflattering, and it is hardly surprizing that it has sparked considerable public unease about how the business world in general operates: an unease exacerbated by a bonus culture seemingly out of touch with reality. If individuals were to exhibit the behaviour collectively assigned to organizations, they would either have the wrath of the justice system descend on them or find themselves being strongly recommended to undergo psychiatric counselling on the grounds that they were a danger to others. Assigning the blame for criminal behaviour as witnessed in recent times to inanimate objects such as organizations is merely an abdication of responsibility by humans for their own selfish behaviour.

One of the critical ways in which that culture was drastically out of touch with reality was in its cavalier attitude towards social responsibility. The ethos of the sector was geared towards immediate gratification, at a personal as much as an organizational level (annual bonuses exerting their considerable pull), and this led to a cut-throat approach to financial trading in which quick gain was all that counted, with no consideration of the consequences this might have on the wider public. The longer-term health of the financial sector itself was disregarded too in the scramble for instant returns on investments. How success was achieved was treated as irrelevant, hence such practices as 'short selling', where traders bet on the share prices of a given company going down, which all too often triggered a collapse even if the company in question was fundamentally quite sound (if perhaps a little stretched credit-wise, as most companies have been in recent years). National currencies too can find themselves caught in this bind. The market can be very irrational, and volatile, thus very susceptible to the action of such predators – generally working for hedge-funds, the least-regulated section of an already very lightly regulated financial marketplace. As many commentators have noted of the financial world recently, greed has very much come into the ascendancy, and greed, of course, recognizes no need for social responsibility, being inherently selfish and lacking in conscience.[3]

Greed is not an exclusively male phenomenon, but it has to be said that the culture of risk-taking it has inspired within the financial community seems to be more congenial to male than female nature. Organizations tend to have a decidedly masculinist cast, and coaching surely has a responsibility to address this when it has brought the business community to such a desperate pass. When risk-taking puts the entire world financial system, and hence the living standards of all of us, in danger of collapse, then it has to be time to think again about the attitudes and assumptions of the management class involved – and this is still overwhelmingly male and motivated by a sense of personal bravado that women only very rarely display. One does not have to subscribe to feminist principles to come to this conclusion. On the contrary, the mainly male-dominated House of Commons Treasury Committee released a condemning report during the time of writing, which strongly suggests that the lack of women on the boards of the financial institutions has played a significant part in creating the group-think which has gone unchecked in these institutions.[4] Summing it up, the competitive instinct, so strong in the male character, simply got out of hand, leaving any notion of social responsibility far behind, and that requires the kind of reassessment that coaching is specifically designed to promote.

We shall also be analyzing closely the notion of group-think as found within organizations and the financial sector in particular, arguing that the destructive effect of it going unchecked and uncontested is at the root of the causes which have led to the meltdown of the banking industry. One of the reasons why such a phenomenon goes uncontested like this is due to the fact that critics of the beliefs and practices which lead to destructive group-think are so often suppressed and silenced. Such critics within the organization are liable to find themselves labelled as 'whistleblowers', who invariably find themselves ostracized from the group and in the extreme, fired and banished from the organization. The sobering question, therefore, is whether the industry has learnt from experience or whether we will observe business as usual once the dust settles.

We conclude our study by suggesting that coaching could become an important factor in reintroducing a strong sense of social responsibility not just into the business community, but into the wider public domain as a whole. That it could play a key role in a campaign to reduce the level of selfishness in our society and the fixation that so many of us have, and are encouraged to have by those in positions of power and social influence, with short-term gain. Coaching informed by critical theory should make us aware of the wider picture, not just our own personal desires, and we intend to explore its potential to have a more prominent public role, and to provide a model for finding a better balance between our rights and responsibilities. Old-fashioned though it may sound to say so, we feel there is a case to be made for deferred gratification – and moreover, a case that is in the public interest if we are to prevent our culture from being undermined altogether by greed. There is a moral point to be made here and coaching must not be shy of adopting such a stance; whatever improves our ethical consciousness has to be seen as a socially desirable activity.

Mapping the argument

The rest of our study breaks down as follows: Part II concentrates on coaching. Chapter 2 is devoted to a survey of the coaching profession as it stands, looking at how it operates and what the relationship is between theory and practice in the many coaching styles that are currently competing with each other for custom. What do coaches do, where do they draw their ideas from, what objectives do the various schools set for themselves, and what is the nature of their relationship to the management that hires them? We also explore the pros and cons the emerging profession is experiencing in a drive to establish unified and regulated practices. Then we move on in

Chapters 3 and 4 to consider both the successes and the limitations of coaching in actual practice, utilizing a selection of case studies which provide us with an insight as to how organizations have chosen to integrate and apply coaching principles within their systems, with varying degrees of success. Within any profession, especially an emergent one, there are potential weaknesses and challenges to its practices which need addressing and we allocate a chapter to raising what we identify as its current shortcomings. Where does coaching work well, and why? Equally, where does it run into problems, and why? It is possible to argue that it seems to have had greater success to date in the public than the private sector: why might this be so, and what might the private sector have to learn from its public counterparts in consequence? It could be argued that there is less of the destructive competitiveness that marks out the profit-driven private sector in the public, a greater disposition towards teamwork and maintaining ethical standards, and we shall be suggesting that coaching can help to bridge the gap that exists between them and disseminate best practice from the one to the other.

In Part III, Chapters 5 and 6, we turn to the history of critical theory in Western culture to map out the main trends that inform current debates in the area, emphasizing the key role played by scepticism. What might coaches appropriate from this intellectually stimulating tradition of thought that could enhance their practice and better prepare their coachees to prosper and grow within their organizations? And then, of course, for the organizations themselves to become more robust entities, less susceptible to crisis. Scepticism is in fact right at the heart of our argument, being for us the attitude that is best suited to arrest the slide into dogmatism that organizations are so prone to experience over time; and it is an attitude that has come to the fore in recent critical theory, which is very much geared towards calling into question the assumptions of received authority – in all walks of life. Dogmatism is neither in the public nor in the organizational interest, and it needs to be combatted on an ongoing basis. Our aim is to demonstrate how coaching can be oriented towards this task such that fundamentalist values are subjected to rigorous scrutiny. Market fundamentalism is no more in the wider public interest than religious fundamentalism is: we are only in our current financial position because market fundamentalism was given its head and allowed to avoid the issue of its social responsibility. What also needs to be brought under review is our tendency to collude with such forms of ideological dogmatism, and the ideas of the cultural theorist Slavoj Žižek, who has a keen interest in this aspect of public behaviour and the psychology behind it, will be particularly drawn on to see how this might be addressed. Difficult though it can be to identify our own blind spots and subject them to analysis, it can be done, and to both our and the organization's ultimate advantage. Again, coaching offers the context in which such a change in perspective can be brought about.

In Part IV, Chapters 7–10, we put the case for a radical new approach to coaching, underpinned by critical theory and particularly its sceptical side, in order to address the root causes of the managerial culture that has led to the credit crisis. The market paradigm is clearly under considerable strain at present: what went wrong, and how can we put it right? Starting from the credit crisis, where do we go next in terms of organizational behaviour? How can we make corporate social responsibility (CSR) something that all employees feel motivated to uphold – even in the face of indifference, perhaps even outright opposition, by their respective managements? How can we instil greater ethical awareness within the business ethos? And how might coaching figure in that process, helping us to redefine what we really mean by corporate social responsibility? Without a strong version of CSR we seem doomed to an existence of boom-and-bust cycles that can threaten the very foundations of our society. The fate of Iceland stands as a grim warning to us all in this regard. Here was a country whose leading entrepreneurs, as one commentator put it, tried 'to buy the world', overstretching their companies, and the banks that were extending them credit, to the point where the country virtually went bankrupt, falling into considerable political disarray in the process.[5] Countries do not go out of business the way organizations do of course, but it is hardly in the international community's interest for events like this to happen: if ethical standards are not scrupulously upheld across all countries, then everyone will be damaged in the subsequent fallout. (As we write, Iceland is still being pursued by various countries, including the UK, for settlement of the massive debts that its banks ran up, leaving a trail of distressed creditors in their wake.)

Overall, our concern is to show how coaching can widen its intellectual range such that it can become a progressively more effective technique within organizational life: a positive force for preventing crises of the kind that have caused such havoc in both the economic and political realms of late, on a truly international scale. There is an urgent need for a radical change in the ethos of the organizational world, and it is time this was recognized and acted upon. There is a radical need, too, as we noted earlier, for a campaign against the culture of selfishness that has taken such a hold on us, in the West particularly (still the financial model to which most of the world aspires, the recent crisis notwithstanding), and to restate the social value of deferred gratification and personal responsibility towards our fellows. We now offer our suggestions for putting that programme in motion.

Part II
Coaching

2
Coaching as Theory and Practice

The roots of coaching can be traced back to the discourses of education, psychology, sports coaching, and organizational development. As suggested by Dianne R. Stober, humanistic psychology provides the philosophical foundation for coaching in terms of the values and assumptions which underpin it.[1] Many of the themes of coaching are therefore based on the humanistic approach. A unifying assumption of the developing field of coaching in both theory and practice appears to be a passion for the growth of people and the nurturing of talent.[2] As Stober summarizes, '[c]oaching is above all about human growth and change', and Anthony M. Grant offers the following definition of coaching: 'Coaching is a robust and challenging intervention, is results driven, delivers tangible added value, is typically a short-term or intermittent engagement, and enables the attainment of high standards or goals.'[3] As a discourse it is very much in its infancy, however, and a definitive description of coaching remains elusive, as Anne Brockbank and Ian McGill have pointed out.[4] It is a patchwork of influencing ontologies, epistemologies, and methodologies each underpinned by different assumptions which means that the practice of coaching is influenced by different schools of thought. It is apparent that each of these approaches places a different emphasis on the directive-versus-facilitative continuum of coaching.[5] Nevertheless, as Bob Garvey et al. suggest, the growth of coaching and its popularity has been exponential over recent years.[6]

There are as many perspectives of coaching as there are proponents contributing to the growing body of knowledge and the construction of the discourse of coaching. On the one hand, there are the pragmatists who argue for the need of coaching to deliver results with an emphasis on techniques. The pragmatist requires the freedom to blend disparate techniques and approaches together without boundary restrictions. On the other hand, are the well-established communities of knowledge supported by clear theoretical and academic identities and which include the adult learning and development community, psychology and counselling, and the study of business. It means that the result of such diversity is that different disciplines and philosophies vie for ownership of coaching and its underpinning philosophies, practices, and principles which may shape and eventually determine the definition of coaching in the future. However, Grant argues that, '[t]he cross-disciplinary aspect of professional coaching is very important. One aspect of this is that no single industry or professional group "owns" coaching.'[7] One could argue, as Miles Downey does, that within any new profession the boundaries and agreed practices will evolve and be determined in time.[8] According to Grant, '[t]he diversity of prior professional backgrounds means that the coaching industry draws on a wide range of methodological approaches to coaching, and a wide range of educational disciplines inform coaching practice.'[9] As suggested above, there appears to be a common theme or unifying philosophy amongst the disparate approaches to coaching, namely a commitment for the growth of people, assuming responsibility for choice and the nurturing of latent talent. In Stober's view, 'the humanistic theory of self-actualization is a foundational assumption for coaching with its focus on enhancing growth rather than meliorating dysfunction.'[10] This assumption places coaching within the realm of growth and supported by an optimistic view of the person being coached.

Some of the identifiable approaches include a focus on the learning and development of the individual with performance improvement, personal growth, and change as the main outcome. This is supported by Elaine Cox et al., for whom '[t]he concept of change, which is at the heart of coaching, is also inherent in the concept of learning.'[11] The underlying assumption is that coaching generates a process of learning which will support the capacity of the individual to grow. In essence, as Garvey et al. emphasize, coaching is about change.[12] One could argue if the individual does not change as a result of the process then it cannot be identified as coaching. Vincent Lenhardt suggests that coaching serves to unite the various approaches of development, providing coherence and meaning to learning and development.[13] Tony Chapman et al. insist that coaching can be defined as both a science and an art, and depending on the preferred discourse of the coach and using psychology as an example, will determine the models and techniques the coach draws on.[14] The art in the practice of coaching will be determined by the skill with which the coach applies the different models and techniques, transcending the scientific knowledge of the particular discourse.

Irrespective of the variety of coaching styles available, one of the key competencies is identified as the ability to listen. The capacity to listen deeply is widely accepted as one of the key ingredients to successful coaching.[15] Laura Whitworth et al. identify the type of listening the coach engages in as not only listening to the words spoken by the coachee, but also what is behind the words and even the spaces in between the words.[16] They also argue that in order to achieve deep listening, it is necessary to draw on one's intuition. They perceive intuition as an intelligence which can arguably be developed. Carl R. Rogers suggests that when he hears not only the words spoken by a client, but her own private and personal meaning, many things happen.[17]

There are proponents of coaching, such as Whitmore, who propose that coaching as an industry is better placed than any other to develop and generate a greater sense of personal ownership within the individual for taking more responsibility for her life. As we go on to argue in subsequent chapters, this sense of ownership and responsibility for our personal actions is not only necessary for the development of a more effective model of corporate social responsibility within organizations, but it could also play a significant role in fostering a renewed sense of ownership for our actions and their impact on others within society at large. This is backed up by Carol Wilson, who states that one of the core principles of coaching is to generate self-responsibility and ownership within coachees for their lives.[18] It is, however, identified as an accountability that is without blame and judgement. Instead, it aims to enable individuals to identify the different choices and options available to them in different circumstances and what they may select to change or do differently. The coaching relationship is therefore seen as a fine balance between support and challenge, as Peter Bluckert has noted.[19]

Whitworth et al. go much further to emphasize that the coaching relationship is unique, and Mick Cope argues that the coach must develop a high level of trust with the coachee.[20] In fact, Tatiana Bachkirova goes further yet and claims that: 'It is the coach as a person, rather than the application of particular techniques or methods, that makes a difference in coaching practice.'[21] The total focus of the relationship is on the person being coached and the encouragement they may need in achieving their personal objectives, both professionally as well as personally. Seth Allcorn reflects on the singular focus of the coaching relationship: 'This appreciation directs our attention to the interpersonal nature of this transaction and, like all relationships, it is the subjective, out-of-awareness, unconscious, and very often hard-to-discuss aspects of the relationship that count.'[22] Unlike other identified methods of intervention, coaching resists the temptation to tell people what to do; instead the motivation is in assisting people in their sense-making activities and providing the support they need in removing any blocks that may prevent them from moving from one state to another, should they wish to do so. Coaching provides the tools and techniques both to aid and challenge the individual in making different choices and decisions in their careers. Rogers, in his personal-centred approach to learning, argues that an absence of judgement on the part of the teacher is when the teacher understands the student from within and with an awareness of the way in which the learner experiences the process of learning.[23] He goes on to state that in the presence of such understanding, the likelihood of significant learning is increased as the learner feels understood from their particular point of view without judgement. A non-judgemental environment supports the decision-making process of the coachee, and as Ernesto Spinelli and Caroline Horner argue, we are in essence the choices that we make.[24]

Numerous authors uphold the special nature of the relationship between the coach and coachee. Mary B. O'Neill, for example, argues that presence is one of the most important principles and tools of coaching; others who subscribe to this notion, such as Brockbank and McGill, Alison Whybrow, and Carol Kauffman, feel that how the coach 'shows up' in the coaching relationship will dictate the perceived value of coaching.[25] The special bond in the relationship is referred to in different ways by different authors. Doug Silsbee suggests that importance of presence within coaching is arguably one of the key requirements necessary for the coach to cultivate real and lasting change for the client. He goes on to identify presence as, 'a state of awareness, in the moment, characterized by the felt experience of timelessness, connectedness, and a larger truth'.[26] The idea of such a state is similar to that of 'flow' described by Mihaly Csikszentmihalyi, namely the ability to be in the moment.[27] Rogers also suggests that the energy created between therapist and client within such a unique relationship transcends the relationship itself to become something larger, which facilitates profound growth and healing.[28]

The special nature of the coaching environment is perceived as being akin to that of a sacred space. The space is seen to include things such as the trusting nature of the relationship, the chemistry between the coach and coachee, nurturing and accepting. It is not necessarily perceived as a physical space, but instead an emotional one because the same state can be experienced in a busy environment, surrounded by other people and sounds. The idea of the coaching space transcending that of a physical space is echoed by Graham Lee for whom it is, 'a psychological space in which coachees feel safe enough to be open with their thoughts and feelings, to be able to share their anxieties, frustrations, aspirations and deepest hopes.'[29] Another way of identifying the special nature of this space is the ability of the coach to be with the client in the moment. Daniel N. Stern describes the 'now' as moments of intensity that may last only for seconds, but these powerful seconds may reveal a deep understanding of the self to the individual.[30] The coaching space appears to facilitate the suspension of time. Through working with the coach in the here and now, the coachee is able to become aware of deep-seated subjective knowledge, which may fundamentally impact on how the coachee lives his or her life. Gunnar Carlberg identifies these moments as 'turning point moments'.[31] Irrespective of how these are identified, it is apparent that the quality of the relationship between the coach and the coachee has to operate at a deep level of trust in order to make these moments possible.

It is however not all about the skills of the coach, with the coachee as only a passive recipient of the chosen skills and techniques of the coach. Instead, a critical factor in the success of the coaching relationship, as Bachkirova insists, is the readiness of the coachee to be coached.[32] The same assumption is to be found within the literature of transformational learning proposed by Jack Mezirow.[33] The expectation of the coaching relationship is that the coach is completely absorbed by the coachee and whatever it is that makes the person tick, what their passions are, and providing the tools for learning to enable them to achieve the results that they want. It would be apparent that the challenge of the coaching relationship is based on mutual trust, allowing the coach to question the sense made by the coachee. Trust as a key element in the quality of the coaching relationship is acknowledged by numerous authors, such as Graham Jones and Kirsty Spooner, Whybrow, and Rogers, who go on to suggest that the educator or coach in this scenario would be much more effective if he were to demonstrate realness or genuineness when entering into a relationship with the learner without front or *façade*.[34] This may mean that the coach enters into a direct personal encounter with the learner, person-to-person. As Rogers describes it, that would mean he is *being* himself and not denying who he is, and therefore coming across as being congruent by the coachee. A further behaviour of the coach which is seen as important is that of expressing true curiosity of the coachee and her circumstances. According to Whitworth et al., such curiosity may lead to some unexpected and significant discoveries on the part of the coachee.[35] As Grant and Stober put it: 'Thus it is clear that coaching is more about asking the right questions than telling people what to do, and it is not necessarily concerned with subject-matter expertise or advice giving.'[36] It is through curious questioning that the coach facilitates the process of self-discovery within the coachee. The process is supported by an overarching assumption of coaching that the agenda of the intervention is driven by the coachee who therefore has the ultimate say in the outcome of the process.[37]

Some practices of coaching suggest that the success of coaching is reliant on the ability of the coach to work with the values and beliefs of the individual. Change and transformation follow when the coachee has an understanding of what it is that drives his or her own behaviour. It is for this reason that the psychology profession argues that the coach needs the knowledge and experience of psychological models to help the client develop self-awareness and an understanding of her personal drivers. Wilson perceives the role of a coach as a person who enables the individual to gain self-knowledge with the assumption that this would lead to a more fulfilled personal and professional life.[38] Self-awareness leads to self-observation which enables the individual to make different choices in relation to her thoughts and behaviours. A significant expectation of coaching is that self-awareness within the coached individual is achieved through skilful questioning.

An assumption of coaching is that personal change will be an outcome of the process, including behavioural changes, and according to James C. Quick and Marilyn Macik-Frey, this is achieved through the deep personal communication which is facilitated by the coaching environment.[39] This allows for the discussion of complicated issues, revealing any personal barriers, fears, and dreams of the person being coached. If an outcome of coaching is to invite the client to expand her world, it is necessary for the coach to exist in the world of the client. If change is to be sustainable, it is necessary for the coachee to learn how to self-coach. As pointed out earlier, learning is an expected outcome of coaching and is achieved through the skilful questioning by the coach. The learning is facilitated using various methods such as metaphors, stories, and questioning techniques, as discussed by James T. Richard.[40] Whatever the desired outcome expected of coaching, there is a multitude of existing and growing models and techniques available with which to achieve these. We move on now to consider some of these in more detail.

Performance versus developmental coaching

One of most widely recognized and adopted models within the coaching community is the GROW model attributed to Whitmore, despite the lack of empirical evidence to support its efficacy.[41] Some of the critique brought against the model is its simplicity and perceived theoretical flaws.[42] Many of the coaching models and techniques employed by coaches can be placed in one of two camps, namely transference on the one end of the continuum, which is based on the assumption of coaching being a process of transference of knowledge, meaning, and understanding.[43] On the other end of the continuum is the assumption that coaching is a process of discovery, helping the client to help herself. The underlying expectation is that the coach does not impart any wisdom or knowledge, instead his purpose is to bring out the best within the coachee. A fundamental expectation of coaching is that it provides the process through which the individual is able to reflect on her own actions and thoughts for the purpose of identifying alternative ways of being and behaving.[44]

The objective versus subjective dimension put forward by Gibson Burrell and Gareth Morgan served as inspiration to Brockbank and McGill, who devised a map through which to identify different approaches to coaching.[45] The authors suggest that coaching is influenced by the philosophy that underpins it and it would appear that the theoretical base supporting most coaching practices is generally implicit. A subjectivist view assumes that social realities like learning and development are fundamentally different from natural phenomena and cannot therefore be captured by objective instruments, which would be the assumption of the objective dimension. Instead, the social world of the coachee is understood to be continuously constructed, reproduced, and transformed through interaction with others. The personal and social world of the client is acknowledged as the basis of the developmental process. This particular style of coaching recognizes the socially constructed nature of reality, highlighting the responsibility of each and everyone in the creation of the reality they experience, which is, of course, the emphasis of this book.

The process of coaching supports the way in which the individual interprets her situations and which in turn influences her behaviour in response to future situations. It could be argued that coaching offers the vehicle through which the coachee makes sense of her world. Through the redefinition of events or the interpretations of these events, the individual expands her repertoire with which to respond to these, particularly if the process is at the conscious level. A person has filters through which she interprets and judges events and situations and if she is able to understand her drivers she may have more choice in terms of responses to any given event. Such reflection will also enable the person to understand her ownership in the creation of the situation in the first place. These filters also give an insight into the beliefs the person has about herself and others and her behaviour and responses in a particular situation. It is argued therefore that if the person is able to change her cognitions she will also be able to bring about changes in her behaviour.[46] This would point towards a psychological understanding of the coaching process. Psychology has been significantly influential in determining the models, processes, and techniques which are used within the coaching repertoire. Some of these are identified and discussed in the following section.

The psychology of coaching

As stated, numerous disciplines have informed the models and techniques used in coaching such as psychology, psychotherapy, counselling, and philosophy. Psychologists would argue that it is their profession that is at the forefront of the development of coaching, and this is supported by the argument put forward by P. Alex Linley and Susan Harrington that any psychological practice is underpinned by a fundamental and deep-seated assumption of human nature.[47] Many feel that coaches need to possess a level of psychological skills and competencies which would equip them to deal effectively across the range of coaching scenarios they are likely to encounter. It is apparent that the term 'psychological-mindedness' has crept into the coaching literature and is described as the top level competency for executive coaches in particular. In summary, it is the ability to go beyond the obvious and to consider the causes and meanings of the behaviour, feelings, and thoughts of the coachee. From a psychoanalytical perspective Allcorn observes, '[t]he approach attends to the executive's unconscious attachments and emotional investments relative to the organization, its workers, and the coach who assists the client in seeing more clearly how his or her internal world affects the organization and its members.'[48] However, due to the need for fast results and outcome achievements, particularly within business and executive coaching, the coach, as Elizabeth C. Thach notes, does not necessarily enter too far into the realms of psychology.[49]

There is much debate as to the suggested overlap between coaching, counselling, and therapy.[50] One cannot deny that coaching and therapy share similar theoretical constructs and practices. The common focus is based on a confidential, one-to-one relationship for the purpose of change. However, in therapy the focus of attention is often on interpersonal health and an identifiable issue such as depression which impacts on the ability of the individual to function. In contrast, the focus of the coach is on untapped potential and the whole person and seeking to maximize her fulfilment in life and work. A further suggested contribution which the psychology and therapy professions bring to coaching is on some of the possible ethical problems encountered and the management of boundaries.[51]

However, as Spinelli points out, the application of psychological models in coaching is not motivated by dealing with dysfunctionality. Instead coaching psychology is grounded in values that support personal empowerment.[52] This is a key theme of person-centred psychology which argues that the coach is not the expert and that the purpose of coaching is to facilitate the self-determination of the coachee with the ultimate objective of optimal functioning by her.[53] This approach also suggests that it is irrelevant to distinguish between coaching and therapy as there is not necessarily a theoretical difference between the two. However, this may provide the coach with a dilemma of keeping the boundaries between psychology and coaching, and when engaged in coaching not to intervene as a psychologist or therapist, especially if that may be the professional background of the coach. Advocates of therapy, such as Erik de Haan and Yvonne Burger, suggest that psychotherapy is influential in providing much of the roots that underpin coaching.[54]

It can be argued that psychology within coaching enhances development in both the personal and professional life of the individual which is achieved through the application of well-established psychological approaches of behavioural science.[55] As with psychology or therapy, there is an exploration of the blind spots and defensive routines of the coachee that may lead to distorted thinking, and which would be a fundamental benefit in challenging the behavioural patterns of the leaders of society as discussed in this book.[56] Coaching psychology is based on the assertion that the individual is autonomous and capable of learning and reflective practice, and that is a fundamental benefit critical coaching could offer business and political leaders in rebuilding their fallen empires.[57] The virtue of coaching psychology is that it allows the coach to support the coachee to reflect on past experiences and bring these to conscious awareness.[58] A cognitive behavioural approach suggests that it enables the coachee to achieve realistic goals whilst improving performance and engendering psychological resilience, preventing stress, and providing assistance to the coachee in overcoming barriers to change.[59]

As will be outlined in future chapters, critical theories provide sophisticated and philosophically informed styles of critical analysis.

This is apparent in an existential approach to coaching, which aims to support the coachee in the meanings they create as well as the relations they adopt in the world. Furthermore, an existential approach argues that human experience is uncertain and therefore always open to novel and unpredictable possibilities. Existentialism shares the arguments put forward by Karl E. Weick that humans are essentially meaning-making beings, and reinforces the proposal in this book that sensemaking is the vehicle through which people reduce the complexity of their environment.[60] In fact, Reinhard Stelter proposes that the core purpose of coaching is meaning-making, suggesting that it is achieved through conversation and a true partnership between the coach and coachee.[61] It is argued that the process of coaching is to support the coachee in the sensemaking activities referred to. Furthermore, Spinelli and Horner claim that the individual who benefits the most from an existential approach to coaching is the person in transition and as discussed throughout this book, critical understanding is necessary to prevent the errors of the past.[62] In essence the existential approach emphasizes the nature of being and meaning as opposed to the doing aspect of the coaching. As Spinelli puts it: 'Paradoxically, existential coaching argues that beneficial change may best emerge via the very process of assisting clients to "stay still" so that they can better explore, evaluate and come to terms with their currently-lived worldview and its experiential consequences.'[63]

Irrespective of the perceived influence of psychology on coaching, it has a long history of well-established theories and practices for the purpose of understanding human development and behaviour. There is also a sense in the psychology profession that its history of statistics and evidence-based research places it in a superior position to take the lead in establishing a meta-model, although it has to be said that such research has not yet reached the practice of coaching.

Constructionism and transformation

One could argue that the dynamic and interactive nature of coaching requires a flexible theoretical methodology which would allow coaches to respond with different skills and attitudes in meeting the different needs of different clients.[64] Such flexibility is provided by a constructionist perspective. The postmodernist philosophies of constructionism and its perception of reality are fundamentally influential in the assumptions that underpin coaching. One underlying belief suggests that the coachee is capable of creating a preferred future. Cox also puts forward an argument that constructionism reflects the values of andragogy introduced elsewhere: 'Many of the aspects of constructivism, such as encouragement of ownership in learning and the emphasis on experiential learning, can be observed within the principles of andragogy.'[65] Social constructionism challenges the taken-for-granted beliefs about the world and the assumption that knowledge about it is acquired through observation. Instead, experience is perceived as the sense made through active interchange between people engaged in reciprocal relationships.[66] The coaching relationship provides the opportunity for a 'communal interdependence' which supports the sensemaking of both coach and coachee. It means that the coach does not impart any wisdom to the coachee, but is there to support the coachee in discovering her own wisdom as identified on the continuum put forward by Cope and referred to earlier.[67] A fundamental belief of coaching from a constructionist perspective advocates that there is a multiplicity of ways in which the world may be constructed and made sense of and rejects any attempt at establishing universal first principles. This is a key principle of postmodern philosophy, as we shall see when critical theory is discussed in detail in Chapter 5. Our mental models dictate how we perceive and respond to the world and as Auerbach posits, '[m]ental models can be useful, or they can get in our way. Mental models usually limit us to familiar ways of thinking and behaving.'[68]

Coaching within organizations

Coaching has gained a strong following in human development, particularly at senior levels within organizations, with Halina Brunning observing that it has become the approach of choice in management and leadership development.[69] Proponents of organizational coaching suggest that competency in psychological methods alone will not suffice. Instead they argue that knowledge and awareness of business, business issues, and leadership is also important, as is an understanding of organizational and cultural discourse.[70] A similar argument is put forward by David Clutterbuck and Gill Lane in relation to situational mentoring.[71] Stephen Gibb suggests that coaching allows the client to explore, discover, and clarify different ways of leading and developing.[72] As observed before, it is argued that one of the reasons for the success of coaching is that it addresses deeply held beliefs and behaviours which inhibit the performance of the manager. As Gibb points out, '[t]here is much in effective executive coaching that is about addressing core beliefs about self and abilities, and experimenting with new ways of being.'[73] The non-judgemental support which coaching provides offers the coachee the opportunity to reflect on critical issues and to explore the complexities that managers of contemporary organizations have to deal with on a regular basis. The coaching relationship provides access to impartial support which is not often available within organizations. Managers do not always have access to open and honest feedback from peers and subordinates, and coaching provides the mirror managers need to understand the impact that they have on others and the organizational environment and how their actions and behaviours are perceived by others. Furthermore, the coach is in the position of being able to ask the questions no one else in the organization would necessarily have the courage to ask. This may be one of the key benefits of coaching as it is able to question the group-think that may exist within an organization; a concept we shall consider in greater detail in Chapter 4.

For the duration of the coaching relationship the coach is seen as a partner of the manager.[74] As no manager operates in isolation within an organization, it is therefore crucial for the coach to understand the manager within the context of her working environment and her interaction with others. It also provides the environment in which managers can be challenged to understand the impact they have on the wider system in which they operate. If some of the banking executives had been exposed to such challenges, then the collapse of the financial sector might well have been avoided. A common theme identified with a coaching approach, as we have seen, is that there is not a standard approach available, and organizational and executive coaching is no different. What works well in one organization or part of an organization, as Alison Whybrow and Vic Henderson note, is not necessarily transferable to another.[75] Instead, the value of coaching is that it addresses the specific needs of an individual, group, or organization. Much of organizational coaching in recent years has been focused on leadership development and based on the collapse of the finance sector, such coaching would benefit from drawing on the critical theories to be dealt with in Chapter 5.[76]

Much has been written about the emotional intelligence of business leaders and coaching is perceived as having the ability to assist leaders in developing their emotional and relational capacity.[77] Auerbach strongly argues for a recognition of the emotional aspect of coaching as follows: 'A coach who neglects the emotional side of the client completely will be shutting out a critical element. Students of emotional intelligence know that feelings are to be attended to as potential sources of useful information.'[78] Emotional competence is increasingly rated as the most important competency to develop *en route* to senior management positions.[79] The ability to recognize and manage one's emotions and the effect they have on others are skills seen as fundamental to being a successful manager. Stephen Neale et al. suggest that the experiential triangle of thoughts, emotions, and actions is present in everything a person does.[80] The power of emotional influence as identified in group-think is an overriding factor in behaviour or the unwillingness to change behaviour. As Manfred de Vries suggests it is a combination of cognition and emotions which determines what the person selects to focus on or ignore.[81] Self-management allows the individual to control and manage disruptive emotions, adaptability, accountability, and the recognition of when to act. The sensitivity and attunement to the emotions of others leads to the ability to demonstrate empathy; competencies which equip the manager to deal much more effectively with conflict at work and the building of collaborative teams.[82] The exploration of emotions allows the person to become conscious of the underlying reasons for the avoidance or attraction to situations or people. It is argued that such self-awareness provides the individual with the tools to manage relationships and situations more effectively.[83] The education that managers are exposed to throughout their careers does not prepare them for the complexities and dynamics of the emotions which they will encounter within the organization. The toxins that result from strained and difficult organizational relationships will inevitably impact on the bottom line of the organization[84] – and beyond, as we have witnessed with the recent collapse of the economy.

Business practices have historically been based on the behavioural models which are supported by rewards and punishment. This may be one of the reasons, Jonathan Passmore proposes, why behavioural coaching, such as the GROW model, is prevalent within organizations.[85] Senior managers tend to be action-oriented and are often motivated by power. This might be the reason why introspection does not always feature highly on their list of priorities and an argument for the critical reflection coaching has to offer as a significant benefit to business leaders. It is also a given that it may be lonely operating at the senior level of an organization with few people the senior executive can confide in or even share weaknesses and fears with.[86] The ability to engage in critical reflection must be deemed one of the most important activities in leaders rebuilding the economy and the confidence in a new dawn.

This is further reinforced by Neale et al. who view coaching as one of the most powerful ways of communicating, arguing that when used effectively it raises self-awareness, cutting straight to the chase.[87] According to Quick and Macik-Frey, we can observe two levels of communication within the coaching environment.[88] The first is the functional level whereby the coachee communicates externally throughout the organization. At this level the manager communicates information and is involved in different external roles. However, within the coaching environment the focus of attention is with communication in the inner tier, which involves a much more personal and intimate level of communication. It is at this level that the person is both given permission as well as challenged to deal with her personal complexities, drivers, and values which influence her external communication. It is by working at this level that the individual is able to develop the self-awareness and management of personal emotions that are vital in building interpersonal relationships and the skill to manage and lead others more effectively. Furthermore, an assumption is that the coach is able to provide a fresh perspective to the analyses of the organization and its processes. This is achieved because of the fact that the coach has no particular stance or agenda in respect of the organization and can therefore offer neutrality. One of the perceived benefits of effective coaching is the resilience which is subsequently developed by the coachee.[89]

It is an accepted fact by both practitioners and theorists of organizations that organizations operate in a continuous sea of change. The inspiration and management of change is expected to come from the senior levels of the organization which requires skills and competencies that go beyond the practical and technical skills of management. Within the coaching environment the manager has the opportunity to envision and explore the nature and consequences of any proposed change before actually embarking on it. Furthermore, it is also a given that managing change is likely to include the crucial skills of managing people and, as discussed, coaching has become a significant tool in the development of senior management and particularly the all important skill of managing people.[90] The intrapersonal competencies necessary in doing so can be identified to include self-awareness, self-regulation, and self-motivation.[91] Despite the diversity and variety of coaches, Stern argues that the common set of characteristics of coaches able to address the specific requirements of management include an efficient and practical, results-oriented approach;[92] precisely the coaching skills that will help a manager to make sense of their organizational environment. One of the most valuable gifts a coach has to offer the client is the ability to step away from the day-to-day business and reflect on the possible routes and choices available to them.

Increasingly organizations are seeking to create a coaching culture which may be perceived as a mechanism to aid in the elimination of issues that have led to the demise of the banking sector. David Clutterbuck and David Megginson suggest that coaching has the potential of setting the tone of how relationships are managed throughout an organization. Creating a coaching culture requires not only investment on the part of the organization, but more importantly a commitment from the leadership. In essence, 'a coaching culture demands a morally rigorous and humanistic approach to work and relationship.'[93] If coaching is to add value to the organization and act as a checking mechanism, it needs to be more than an add-on within the organization. Instead it should be integrated and supportive of various HR systems within the organization. Above all, there has to be a culture of true dialogue within the organization where the ability to voice an opinion or to dispute policy openly is explicit and accepted. Where this is present, Jennifer Joy-Matthews et al. suggest communities of practice may develop within the organization with the following four characteristics in evidence:

Learning is grounded in the actions of everyday situations;
Knowledge is acquired situationally;

Learning results from social processes including ways of thinking, perceiving problem solving, and interacting;
Learning is not separated from the world of action but exists in robust, complex social environments.[94]

These concepts reflect the type of organizational culture necessary in which a coaching culture would grow and develop. How prevalent a true coaching culture is or is likely to be within organizations remains, however, questionable.

Coaching as learning

As mentioned earlier, the roots of coaching can be traced back to sports coaching and according to Downey coaching owes much to the book by Timothy Gallwey, *The Inner Game of Tennis*.[95] It proposes that the coach works with the capacity of the individual to learn and coaching is thus about facilitating learning and development. Although there is not any single theory of adult learning, transformational learning theory and critical reflection have been applied to adult learning within the coaching context.[96] Stober and Grant concur and claim that, '[u]nderpinning the coaching process are the principles guiding effective adult learning'.[97] Joy-Matthews et al. suggest that learning can be understood as a change in the behaviour of the learner as learning facilitates a modification or addition to existing behaviour. The same could be said of coaching. One could argue that coaching does not take place if there is no learning, and an outcome of coaching both implicit and explicit is that the person being coached will develop a greater sense of their own frame of reference and the capacity to reframe their references if it is more enabling, resulting in different outcomes. Cox succinctly compares the elements of coaching and adult learning to observe: 'It could be argued, therefore, that andragogy, as well as providing the core principles that underpin adult learning, also, since coaching is an adult learning situation, too, offers the philosophy for coaching.'[98]

This is supported by Mezirow who argues that learning is not merely adding more knowledge, but instead it is also about the transformation of pre-existing knowledge.[99] The traditional approach to learning defined it as a process whereby the individual gained knowledge and skills and possibly also attitudes and opinions.[100] However, in recent years learning has increasingly been seen as a social process which takes place in the interaction between people, resulting in the constructionist view of learning put forward by such as Vivien Burr and Kenneth J. Gergen.[101] Malcolm S. Knowles distinguishes adult learning from pre-adult learning and defines it as andragogy, 'the art and science of helping adults learn', which is in contrast with pedagogy, the art and science of helping children learn.[102] There are five assumptions underlying andragogy which describe the adult learner as someone who (1) has an independent self-concept and who can direct his or her own learning, (2) has accumulated a reservoir of life experiences that is a rich resource for learning, (3) has learning needs closely related to changing social roles, (4) is problem-centred and interested in immediate application of knowledge, and (5) is motivated to learn by internal rather than external factors. It could be said that these assumptions equally apply to coaching. Coaching guided from a transformational perspective implies the partnership between experiential and transformative learning which allows the client to examine their experiences as well as their frames of reference.

Coaching supports the client in the critical examination of particular issues and in the adaptation of both cognition and behaviour. There are numerous theories on different learning styles, but irrespective of how the individual prefers to learn de Haan and Burger suggest that coaching can facilitate learning within any of the learning preferences.[103] De Vries argues that transformation is key in helping the individual to move beyond a reductionist formula of change to one of sustainable change.[104] The purpose of transformational learning is to develop a critical awareness of deep-seated assumptions, which may prevent further learning within the individual.[105] A key role of the coach is to challenge the assumptions of the coachee, providing feedback, and offering support in exploring and creating options as well as identifying the consequences of those options. In summary, coaching is in essence self-directed learning which is achieved through the art of questioning, directing the attention of the individual inwards.[106]

Conclusion

Brockbank and McGill succinctly summarize the purpose of coaching and state that, 'coaching has one clear purpose, the learning and development of an individual, a process that involves change'.[107] They go on to say that deep learning leads to a shift in habits and the capacity to adopt new habits, leading to new capabilities and skills. It is apparent that the quality of the relationship with the coach is critical to successful coaching and the depth of the conversations is identified as one of the key factors. For de Haan and Burger such conversations are powerful as they deal with issues that are of real importance to the coachee.[108]

Another way to describe the depth of the coaching conversation is to turn to the concept of dialogue. As with the coaching conversation, dialogue does not introduce boundaries. Instead it is ongoing, seeking, and encouraging multiple meanings to unfold for the purpose of exploring meaning and understanding. Dialogue reflects the emancipatory nature of coaching as it resists the need or temptation to persuade or convince the participants of a single or meta-perspective (the notion so disliked by Lyotard). It is through dialogue that the participants make sense of the world and their experiences. Garvey et al. suggest that the coaching conversation is another vehicle for meaningful dialogue, providing a powerful opportunity for learning.[109] Anne Deering and Anne Murphy identify dialogue as a means of conversation that allows the many voices and disparate views to be heard, which reflects a fundamental premise of postmodernism.[110] For participants to be engaged in dialogue David Bohm identifies a number of conditions that have to be present. Participants must suspend their assumptions and perceive one another as colleagues requiring a sense of equality and a shared quest for deeper insight and clarity.[111] According to Peter Senge, hierarchy and power are seen as antithetical to dialogue.[112] Finally, there must be a facilitator who is able to hold the context of dialogue; it is not a state achieved by an individual in isolation. These conditions allow for the free flowing of meaning to pass between the coach and coachee.

Bohm posits that it is only through dialogue that we can engage in the inquiry and reflection which precedes transformation, as dialogue allows us to become observers of our own thinking.[113] This is a critical aspect of the development sought in coaching, supported by Berger: 'From a developmental perspective, real growth requires some qualitative shift, not just in knowledge, but in perspective or way of thinking.'[114] Through dialogue we support each other in becoming aware of the incoherence within our own thoughts. Dialogue allows us to transcend individual understanding and Bohm is of the opinion that it is only through collective learning that we are able to realize the potential of human intelligence. He describes dialogue as a 'stream of meaning' that flows among and through the participants as well as between them, out of which new, shared meaning emerges.[115]

It is apparent from both the theory and practice of coaching that there are many different perspectives as to what could be labelled as coaching. As with any newly emerging field it is also clear that different theoretical bodies of knowledge are vying for ownership. Irrespective of the disparate views of coaching one could conclude that the ultimate outcome and purpose of coaching is developmental. Furthermore, coaching appears to be synonymous with learning, and learning that includes reflection on and change to assumptions and existing frames of references. The focus of the coaching sessions and the conversations is therefore on the future and who it is the coachee wants to become and what it is they want to achieve. The importance of reflection is emphasized by Cox, who argues that, '[r]eflection, then, is where professionals come to terms with their feelings, learn from their mistakes, explore their successes, and develop empathy and understanding'.[116] Whitworth et al. propose that it is through the cycle of action and learning that sustained change takes place.[117] It is apparent that the fledgling profession of coaching remains in a state of flux with no clear boundaries as to what constitutes coaching and as Stephen Gibb and Peter Hill suggest, the time of turbulence in the coaching community is no different from any other newly formed professional development.[118] It is a period of social construction of the emergent identity of the coaching community. How this has played out in terms of actual outcomes is what we shall go on next to consider.

3

Who Benefits from Coaching?: Case Studies

The motivations for individuals or organizations in seeking coaching are as varied as the approaches to coaching itself. Historically, coaching was used as a developmental tool for senior executives, but having realized its benefits organizations are increasingly cascading it down to all levels. Some organizations are endeavouring to establish a coaching culture to integrate coaching as part of a management and leadership style. Coaching is also seen as a powerful tool in aiding individuals as well as the organization in managing ever-changing landscapes. At the senior level of the organization, in particular, the ability to manage change requires skills and competencies beyond the standard practical and technical skills of management and is guaranteed to include the crucial skills of managing people.

Coaching has become recognized as the most appropriate tool to develop the skills required of senior managers to enable them consistently to deliver sustainable business results. A common theme as to the benefits of coaching amongst senior managers is its ability to support them with the sense of isolation they find themselves in as leaders of their organization. The coach is an independent person who can offer both support and challenge in dealing with organizational issues without bringing any personal agendas into the relationship. In essence coaching provides the time and space for reflection detached from the day-to-day activities. The opportunity to view the organization from a distance allows for clarity and insight. A coach acts as sounding board for testing new ideas and solutions in a way that would be difficult for executives to obtain from those close to them for various reasons such as trust and confidentiality.

Organizations must be able to rely on their senior teams consistently to deliver, therefore, and at the heart of performance delivery is an attitude capable of generating and handling innovation and change in a complex and continuously evolving commercial and cultural landscape. However, the challenge for individuals and organizations is to sift through the plethora of available coaches and coaching styles to find the coach that is right for them, their team, and their organizations. We share some case studies of individuals and organizations with whom we have been involved in the provision of coaching support, as well as some case studies documented by the Chartered Institute of Personnel Development (CIPD) and available on their Web site.[1] This is a very valuable resource for individuals and organizations wanting to understand how organizations are applying and integrating coaching practices. The value of coaching is not only sought by the private sector, the public sector has also wholeheartedly embraced it, not only for individuals and teams, but also in creating a coaching culture. However, at the time of writing, the economic downturn has meant that many organizations, both public and private, have reduced their investment in coaching, although it could be argued that it is the time when leaders of organizations need its assistance the most. Furthermore, during testing times if any activity does not directly impact on the bottom line in the private sector, it is often the first thing to go. The challenges the public sector faces are different and the pressure on these organizations is to improve efficiency and to cut costs rather than to increase profits.

Local Authorities

Creating a coaching culture

Many organizations, including Local Authorities, are committed to creating an internal coaching capacity for the purpose of providing coaching support throughout the organization. One of the drivers for doing so is the cost of using external coaches which prevents it from being available beyond the senior teams. One of the ways Local Authorities develop their internal coaching capacity is through internal programmes offered by local Universities or coach training providers. A group of Local Authorities in the North of England, for example, have collaborated to create jointly a coaching programme for the purpose of developing an internal capacity. The obvious benefits are the immediate financial savings as well as establishing a shared public sector coaching model which, if successful, could become a template of best practice to other Local Authorities and public sector organizations. Creating an internal coaching capacity has a number of advantages as well as disadvantages. The obvious advantages as suggested are the cost implication and the control of the process. Some of the immediately apparent disadvantages are issues of confidentiality and trust on the part of the coachee. There is the added question of whether a manager is capable of coaching his or her own staff and if the intervention could actually be defined as 'coaching' rather than just 'training'.

A further problem is the issue of time and how busy individuals may find this to include the provision of coaching whilst focusing and delivering the expectations of the role they are employed for. This in itself raises questions of job description. In our experience organizations also do not consider the ethical implications of internal coaching and issues of supervision. Developing a consistent internal coaching offering, taking into account some of the issues raised, is still some way off. During difficult economic times, nurturing incentives such as these are often neglected and left to wither before being established as the norm. Organizations often underestimate the time and commitment required in establishing a change of culture.

The acknowledged experts on creating a coaching culture, Clutterbuck and Megginson, caution that creating a coaching culture is testing and that it will take time to establish. Furthermore, '[i]t requires a sustained, thoroughgoing approach that addresses all of the critical drivers of the business, all of the key systems and most, if not all, of the activities people do. In essence, it is like genetic engineering – using the coaching virus to affect and bring about subtle changes in the operation of every cell in the corporate body'.[2] An organization will know it has been successful in establishing a coaching culture when it becomes the normative way of doing business within it.

A social focus

Coaching is traditionally associated with business and for the development of individual and team performance. However, one innovative Local Authority took the risk to provide coaching support in the development of a newly formed team. The express purpose of the team was to address the child poverty agenda of the government. The intention was to facilitate the establishment of a coaching culture within the team to enhance the work they do with the communities they operate in. A key assumption of coaching is the development of ownership and a responsibility within the coachee for the decisions and choices they make. In working with the individuals and families the team uses the tools and assumptions of coaching to engender a sense of opportunity and choice being available to them. A research project is underway to determine the possible benefits that coaching has had on the team and the possible impact it may have had on the individuals and families which are supported by the team.

Change and innovation coaching

In 2004, Sir Peter Gershon produced a report based on his review of public sector efficiency for HM Treasury.[3] In it he identified opportunities to embed efficiency across the sector and it is in response to his report that one such Local Authority decided to rise to the challenge using a coaching approach. The continual demand of a consumer market requires increased innovation and creativity and the public sector is not exempt from these pressures to find better and more efficient ways of delivering customer value. However, innovation and creativity are not traditionally associated with local government. It is also at the mercy of political pressures and particularly the need for change in the services agenda and the way in which it responds to such change. As with many organizations, Local Authorities have traditionally abdicated responsibility for change by employing external consultants to do it on their behalf. The result is that the embedded culture of the authority remains unchanged. The senior management team of the Local Authority in question, having experienced personal and team coaching, decided to use a coaching approach to change. The decision was to apply the support of coaching to facilitate change through action learning.

A pilot programme was established and if completed successfully, would create a model for best practice. The project team initially experienced high levels of frustration at what they saw as a delay in finding solutions and taking action. They were learning one of the fundamental approaches to coaching, namely that of dialogue and reflection to build a thorough understanding of their situation before exploring possible solutions. Traditional approaches to change are often driven by an unrealistic need to identify solutions immediately without clearly defining or understanding all aspects of the change situation. In this example the coaching process forced them to understand the drivers and values of the authority which have influenced past and present assumptions and behaviour. These tensions were not only apparent with the project team, but also the senior management team who ultimately had to approve the solution and project plan identified by the project team. The balancing and meeting of these complex layers of needs require high level coaching competencies and skills. The complexities also manifested themselves in collusion between the project team and the hierarchy. One of the challenges for the coach was to try and shield the coaching environment from the political and personal agendas threatening to derail the process, whilst at the same time challenging the project team. Upon reflection, the coach commented that at times all he could do was to rely on and have faith in the coaching process to deal with the barriers and resistance in response to the difference in approach to change. As well as developing a sense of ownership for the project, the team also developed a much greater sense of pride in the service being offered to their customers.

One of the factors which contributed to the success of the project was the selection of a dedicated team to focus exclusively on the change project, removing them from their day-to-day responsibilities. This went some way in lessening the tensions of dealing with business as usual whilst at the same time learning to do things differently. It was also a multi-disciplinary team, again a break with tradition. A requirement for learning is the ability to build collective pictures of a new future, thereby fostering a commitment to change versus compliance, which is often the case when change is imposed. This is exactly the process the project team went through. The initial framework was provided by the senior management team, but it was the project team, with the aid of coaching, that had to build that collective vision of what the structure of the service provision should look like and how the services would be delivered. Feedback from both the project team as well as observers of the project identified coaching as a key factor to the success achieved by the project team. The coaching intervention kept the team on track and prevented them from being distracted by external issues.

Another key to success was the fact that those who were responsible for the implementation of change were also empowered to provide the solutions. The responsibility initially caused the project team anxious moments as they had been stretched beyond their comfort zones. This was also the experience of the senior management who had their authority to impose solutions thwarted. The team started with more or less a blank sheet of paper and this in itself generated fear, exhilaration, and scepticism within the group not to mention a similar response from some members of the senior management team. The difficulty the senior team faced was resisting the temptation to do what they had always done, namely handing down instructions and imposing solutions on the project teams; the challenge was to trust that the team was going to design a structure to meet the community's services needs by delivering sustainable solutions.

Upon reflection, the learning they identified was both at a personal as well as a team level. They went from a group which had never made presentations to an audience within or without the organization to a team that formulated and designed the vision and plan for an innovative project, delivering their recommendations to the senior management team for approval. The successful outcome was the acceptance of their recommendations by the Board. One successful project team will not, of course, constitute a radical change to the culture of an organization, especially one which is permeated by layers of tradition and hierarchy. It has, however, demonstrated that coaching has the power to act as a catalyst for change.

Leadership programme

Our experience of coaching within Local Authorities included a request by another Authority to support an organization-wide leadership development programme for a tier of senior managers. The programme included workshops over a period of time as well as a 360-degree feedback questionnaire. The results of the feedback questionnaire were interpreted and an action plan was determined with the help of a coach. Each manager had two confidential meetings with an external coach. This was highly successful in challenging the perceptions often associated with a 360-degree feedback questionnaire through offering support in identifying how to integrate the feedback into their personal development plan.

Overall the coachees were cooperative and willing to learn, given that the decision for coaching was made on their behalf. The review of the process suggested initial cynicism as to the benefits of the coaching sessions, but an overriding feeling was that it had been more beneficial than they had at first anticipated. Some felt a third coaching session after the completion of the leadership programme would have kept the momentum and focus going and reinforced responsibility in achieving the agreed outcomes. The general consensus was that coaching offered a valuable space for reflection, weighing up the pros and cons of further development opportunities. The coaching intervention supported the managers in going back to respondents where there were concerns or a lack of clarity in the scores, and for the purpose of understanding how they are perceived and what they can do to develop those particular areas identified as in need of further development. It is safe to say that this would not have occurred without the input of the coach. Some individuals applied for new roles and saw coaching as providing the time to explore the possibilities and the consequences of doing so as well as providing them with the confidence to see it through.

Local Authorities are not different from other organizations, public or private, and there is a distinct absence of support given to newly appointed directors in coming to grips with what it means to be a director and how to let go of the operational role, no matter how successful they might have been in it. Some newly appointed directors naturally fit into the new role and its responsibilities. However, the majority experience a tension between letting go of the old and embracing the new. The inability to delegate and manage this tension may lead to high levels of stress and eventual burnout if it is not addressed. An unintended outcome for some of the participants on the leadership programme was the help coaching gave in facilitating a transition from an operational to a strategic role.

The NHS

Not only is the NHS the biggest employer within the UK, but it is also one of the greatest advocates and users of coaching. Coaching within the NHS is seen as a tool through which to develop its people to enable them to rise to the challenges the organization faces and the ability to maximize performance. Executive coaching is one of the core elements of the NHS Institute's support offered to Chairs, Chief Executives, and Executive Directors. The NHS is fully aware of the need to provide such a resource for newly appointed Directors as they confront the challenges of the job, particularly at the time of writing. At that time the NHS faced tremendous pressures for improvement and efficiencies as a national election loomed, and the cuts in spending to be expected of it regardless of which party emerged victorious. The NHS recognizes that it is especially during trying times that the productivity of the Board plays an exceptionally important role in the performance of their organization. The NHS Institute has commissioned a register that provides the opportunity to Board members in working with highly specialist individual coaches to drive performance improvement, tackle difficult governance issues, and explore development initiatives for whole teams. The focus in selecting coaches is on work and performance issues and to enable senior individuals in the NHS to maximize the deployment of their own skills and talents, as well as those of their teams. In addition to external coaching support offered to board members through the registers, the NHS is also committed to grow and develop its internal coaching capacity. Individuals who put themselves forward as internal coaches are given the opportunity to undergo a training programme to develop a competency in coaching.

In supporting the drive to establish a coaching culture within the NHS the National Leadership Council and the NHS Institute for Innovation and Improvement, aided by the European Mentoring and Coaching Council (EMCC), hosted the first NHS coaching conference in 2010. The purpose was to promote the value of coaching in dealing with the challenges faced by the management teams in the NHS and to experience how coaching is able to encourage cultural change in finding solutions to these. Coaching is identified as having the power to impact positively on relationships which enhance the effectiveness of the Board. The target audience included Board members and senior leaders, as well as clinicians, emergent leaders, HR and OD professionals, and internal coaches. The conference provided a mixture of expert speakers, workshops, and interactive sessions to generate ideas on the future of coaching within the NHS and how it can make a positive difference on performance, quality, and innovation across the whole of the system. Feedback from the delegates suggests it was a tremendous success with calls for it to become a regular event in the annual calendar. The challenge for the NHS is to sustain and build on the momentum created at the event.

The BBC

The interest in coaching originated during the time of Greg Dyke as Director General (2000–4). He asked the staff to make things happen rather than wait to be told what to do. This provided Liz McCann with the opportunity to follow her passion to bring coaching to the BBC. At the time of writing, they have 70 internal coaches with more going through the training programme which will allow them to become internal coaches within the organization. As with the Local Authority mentioned above, the internal coaches within the BBC have a day job in addition to that of being a coach. Furthermore, the internal coaches do not receive any financial rewards for being a coach. One candidate commented on a common problem facing internal coaches, namely combining coaching and their responsibilities as managers: 'I don't have enough time for the day job but I make this a priority – because this has a significant impact on my job as a manager.'[4] Managing the process and keeping the momentum maintained is sometimes difficult. Candidates interested in becoming an internal coach have to take part in a rigorous selection process which also requires them to be involved in a continual process of development, which includes group supervision sessions. To avoid some of the downsides of internal coaching identified above, the BBC has a rule that no coach is assigned a coachee from their own BBC division. Coaches also need to demonstrate significant coaching experience before they are able to coach anyone in a position more senior to that of their own. The benefits identified are numerous with an overall sense that they are in a position to be much better managers having undergone coach training. It also acts as a significant feedback mechanism for the organization.

Nokia

The giant global manufacturer of mobile devices and mobile multimedia places a high priority on development opportunities for all employees, with a strong support for continuous learning. Although Nokia actively facilitates coaching, unlike the approach of the BBC, it has chosen not to put rigid processes in place to manage its activities in this area. The company makes a substantial investment in coaching and encourages all managers to coach their teams by providing them with appropriate training. Nokia also employs the services of external coaches, but internal to a lesser extent, sharing the belief of other organizations that coaching enhances leadership capability as well as supporting the development of a coaching culture. It identifies a further benefit, namely that of employee retention and engagement. One way in which line managers will employ their skills of coaching is within the context of agreeing the personal development plan (PDP) of their subordinates. The focus will be on the development needs, learning styles, and future career aspirations of the individual. Coaching also forms part of some of the leadership programmes used to develop the leaders of the organization.

Career coaching at Orange

There seems to be different stages in the acceptance and evolution of coaching and its applications. In the early stages individuals or organizations perceive coaching as being remedial by nature. Once the benefits become apparent, coaching is then part of the process to develop the performance of the individual or team, especially when there appears to be a plateau in performance or relationship issues in the case of a team. However, as with any form of intervention, coaching adds value at different levels of development of both the individual and organization. One organization that has recognized this is Orange. Not only do they integrate coaching into the leadership and personal development programmes, but they have also included it as a key factor in their talent development strategy. A group of volunteer line managers have been trained as career coaches providing support to employees who do not directly report to them. In keeping with the essence of coaching, Orange is keen to encourage employees to take responsibility for their own careers. Being in a competitive market, it is important for Orange to develop and retain the talent that they have. The career coaching programme is a result of feedback from the employees who welcomed the opportunity to explore their career choices within Orange before looking outside of the organization. Not only does this approach develop and retain talent, but it also helps to ensure that the right person is in the right job. This programme is available to anyone in the organization, irrespective of level or grade. The uptake for career coaching came as a surprize with 10% of the employee population expressing an interest.

General conclusions

Many individuals and organizations seek the support of coaching for the purpose of grooming talented managers for more senior positions. This is true in both the public and private sectors. In our experience the result may also be that as part of the process the individual manager may realize that future opportunities lie outside of his or her current organization. This can be a positive aspect both for the individual and the organization as growth sometimes means a change of environment. The outcome will depend on the motivations of both the individual as well as the organization, as our experience with one organization will testify. We worked with a large American multinational organization for the purpose of developing some of their up-and-coming leaders of the future. One such individual was a highly qualified and capable German woman who was being groomed to replace the existing Vice-President of Europe. The brief was that her Germanic approach was seen as unpalatable by some of her American bosses. The outcome of the coaching intervention was that she realized the changes expected of her in style and approach would have resulted in an incongruence with her personal values. In consequence, she left the organization for one which more closely reflected her own values and beliefs. This story is not uncommon and as Michael Cavanagh reflects: 'It is not unusual for individuals to be referred for coaching in the hope that they will be "fixed" and that their negative impacts on team or group performance might be alleviated.'[5] The coach has the challenge of balancing the needs of the different stakeholders and it is not always entirely clear as to who the client is. If done well, coaching can act as catalyst in solving entrenched relationship issues within the organizations. Although our experience suggests that most individuals as well as organizations who seek out coaching do so for the purpose of investing in the potential of the individuals or teams. There are, however, occasions when coaching is perceived as remedial or seen as a possible exit strategy for someone the organization may want to shed.

Furthermore, coaching is also effectively employed by organizations during a time of redundancies. Every individual is affected by redundancy in different ways. It can lead to feelings of failure and an inability to understand that it is the job that is redundant not the person. Coaching establishes a bridge between the employee facing redundancy and the current job market and aids the individual in developing a more positive attitude to the situation. Coaching is also able to explore the initial sense of loss the individual will experience, whilst at the same time encouraging him or her to celebrate their successes and good times they have had in their career with the organization. This helps to bring closure on the current situation before focussing on future goals and career objectives. It offers employees the support, encouragement, and advice they need as they prepare to leave the organization. Coaching within this situation is used to explore new avenues, aid the individual in identifying what to do next, and to create a strategy on how to achieve it. It also helps the individual in building confidence that might have been destroyed through the redundancy process, highlighting opportunities, and increasing self-awareness of the skills they have to offer the marketplace.

These are just some examples of the applications of coaching in our experience and some of the case studies collected by the CIPD. No doubt there are numerous different ways in which coaching benefits both individuals and organizations in the private and public sectors. As discussed in Chapter 2, there is a strong drive from both industry and the coaching community to regulate the emerging profession through the provision of training, development, and accreditation for the purpose of developing and maintaining the reputation of the emergent profession. It is interesting to note, however, that one of the largest and most successful retail giants in the UK, in their application brief for the selection of external coaches to work with their senior teams, stated that their experience has been that neither paper qualifications nor client recommendations are necessarily to be taken as reliable guides as to the quality of what is on offer in the executive coach marketplace. Instead, they have found that coach assessment centres are the best way through which to determine competencies, ethics, and a best fit with their organizational culture. This raises a very important point mentioned in Chapter 2 that coaching is a very personal intervention and different organizations will require different approaches. The question which remains unanswered at this stage is whether individuals and organizations are able to determine objectively the type of intervention that would benefit them at a particular time in their evolution.

Reflecting on the many organizations which develop internal coaching programmes for the purpose of creating their own capacity to coach, from a critical perspective we feel moved to question the motivations for doing so. Are organizations mainly motivated by the savings made from not being reliant on external coaches? It is understandable, as external coaches are expensive, but what might be the price to the organization? One of the case study organizations also confessed that they were hoping to see an improvement in the annual staff feedback survey, which leads to a further questioning of the motivation for introducing coaching in the organization in the first place. As we have seen from all of the case studies in this chapter, every one of the internal coaches is expected to coach over and above normal duties without any compensation – either monetary or time in lieu. Are organizations doing coaching on the cheap and therefore denying themselves the full benefit of what it is capable of offering? There are many potential pitfalls with internal coaching such as shared blind spots and culturally driven behaviour. How effective or willing is an internal coach fundamentally to confront the dominant assumptions and paradigms of the organization if they are an integral part of it? Would internal coaching have had the credibility and power to question the mindsets of the banks and prevent the behaviour that has led to their demise? We would argue it is questionable.

There is also the issue of the quality of coaching being developed. Many of the programmes aimed at developing internal coaches are often of only two to three days' duration, and the level of expertise a coach can develop in such a short space of time must seriously be doubted. Furthermore, not all organizations take into account the ongoing development of coaches, nor the need for regular supervision. Where supervision is part of the process, it is also provided internally and the same questions as to the level of quality and challenge apply. Private sector organizations, in particular, have traditionally chased the holy grail of management and organizational fads for the purpose of finding solutions to their problems. More often than not these fads do not result in sustainable benefits and only serve to increase the wealth of the consultants and gurus who peddle the miraculous cures. Furthermore, they create change fatigue within the rank and file who have to implement the latest fashionable solution. Often the reasons why these interventions do not produce the expected results are due to the short-term view of many organizations and a perspective that the latest fad will act as a magic bullet. If results are not immediately forthcoming, enthusiasm wanes and is replaced by the next fad, whatever that may be. The challenges organizations face are complex and one solution can never provide answers to all. There is a danger that coaching might fall victim to the same fate as other valuable interventions and not be given the time and commitment in being developed as part of the organizational culture. There is also a danger that it is introduced and mechanically practised, becoming merely another tick in the box. We shall go on next, however, to consider where coaching runs up against barriers that can curb its potential quite severely.

4
The Limitations of Coaching

Organizational practices and discourses are prone to suppressing voices that raise doubts about the validity of their taken-for-granted beliefs and ideologies. John O. Ogbor asserts that organizations are socially constructed ideologies that, 'legitimize the power relations of managerial élites within an organization and society at large'.[1] It could be argued that organizations seen from a postmodernist perspective may be perceived as institutions which suppress conflicting interests and thereby fuel corporate hegemony. A postmodernist epistemology encourages different perspectives which may therefore offer new possibilities. The same would be true of a critical approach to coaching and its ability to offer a challenge to the entrenched worldviews of the individual or organization. A perceived weakness not of coaching, but of the recipients of coaching such as leaders and organizations, is their unwillingness to engage in a critical analysis of personal values, group norms, ideologies, and associated behaviour. This scepticism is borne out by Vega Zagier Roberts and Michael Jarrett in a discussion as to how clients select coaches and how irrational the process may be at times:

> Furthermore, what people hear when given information about a potential coach is filtered through a complex set of desires, fears, and prejudices, some conscious and others unconscious, which vary over time. Clients may make a choice based on what they believe to be rational criteria, whereas in fact they may be influenced by the unconscious desire to find a coach who will not take them too far out of their 'comfort zone'.[2]

De Vries et al. also note the lack of deeper reflection involved: 'Too many leadership coaches and executive education providers only see the obvious. They are too quick to jump to conclusions that lead to superficial solutions.'[3] As we will go on to discuss in subsequent chapters, the destructive practice of group-think goes to extreme lengths to protect itself from possible challenge and scepticism.

One could argue that organizations continue to be dominated by a modernist philosophy which reinforces a hierarchical structure and a mechanistic command and control culture often referred to as *Fordism*. Such a culture takes pride in its perceived logic and reason; a notion to be called into question by our study as a whole. Many of the models which underpin coaching are sympathetic to a modernist philosophy which regards a successful outcome of coaching to be the achievement of measurable goals and objectives. This is questioned by Clutterbuck, who points out that there is a danger of the coach manipulating the relationship in favour of her own agenda: 'This is especially true with regard to goal setting, where our researches indicate that fixing upon specific goals at the start of a relationship can sometimes be a crutch for the coach, rather than for the benefit of the coachee.'[4] Much of the literature on coaching is driven by tools and techniques, rather than an underlying philosophy to support the tools and techniques. Brockbank and McGill back up our critique of a lack of a coaching philosophy underpinning the practice of many coaches, and caution as follows: 'Because the philosophy that underlies any approach will impact on its outcome, we recommend that practitioners take time to examine their philosophy, however embedded it might be, and make this known to prospective clients.'[5] One such model which has dominated the understanding and practice of coaching is the GROW model put forward by Whitmore, which, as we have noted, has been criticized for its simplicity. Clutterbuck concurs: 'Some of the dangers we observed in this one-model approach were that: coaching becomes mechanistic; critical clues to the client context are missed or ignored; and – whatever may be claimed to the contrary – the client can easily become manipulated to fit the coach's agenda.'[6] We will argue throughout the book that in principle critical coaching is best placed to challenge these taken-for-granted beliefs and ideologies of organizations and their leaders. However, the current literature on coaching, particularly performance and leadership coaching, is based on the positivistic paradigm which has dominated management literature since Taylorism and its underlying need for measurable outcomes. The success of coaching is dependent on numerous factors, such as the willingness of the coachee to be coached.[7] The quality of the relationship between the coach and coachee is paramount to the success of coaching. The person-centred coaching psychologist argues that by accepting the coachee in a non-judgemental and authentic space, she will be self-determining and motivated to achieve her optimal level of functioning.[8] This raises some interesting questions as to the ethical guidelines of coaching. How willing or effective will the coach be in encouraging reassessment of behaviour that may have a detrimental effect on others as well as the wider system within which the individual operates?

A deep-seated view of positivism is that of order and pattern and it seeks an explanation of what is observed. It stands to reason that if the management discourse is dominated by assumptions of positivism then the practice of coaching within organizations will follow the same pattern. The claims associated with many of the coaching models are queried, with Kemp, for example, pointing out that despite the popularity some of these models may have gained among coaches and coachees alike, many make erroneous claims of validity; claims supported by tenuous evidence which remain unfounded.[9] He goes on to argue that the purpose of these claims is to help coaches in differentiating themselves in an increasingly crowded marketplace. These criticisms are echoed by Garvey et al., who complain that the breadth and quality of available research in coaching remains fragmented and rudimentary.[10] The eclectic mix of books available on coaching clearly indicates the diversity of approaches and models to coaching. There is therefore an absence of an overall framework as to what constitutes coaching and how the value and effectiveness of coaching is to be measured. Measurement within organizations tends to favour quantitative data which reflects the dominant positivist paradigm, yet the complexities of the coaching approach means that qualitative measures are possibly better suited in identifying the value of coaching.

In Chapter 3, which presented case studies of where and how coaching is applied, we mentioned how a number of organizations are endeavouring to introduce a coaching culture into their organizations, but with varying degrees of success. As Clutterbuck and Megginson warn organizations attempting to establish a coaching culture: 'Achieving a coaching culture, however, is an on-going commitment far more difficult to budget for. The financial cost is implicated by the need to change attitudes and practices that relate to just about every aspect of the business.'[11] A further difficulty is, as observed above, the eclectic mix of what is perceived as coaching. This means that even within one organization there could be numerous interpretations as to the nature of coaching and therefore vastly different applications. One such example is the NHS, as discussed in Chapter 3. The NHS is committed to embedding coaching as a means of developing their staff, but if each Trust approaches it from their own particular brand and interpretation, then there is no consistency across the organization. This could very well lead to confusion and a possible cynicism as to the value of coaching in developing the coachees. As is emphasized throughout this book, however, a metanarrative of coaching is also not necessarily the answer.

Another growing product offering of coaching is that of team coaching. It could be argued that the motivation is financial as the cost of coaching a team is considerably less than coaching the individuals of the team. However, team coaching could possibly better address some of the relationship issues within a team collectively than only working with team members individually. The boundaries between what is identified as action learning, facilitation, and coaching become blurred with group coaching and the jury is still out on whether team coaching actually exists and whether it is not merely another label for other forms of action learning. Commenting on an attempt at establishing a theory of team coaching, Garvey et al., strike a sceptical note:

> [I]t is by no means clear that the authors have succeeded in developing any form of team coaching that is distinct from other forms of group intervention or other forms of coaching. We are doubtful, as things currently stand, if there is any evidence that can be stretched to develop a theory of team coaching.... [T]he empirical research base to support team coaching as a distinct form of coaching is extremely thin.[12]

Practitioners find it difficult to articulate exactly what coaching is and how they go about it. This makes the evaluation of coaching that much more difficult and as Elouise Leonard-Cross notes: 'It is questioned whether coaching offers a valuable return on investment (RoI) for organizations and studies have identified different figures for this.'[13] Adding to the debate of measuring the impact of investment in coaching, Clutterbuck and Megginson point out that this 'is much more difficult, because like investment in customer care, or employee welfare, the organizational benefits are often indirect'.[14] Instead, as Maj Karin Askeland observes, '[i]n my experience from the coaching community, coaches often turn to the mystical in explaining what it is they actually do.'[15] They argue that it cannot be explained and, instead, has to be experienced. Askeland delivers a sharp criticism when he adds that, '[t]his shows a lack of critical reflection in the coaching community on what it is we actually do as coaches, where it comes from and what the theoretical assumptions are.'[16] The lack of critical reflection prevents the practice from measuring its successes as well as its limitations. This may be due to the fact that coaching has attracted professionals from a wide variety of disciplines and their numerous sub-disciplines such as psychology, counselling, and therapy, as well as various disciplines within business and management. There are those proponents who suggest that the confusion as to the nature of coaching is damaging to the professionalism of coaching. On the other side of the continuum are those proponents who insist that coaching should not be judged on a common definition, but claim it is the outcome of the intervention that is important. The absence of clarity also makes it difficult to determine the criteria by which one would judge a reputable coach.

There is much reference made in the literature of a need for regulation and a consistency to the coaching practice. The blurring of boundaries between the different disciplines add to the difficulty of a clear definition and practice of coaching. As Peltier poses in the introduction to his latest book on the psychology of executive coaching: 'What is real? What is bogus? What is coaching and what is psychotherapy? Where does psychology fit into coaching practice? Who should coach? And how? These questions remain without a definitive answer.'[17] An added complexity is clarity regarding the different therapies as highlighted by Brockbank and McGill: 'The literature can be confusing, as neither counselling nor psychotherapy is a clearly defined concept'.[18] However, we contend that the emerging profession would do well to consider the scepticism of critical thinking, as put forward by thinkers like Lyotard, and to be outlined in

Part II. A critical approach would allow the emerging profession to be clear as to the consequences of creating a metanarrative of coaching. The benefits coaching provides through the many 'little voices' that Lyotard refers to, and the diversity of practices and models, in turn reflects the diversity of individuals and organizations who seek the support of coaching. Such a criticism is added by David B. Peterson, who argues that humans are complex and multifaceted, and reinforced by Garvey et al.: 'One size does not fit all'.[19] Peterson also suggests that the multifaceted life of the coachee includes their interaction with their equally multifaceted life; past, present, and future and their interactions with everyone and everything around them. He concludes, '[t]herefore, behavioral approaches that reduce complex human behavior to mechanistic stimulus-and-response chains will not succeed.'[20]

An inherent weakness of the humanistic philosophy which underpins coaching may lead to a coach becoming too close to the coachee and their personal development needs. This may result in the coach colluding with the coachee in their reality and therefore failing to provide one of the key benefits of coaching, namely the ability to question one's assumptions, values, and behaviour. The value of scepticism and critical thinking is therefore not only for the benefit of the coachee and the organization, but for coaches too, inviting them constantly to reflect on their approach to the practice of coaching. The result is that the coach will then be able to provide the *tough love* which is associated with the value of the coaching intervention. The coach is not the friend of the coachee, as friends conspire with each other and may reinforce their particular worldview without question for fear of upsetting the relationship. In its purest form, coaching is not blind to the weaknesses of the coachee and through non-judgemental support is there to inspire the coachee to develop a balanced self-awareness which includes both her strengths and weaknesses. The coachee is then able to make different choices, if she so wishes.

The lack of clarity as to the exact nature of coaching also means that both coaches and coachees sometimes have trouble in identifying the boundaries between coaching and other interventions such as counselling or therapy. This becomes even more problematic when distinguishing between organizational and life coaching, which could possibly have a greater overlap with therapy as coaching is likely to focus more explicitly on the personal issues of the client. This means that coaches might inadvertently stray into areas and situations they are not equipped to deal with. John Price offers a general description by way of separating coaching from therapy, which suggests it is short term, future focused, less deep, and focused on achieving specific goals or objectives.[21] There is also a general assumption that clients of coaching are mentally healthy. Categorizing people in this way is problematic in itself and a constructionist philosophy would argue that such a label would be socially constructed and could potentially be damaging to the individual. The temptation to assign labels of one kind or another to a client should therefore be approached with sensitivity and caution. The converse may also be true if a therapist makes a transition into coaching, the temptation may be to approach coaching from a therapeutic perspective, which may not necessarily be appropriate for the client. This situation highlights the need for the coach to enter an explicit contract with the client which will meet her specific needs.

Gergen writes extensively on the subject of mental illness to illustrate how a community's understanding of what constitutes this condition influences what becomes the *reality* of mental illness and how it is socially and culturally created (a point established earlier by Michel Foucault in his controversial book *Madness and Civilization*[22]). By current definitions of 'mental deficiency', the assumption is that the person suffering from such a deficit is the victim of an external force over which they have no control. Psychology as a profession absorbs and transforms the everyday language of a culture and 'technologizes' it, making it the possession of the profession. The claim to knowledge then shifts from the everyday realm to that of a body considered to have superior knowledge, disqualifying the knowledge of the layperson. The common language is devalued and silenced thereby stifling its pragmatic potential, and the profession disseminates deficits into the culture which get absorbed and incorporated into daily life – such as *stress*, *depression*, and *identity crisis*. Once such terms become part of everyday vocabulary they gain a status, and thus a hold over our thoughts and actions, when they may otherwise have gone unnoticed. In turn, such knowledge informs future behaviour and beliefs: 'In effect, the culture learns *how to be* mentally ill'.[23]

The coaching relationship is also in danger of potential abuse and the exercise of power. It could be that the executive being coached feels it necessary to exert his authority over the coach and intimidate her in the same way as he might his subordinates. Conversely, the coach may use her specialist skills to manipulate the coachee. As Peter Welman and Tatiana Bachkirova concede, there is inherent within everyone the potential desire to impose our will on someone else.[24] Power can be very seductive and Foucault argues throughout his writings that it is the source of most of the evils to be found within society.[25] Garvey et al. dedicate a whole chapter in their book to issues of power as they relate it to coaching, and proffer the following warning: 'We should recognize that, as coaching becomes a more commonplace activity, issues of power, voice and discourse will become more important'.[26] Power as a concept permeates organizational theories and practices. The power dynamics between the coach and the coachee are particularly significant in the successful outcome of the coaching relationship. Rowan offers an alternative approach which eliminates the need for the expression of power: 'From a transpersonal point of view, the role of the coach is that of a companion along the way. There is no assumption of expertise, or leadership, or superiority in any way'.[27] The debate on power within the coaching relationship extends beyond that encountered between the coach and coachee to include the dynamics with and within the organization. The coaching contract needs to identify from the outset who the client is and whose objectives will be the focus of the coaching intervention. As has been suggested earlier, the tension arises when the objectives of the coachee are in conflict with the objectives of the organization. A critical skill of the coach is also to recognize the power dynamics of the relationships the coachee is involved in beyond the coaching relationship and which enter into the coaching space with the coachee. As we shall go on to discuss in Chapter 8, this can be a case of identifying the particular 'grammar' of the organization in question, the various codes, often implicit, that its employees operate by in their professional lives.

As mentioned earlier, at the heart of psychology is the need to fix that which is broken about an individual. Positive psychology has in recent years emerged as a counter-balance to the deficit mindset of traditional psychology and has gained significant popularity amongst coaches. Instead, of focusing on what is wrong or needs mending, the focus is on the strengths of the individual. This in itself is not particularly new as Aristotle believed that each individual has a unique spirit within herself which acts as a guide for the person to pursue what is right for her.[28] During the twentieth century, Carl Jung put forward his own concept of individuation, or the notion of becoming all that one is capable of being.[29] The humanistic psychologists were also critical of a pathological approach to human beings with the most famous being Carl Rogers who introduced the concept of the fully functioning person.[30] The person who has almost become a household name and the first psychologist to use the term 'positive psychology' was Abraham Maslow, who identified a hierarchy of needs which culminated in the self-actualization of the individual.[31] Its purpose is described by Kauffman as follows: 'The mission of positive psychology is to develop sound theories of optimal functioning and to find empirically supported ways to improve the lives of ordinary and extraordinary people.'[32] The focus on strengths in positive psychology holds out the promise that knowing your strengths will encourage an optimistic perspective to one's life which provides a sense of direction. Furthermore, it is suggested that such a focus helps to develop confidence and generates a sense of vitality which ultimately leads to a sense of personal fulfilment. There are, as is to be expected, the sceptics of positive psychology who suggest that it is an American Pollyanna approach to life and not reflective of a European mindset.[33] However, positive psychology claims rigorous empirical research to back up its hypotheses. Even if there was no validity in their arguments, one could argue that from a constructionist perspective, embracing its principles as *true* will lead to a more positive self-fulfilling prophecy which has to be more empowering to the individual than a truth based on a deficit mentality.

Regardless of the particular approach taken by a coach, the absence of critical reflection on the ideologies and assumptions that underpin their coaching will mean coaches are not equipped rigorously to offer a challenge to the ideologies and assumptions of their clients. A constructionist model, representing possibly the newest and most controversial theoretical model of coaching, gives a coach the opportunity to understand the approach to coaching they have constructed. From the social constructionist perspective, it is through the social interactions and symbolic frameworks within which one interacts that the social identities of the person are assembled. A constructionist paradigm contests the idea of a reality external to the individual and therefore the existence of an objective knowledge. Instead, an appreciation of the world is seen as being dependent on an understanding of how an individual shapes the world internally. Through the engagement with the coach in the coaching relationship the coachee creates and constructs her identity as opposed to discovering it.

Constructionism also supports the underlying philosophy of postmodernism, namely the notion of many little voices as opposed to a grand or metanarrative. This philosophy will also take issue with the school of thought that aspires to creating a clear definition and framework of coaching. From this perspective, the emphasis would be on the coach to develop a clear and transparent message as to the coaching they offer and, equally, do not offer. This caution is supported by Bachkirova and Kauffman who warn that, '[t]he ambiguity of the term "coaching" should not be a good excuse for coaches to be vague and overambitious about what they can offer.'[34] Taking a position against a metanarrative of coaching, translated into the practice of coaching, would mean that the coach would therefore be in a position to challenge both the individual and organizational grand narratives where she may find them. It also means that the need for an overall definition of 'what constitutes coaching' is counterproductive as one size will never fit the requirements of everyone; instead coaches will represent the *little voices* referred to by Lyotard. This may very well lead to a sense of dissatisfaction with the organization and a scepticism on behalf of the coachee as to the beliefs, values, and practices of the organization. This could create a possible conflictual relationship between the coachee and their organization. Where does this leave coaching?

This is an example of the possible ethical dilemma faced by a coach, namely to balance the needs of the individual client with that of the organization. It is not always clear-cut as to who the client actually is and therefore whose needs must come first. The waters are further muddied by the principles of CSR. In the last 20 years there has been a shift from an emphasis on the shareholder to that of the stakeholder within business. The transition has meant a greater engagement with stakeholders through dialogue and increased transparency in organizational activities and reporting structures. A significant expectation of CSR is an increased expectation on behalf of the public for companies to act as good corporate citizens. An underlying assumption is that organizations should focus on activities other than just making money – such as caring for the employees, suppliers, and society at large. However, judging on the basis of the behaviour of organizations in recent years, not to mention that of the banking sector, that raises questions as to the sincerity of organizations to take CSR really seriously.

In most caring professions, the needs and interests of the client takes precedence. However, it is more complex within an organizational setting where it is necessary to include the needs of different stakeholders. Adding to the complexity is the fact that the organization will often pay the bill of the coach, which then begs the question as to who is the client and whose interests does coaching serve? The coaching contract has to establish the rules of engagement from the outset, which should include confidentiality and reporting of progress and the raising of any emergent issues. It may be that maintaining an open mind as to what coaching is, or should be, will equip the coach better in meeting the diverse needs of the client and the complexity referred to. To call for a metanarrative of coaching raises all the questions of power and control that Lyotard spent much of his life confronting.

As a new and unregulated profession, an ethical framework is patchy and unless the coach is a member of one of the coaching associations, it is likely that she would be unaware of any ethical guidelines. Such frameworks and guidelines are merely advisory as they are not enforceable. Yet the nature of coaching dictates that sooner or later the coach is likely to face a dilemma which will require the support of an ethical framework to resolve the issue. Despite ethical frameworks, evidence from other caring professions suggests that clients rarely bring a complaint against their therapist. Instead, they vote with their feet and end the relationship. However, this approach does not support a case for the removal of unethical practitioners. In the absence of regulation, this would not be possible in any event. There are common themes to be found within the ethical frameworks of the various coaching associations. On closer inspection, however, these frameworks are inadequate in dealing with some of the complexities the coach is likely to face throughout her coaching career. One such theme is that the needs of the coachee are considered above those of anyone else. As raised earlier, this poses problems if the needs of the coachee are in competition with those of the organization, especially if the organization is footing the bill.

Another theme fraught with complexity is that of confidentiality and the question the coach will have to deal with at some stage is at which point is she obliged to break such confidentiality? In Chapter 9, we introduce a controversial concept of coaching leading to whistleblowing, and the same debate could be had in relation to coaching and confidentiality. How does the coach treat the information and knowledge they become party to within the confines of the coaching relationship? One route is for the coach to develop a heuristic based on a philosophical framework with which to underpin her coaching practice. A possible framework is the focus of this book: to develop scepticism which flows from critical theory. The sceptical coach will be willing to scrutinize the assumptions and ideologies not only of the coachee but also of the organization, for the purpose of deepening understanding and awareness of the behavioural drivers involved.

One way of overcoming some of the ethical dilemmas is by ongoing development of the coach through supervision. However, research seems to indicate that very few coaches actually engage in regular supervision sessions. There appears to be an implicit assumption among newly qualified coaches that once they have completed their chosen programme of study then further development and supervision is no longer necessary. Yet supervision provides invaluable support to the coach in dealing with the ethical complexities raised above. Coaching supervision is pivotal in the ongoing development of the professional coach and in providing the basis that coaches need for raising their self-awareness and awareness of their practice. It may very well be that the term 'supervision' is off-putting due to possible negative assumptions and images of control, monitoring, and judgement associated with it, particularly for coaches from a business background.

However, the increased knowledge of coaching on behalf of clients suggests it is the coach who can demonstrate and provide evidence of regular supervision who will have the competitive edge when tendering or competing for coaching assignments. Not only does supervision provide an individual coach with professional development, it also offers opportunities for reflective learning. Supervision is a formal process that can be pursued either on a one-to-one basis, group, or a combination of both. Peer supervision facilitated by an experienced coach allows participants to learn from each other and to explore what works and what does not. Both approaches allow coaches consciously to spend time on developing their practice and their particular brand of coaching. Unless an individual coach is part of an organization or a group of associates it can be lonely, and there will come a time in the career of any coach when she may be uncertain as to how effective she is being in meeting the needs of her clients. In order for the coach to gain benefit from the supervision, it has to take place regularly so that the breadth and depth of the coaching practice and framework can be systematically reviewed and developed. Supervision also provides assurance to the organization that any unethical or poor coaching is identified and improved upon. The supervisory approach inspects the practice of the coach and identifies ways in which she can best meet the needs of her client and the organization. A coaching client is always part of a wider system and complexities that surround their various relationships and roles. The supervisor is a valuable and impartial support to the coach in working out the dynamics and the influence on the client, and how the client presents these during the coaching sessions. As referred to above, complex ethical dilemmas also form part of the milieu of coaching and the impartial perspective of the supervisor provides support in understanding the complexity and sensitivity surrounding such situations. Irrespective of the approach by the supervisor, it offers a supportive space in which the coach can 'off-load' her own issues with the same degree of non-judgemental acceptance afforded to the coachee. It is not an optional extra but a competitive necessity.

Any new and emerging profession is likely to attract a range of advocates claiming to be equipped to practice and coaching is no exception. In some cases, as Passmore notes, counselling is seen as a proxy for coaching, and a cynic would suggest it is because coaching can demand a higher fee than counselling is able to do.[35] It is also much easier to offer one's services as a coach than as a counsellor since the coach is not required first of all to undertake formal training. In the absence of a professional body to regulate the profession, training and development is also *ad hoc* and as varied as the suppliers of such training. Courses vary from one day to a 2-year Masters degree and with many options in between. Brockbank and

McGill share this concern regarding the quality of training, observing that, '[a] vast choice of training is on offer, as more providers enter the field, not always of high quality.'[36] It is chilling to note the claims made by some providers who confidently assert that their programmes will lead to a lucrative income for newly qualified coaches. Various disciplines are also sold as being the 'holy grail' of coaching and as Clutterbuck warns, '[t]he aficionados of these philosophies or disciplines are often highly enthusiastic, but this enthusiasm may at times hide a dangerous trap – the implicit assumption that this philosophy, powerful as it may be, is always the best approach for every client.'[37]

As is to be expected of a new and evolving profession, there are numerous bodies of knowledge and communities of practice who will not only influence its practice, but who will also want to lay claim on its ownership. The lack of evidence-based research of coaching and an overall code of practice leads to criticisms such as those posed by Grant, who questions whether coaching is not merely a more socially acceptable form of therapy, particularly within organizations where the revelation of any form of internal conflict may be perceived as a weakness.[38] In the absence of an agreed model, Stewart et al. argue that it is difficult to evaluate the specific effects and outcomes claimed in the name of coaching.[39] Furthermore, it could be said that coaching will be subjected to the need for control, prediction, and uniformity of positivism, which as we noted earlier, has dominated management discourse since Taylor. This is further evidenced by Downey, who observes that the effectiveness of coaching tends to be measured by the achievements of those being coached.[40]

Furthermore, the lack of *evidence* associated with current coaching practices is problematic in itself as it would mean different things to different researchers just as the word *truth* has different interpretations, depending on the particular philosophical stance the researcher positions herself on. As things stand, coaching clearly does mean different things to different people and each coach approaches coaching with her own preference for a particular style, depending on her own experiences, education, and biases.[41] In the absence of a standardized approach to coaching, coaches have to adapt their style according to the needs and circumstances of the coachee. No matter what approach is adopted by the coach, it is dependent on one-to-one conversations, which is not necessarily a new phenomenon.

Furthermore, it has traditionally focused on a dyadic relationship between the coach and the coachee for the purpose of developing the personal performance of the client.[42] The same difficulty in defining the 'nature of coaching' applies to the task of identifying a reputable coach. Coaches come from very diverse backgrounds. Some have come through the psychological or therapeutic professions. Others were business consultants in a previous career. Some might be directors who have taken early retirement, and due to their knowledge of business see it is an opportunity to make their experience available to others; and so the list goes on.

On the other side of the argument, Grant suggests that the diversity of the profession is both a strength and a liability.[43] As we discuss elsewhere, postmodernism strongly advocates diversity and the promotion of difference, and opposes the metanarratives associated with many of our institutions and the power and control this leads to. Coaching as a profession would therefore do well to heed the scepticism of critical thinking and be aware of the consequences of creating a metanarrative of coaching. It may very well be that the benefits coaching provides need to reflect the diversity of individuals and organizations who seek the aid of coaching by equally diverse practices and models, without falling victim to the false illusion of a metanarrative.

An approach which may well provide a framework without imposing a narrative is that of andragogy. Travis J. Kemp puts forward a credible argument that all coaching intervention is encompassed within a broad, generic experiential learning process, or the theory of adult learning, and supported by a significant evidence-based body of knowledge.[44] The root theory of andragogy is a discipline of adult learning and development which is underpinned by deep reflection and introspection, scrutinizing assumptions for the purpose of creating new insight and awareness.

There are numerous claims made, some of a dubious nature, as to the outcomes of coaching which include a reduction in the experience of stress, improved leadership skills, and behavioural change. Furthermore, coaching seeks to influence and bring about changes in behaviour which will change and improve performance. However, Silsbee argues that performance coaching has its limitations and argues that it is often driven by organizational objectives, which may lead to a tension between the objectives of the organization and that of the client.[45] Change may require the client to discover new ways of seeing and interpreting events, which may also lead to changes in behaviour. A further challenge to the claims of coaching is how longer-term, sustainable change can be attributed to the coaching intervention, especially if some time has elapsed between behavioural change and coaching. Silsbee goes on to suggest that for new skills and competences to be sustained, they must be grounded in self-awareness and self-generation.[46] The focus of developmental coaching is on learning rather than performance. If, as we suggest, the influence of the modernist paradigm which dominates organizations permeates the practice of coaching, it would mean that it will be driven by the need for measurable outcomes and solutions. Performance coaching is also in danger of reinforcing existing paradigms and will not necessarily lead to the transformation often claimed by some schools of coaching.

As we have noted, many organizations that have benefited from a coaching intervention are endeavouring to instil a coaching culture by creating an internal coaching capacity. How could an internal coaching framework ever hope to challenge the mindset that has led to the meltdown of the banking industry? The critical coaching necessary to deliver such scepticism can only be achieved externally. Brockbank takes a similar line and states that '[s]uch a scheme is less likely to stimulate transformation, innovation and creativity'.[47] Based on the model by Burrell and Morgan identifying a reality dimension along a subjectivism/objectivism continuum, Brockbank argues that for transformation of an individual or organization to occur, it will only be achieved if existing views and the *status quo* is challenged.[48] Through the reflective practice of coaching, coachees are able to question both their own prevailing paradigms as well as that of the organizations within which they are embedded. It is difficult to see how an internal coach, paid by the organization, will be able to achieve this effectively.

On a larger scale, coaching could offer the same degree of development and change at the organizational level which is achieved at the individual level and serve to confront the assumptions and ideologies of the organization. However, as Garvey et al. point out, '[c]oaching and mentoring are essentially one-to-one practices and so those studying, researching and working in the area tend to ignore the wider, social and organizational implications of their work'.[49]

Coaching beyond the individual level to include the organization may prevent the group-think and illusion we have observed as so prevalent a factor within the bank sector. If coaching is to continue to gain credibility as a tool for leadership and organizational development, it should guard against falling victim to the illusion of quick fixes. There are overwhelming arguments to suggest that coaching is a powerful method for the development, growth, and learning of the individual, team, or organization. Identifying the overarching assumption as to what coaching is, Kemp states it is 'a human development methodology'.[50] This reflects a fundamental core value of coaching which has its origin in the caring professions, such as psychology, therapy, and counselling, or a humanistic approach to organizations, which means much of the coaching relationship is grounded on the support offered to the coachee. Coaching which includes a more thought-provoking approach advocated by a critical perspective may be better equipped to provide the sense of challenge and scepticism organizations and their leaders need to remain open to their own blind spots. The range of critical theory that is now available to us, and how it might be brought to bear on the coaching process, forms the topic of the remainder of the book, beginning with a survey of the theoretical realm in general in Part III.

Part III
Theory

5
The Rise of Critical Theory

The theorization of analytical principles has been an increasingly important concern of those working in the fields of the humanities and social sciences in recent years, leading to far more sophisticated and philosophically informed styles of critical analysis being developed. In this chapter, we shall be surveying the rise of critical theory from the later nineteenth century onwards, from Marxism and structuralism to poststructuralism, postmodernism, and feminism, and considering its impact both on academic disciplines and public life. The basic principles of the main schools of critical theory will be mapped out, as well as their rationale for adopting these, with close attention being paid to the social and political contexts involved in each case. The sceptical bias of the more recent critical theories, namely poststructuralism and postmodernism, will be emphasized, and the implications of such attitudes for coaching will be touched on, prior to a more extended treatment of the topic of scepticism, and its role in public life, in Chapter 6.

Critical theory in academic life and public life

Critical theory is an analytical tool that enables academics to construct a range of methods of interpretation. The same phenomenon can look very different indeed if viewed from a Marxist, feminist, or postmodernist standpoint – to cite just some of the many possibilities available to practitioners these days. Interpretation of phenomena is, of course, one of the primary concerns of an academic discipline, and critical theory as a body of work serves to expedite this. In terms of business studies, critical theory provides a means of interpreting organizations, and depending on the theory used, different insights can be gained about the effectiveness and efficiency of any given organization. Clearly, this has important implications for how coaching is conducted; especially since, as we noted earlier, organizations can vary quite considerably in what they require, or expect to receive, from coaching.

As its application to business studies shows, critical theory can reach out well beyond the academic ghetto with its essentially intellectual concerns. Critical theory has something to contribute to the way we live in the most general sense, and we wish to develop that aspect of it in terms of coaching. There are few things more public after all, than the world of work; almost all of us are involved in that at some point or other of our lives, and how we relate to, and operate within, our own particular organization is a matter of some social importance. It is not just a question of making ourselves more efficient at tasks delegated to us from above (still many people's experience in the workplace), but of how our input can help the organization to adapt and develop in response to a constantly changing socio-political climate. And the credit crunch has put a premium on such flexibility, demolishing many of our long-established assumptions about how the business world should operate. New models are urgently needed if we are to reconstruct this sector such that it regains not just the trust of the general public, but of its own employees as well. As the financial crisis has starkly revealed, we are all stakeholders in the business world: what happens there affects everyone.

Critical theory: A history

Critical theory has its roots in the history of Western philosophy, which means that we can trace back many of its concerns to classical Greek thought; in particular, as far as current trends go, to the tradition of scepticism that grew out of that cultural milieu. Critical theory might be broken down into two main groups: system-building and system-challenging (a further division that is made is between the formalist and the sociological, and we shall come back to that). The more recent critical theories tend to be less concerned with system-building, which was the focus of many of the earlier movements in the modern period, than with conducting a critique of systems in general. That is exactly the attitude we find embedded in classical scepticism, where the grounds of our knowledge are consistently being called into question. We shall be returning to scepticism later, but first let us consider the system-building theory *par excellence*, Marxism, to get a sense of the cast of mind involved.

Marxism is one of the most influential theories of the modern age, and it has infiltrated into pretty well every area of human experience. At base it is a philosophical theory, building particularly on G. W. F. Hegel's concept of the dialectic, but it quickly transforms itself into a socio-economic theory of the most ambitious kind, concerning itself with nothing less than the future organization of the human race. It is very self-consciously a 'theory of everything', claiming to cover all aspects of human existence, to be a 'science of society' that tells us how to plot social change in accordance with the operation of physical laws. As such it is also a quintessentially *sociological* critical theory. Hegel had argued that every thesis gave rise to its antithesis and that the struggle that ensued between the two entities was resolved by the emergence of a synthesis, which in its turn gave rise to a new antithesis as the process kept unfolding over time. For Hegel, in terms of human affairs this was a case of the World Spirit progressing to its highest stage of realization, which in his view was to be found in the Prussian state of his lifetime (Hegel being a high-profile figure in Prussian public life as a professor of philosophy at the University of Berlin).[1]

Marx took over the dialectical method but reached a very different conclusion as to what that highest stage was supposed to be. He too saw a struggle taking place, but this time over the course of human history between social classes, with the dominant one generating its antithesis which eventually overtook it in a new synthesis – that is, power structure. The final stage of this process, as far as Marx was concerned, would be the dictatorship of the proletariat, where that class would overcome its oppressors, the bourgeoisie (who had overthrown the feudal system at an earlier stage), and establish a classless social system where all goods would be held in common and economic exploitation would cease; in other words, a communist society, as argued for by Marx in *The Communist Manifesto*.[2] Hegel was propounding a metaphysical conception of human history, Marx on the other hand saw it in materialist, economic terms, thus the development of the analytical method of dialectical materialism.

In Marx's much-quoted observation, 'philosophers have only *interpreted* the world, in various ways; the point, however, is to *change* it'.[3] This was critical theory with a specific political mission, and that is how it has been received ever since by Marx's followers.

The whole thrust of Marxist theory is towards overcoming class antagonism and instituting a new social order, and although it does not think this will happen of its own accord, it does see an inevitability about the process once the working class comes to realize the extent of its exploitation and develops the appropriate sense of class consciousness to contest this condition and change its circumstances of existence. A major problem that Marxist theory had to face, however, was that after the Russian Revolution that class consciousness seemed to be very slow in developing elsewhere. The expectation had been that capitalism would collapse once its contradictions were properly exposed, and that would kick-start a global revolution. But capitalism proved to be more resistant than Marxist theory ever thought it would be, hence the recourse of the latter to the concept of hegemony to explain why this was so. How could it be that even the Wall Street Crash of 1929 and then the Great Depression it gave rise to were not enough to bring about mass rebellion?

Hegemony claimed that the ruling class contrived to embed its values in the rest of the population through indirect means, such as the education system, the media, and the arts. In that way we began to think those values were natural and that we should all be living up to them in our daily lives. We internalized them to the point where it was unnecessary to use force to keep us in line, thus entrenching the ruling class in power. Dissent was largely quashed and the working class prevented from reaching its destiny as Marxism perceived it. In effect, mass group-think set in.

Marxism soon generated several distinct schools, such as Western Marxism, which was more philosophically oriented than the Soviet form where economic factors loomed largest. Western Marxism is generally traced back to the early work of Georg Lukács, such as his controversial book *History and Class Consciousness*, which went on to inspire several generations of thinkers, such as the highly influential Frankfurt School.[4] The School's most acclaimed thinkers, Theodor W. Adorno and Max Horkheimer, devised an analytical method which they dubbed 'critical theory' (nowadays the term is used, as here in this book, to describe cultural theories in general), which combined the techniques of philosophy and the social sciences to study modern cultural phenomena. They applied the method to the Soviet Union as much as to Western society, and were among the few Marxist thinkers to be critical of the former during the 1930s and 40s, when it was presenting itself as the new hope for humankind. Their view of the world as Second World War came to a close, as outlined in *Dialectic of Enlightenment*, was very pessimistic.[5] Both the West and the Soviet Union were described as 'administered societies' allowing little real freedom of thought, and guilty of imposing a conformity of belief in their respective systems on their largely cowed citizens.

Another important thinker to emerge from the Frankfurt School tradition, Herbert Marcuse, who had settled in America after the war, held that his adopted country had become a 'one-dimensional' society, where political opposition to the capitalist system was effectively being stifled.[6] Again, this raised doubts as to the continuing validity of classical Marxist thought in a changing world order. Marcuse went on to query whether the nature of class struggle had altered in the new cultural climate, suggesting that the student movement of the 1960s, as well as various ethnic minority groupings (the black community, for example), were more likely to change society than a now fragmented working class which had largely lost its cultural identity.

Marxism politicized all human activities, giving it a clear agenda as a critical theory. Everything could be interpreted in terms of its ideological position and ideological impact, enabling commentators to make class-based judgements on whatever it was they were analyzing. The fact that it considered itself to be a universal theory meant that its methodology could be applied in any area of human endeavour. But it is precisely this claim to universality that has come under attack from the later twentieth century onwards, as theories such as poststructuralism and postmodernism have made such a point of emphasizing the limitations of human reason. Universalizing theories are no longer so much in vogue, and Marxism has suffered in consequence from the turn towards scepticism amongst not just intellectuals but the general public as well (although it has to be conceded that religion has been making a comeback in public life, thus countering the rise of scepticism to quite a significant degree in recent years).

The turn against Marxism is very symbolic, representing a growing suspicion of theories of everything amongst both intellectuals and the general public. The later twentieth century no longer has the same degree of belief in human reason (which also explains the rise of religious fundamentalism to a large extent, since it lays greater store in faith than reason), therefore not in system-building either. Before investigating what the retreat from rationalism involved, however, let us consider another universal theory which had a huge influence on twentieth-century thought – structuralism.

Structuralism, like Marxism, can be applied to any area of human activity, although it does not have Marxism's explicitly political agenda. In this case we are dealing with a formalist theory which explains how systems work, and the assumption is that the world is made up of a myriad of interlocking systems. Structuralism's roots lie in linguistics and it treats systems as being governed by an internal grammar that analysts can pin down with considerable precision; this is the 'linguistic model' popularized by theorists such as Roland Barthes, drawing heavily on the pioneering work of the language theorist Ferdinand de Saussure.[7] Chess, for example, has a set of rules which dictate what players can do within the game, thus constituting its grammar. Those rules must be followed by all participants, although they could be changed, as long as they then become the new convention everyone abides by: there could only be one set of rules in play at any one time, otherwise the game would descend into chaos.

Structuralism's goal was to catalogue the grammar of all the systems that human beings were involved with, and in that way we could build up a comprehensive understanding of our world. We responded to all systems as collections of signs, which prompted predictable reactions in us (much as traffic lights, one of the most rudimentary of sign-systems, do). Sign-systems, as Barthes pointed out, generate narratives, and our world is in fact saturated by narrative, from the very simple to the very complex:

> The narratives of the world are numberless. Narrative is first and foremost a prodigious variety of genres, themselves distributed amongst different substances – as though any material were fit to receive man's stories.... [N]arrative is present in myth, legend, fable, tale, novella, epic, history, tragedy, drama, comedy, mime, painting (think of Carpaccio's *Saint Ursula*), stained glass windows, cinema, comics, news item, conversation.[8]

Why those narratives have the effect on us they do is what structuralist analysis reveals: the more we delve into the inner workings of their respective grammars, the more knowledgeable we become about human behaviour in general. Organizations clearly each have their own particular grammar, and working out what this is and how it manages to induce reasonably predictable responses in the organization's members, helps one to orient oneself within the system and to realize one's goals within it. It can also point out where the grammar is possibly working against the system's best interests and needs to be altered (as all such sets of rules can be). Structuralism remains a powerful theory when it comes to understanding the form that systems take, and there is still mileage to be had in analyzing systems from this perspective, as we shall go on to demonstrate in Chapter 8.

Structuralism does have some political implications in terms of its conception of the individual. One of Barthes' most provocative concepts is 'the death of the author', which held that authors of texts could not control them once they passed out into general circulation.[9] Individuals were not bound by the particular interpretations that an author had put on his or her text, and could adapt it to their own concerns and experiences instead (as Barthes saw it, the reader took over from the author). In other words, the meaning of the text was not fixed, and could change over time depending on what individuals read into it, drawing on their own experience. Interpretation was always occurring and authors could not stop that from happening; the text took on a life of its own once it passed into general circulation. In terms of organizations, that could mean a greater diversity of opinion being present within their ranks as to the validity of their objectives, or official policies, than the managements involved might think there was, or even wanted there to be; organizational narratives being no less open to multiple interpretation than their fictional counterparts are.

Poststructuralism came to regard structuralism as an overly predictable method which imposed an order on phenomema that was not really there. Thus Jacques Derrida's deconstruction set out to demonstrate that structuralism was based on false assumptions, including a belief that linguistic meaning could be unproblematically communicated between individuals. Words, Derrida would argue, were always in a process of flux as regards their meaning, and there was consistent slippage in discourse. Meaning was never absolute or precise; it was more a case of there being a range of meanings and nuances present at any one time, and for these to be different for each person involved in the linguistic exchange, since their personal experience differed. Traces of other discourses were ubiquitous in any exchange, rendering the notion of absolute meaning impossible; the supposed purity of meaning was always being contaminated, a process that could not be arrested (rather like the 'death of this author' in this respect). Western thought was based on a 'metaphysics of presence', which assumed that the meaning of any word or phrase was present in both the speaker's and listener's mind, and that these meanings were identical.[10] Derrida opened up the possibility of communication being a far more anarchic affair than it had previously been considered, and for there to be far more gaps (aporia) in the process than we were prepared to admit. Meaning was always being deferred, we were constantly in a state of becoming rather than being (a long-running philosophical debate in itself). From a Derridean perspective, we could never have total understanding of the world around us, which was characterized by difference and thus highly unpredictable. It is a typical claim of the poststructuralist–postmodernist movement: that there are limitations to the power of reason, and that we delude ourselves to think otherwise. As we shall go on to find when we consider the work of Slavoj Žižek, however, we are rather good as a species at deluding ourselves.

Michel Foucault's historical researches concentrated on power relations. He was particularly concerned with how certain discourses came to dominate in the social sphere, exploring how, for example, homosexuality, an unexceptional practice in most of the classical world, had come to be marginalized, and even criminalized, by the rise of Christian society and its insistence on heterosexuality as the norm.[11] (Foucault's work has been very influential in the development of queer theory, which is yet another system-challenging venture, confronting discrimination over sexual orientation.[12]) Equally, he argued that mental illness came to be regarded by the ruling classes, from the early modern period onwards, as a condition to be hidden away from society in institutions.[13] Again, the notion was that a normative code of behaviour had to be imposed. Foucault saw the modern era as obsessed with establishing standards for social behaviour, and with policing these strictly – the hospital and prison systems were yet other instances of this drive by the ruling authorities to impose order and control on the general population.[14] Hierarchies were built on nothing stronger than the possession of power, and had no other intrinsic dynamic. That power could always be challenged therefore, and as far as Foucault was concerned, always should be, to promote the cause of the marginal and oppressed that every society had in its midst – the different, no matter how invisible the authorities had tried to render them.

What came to be emphasized increasingly in poststructuralist thought was the importance of difference. For poststructuralist thinkers, the world around us was characterized more by difference than anything else, and those in power did not like this, since it threatened their ability to control – homogeneity was preferred instead. For Derrida, as we have seen, difference could be traced right down to the level of our everyday use of language. He coined the term *differance* to indicate how words could carry multiple meanings, often depending on their sound quality, for example, echoing other words.[15] Any attempt to construct a theory of everything was thus doomed at source by language's inherent instability.

Postmodernism is a similarly sceptically minded theory (in fact, we might subsume poststructuralism within the broader movement of postmodernism) that seeks to undermine the grand narratives of our culture; in effect, the dominant ideologies by which we live. Jean-François Lyotard in particular encouraged us to reject institutional authority, arguing that it invariably involved the suppression of opposing viewpoints and dissent in a general sense. His first target in this respect was Marxism, which he argued had failed to take account of the extent of difference in the world, favouring instead a one-size-fits-all approach, in which all countries were seen to share common characteristics such as the class struggle and to require the same solution, the establishment of a thoroughgoing communist system. In his writings on Algeria during the 1950s and 60s, when the revolution was taking place there against French colonialism, Lyotard was adamant that the local situation did not, and could not, conform to standard Marxist analysis: 'It is in a completely *abstract* way . . . that one can speak of *a* proletariat, *a* middle class, *a* bourgeoisie in Algeria.'[16] Poor developing world countries like Algeria had their own special needs to resolve and should not be treated as if they were socially and technologically advanced European nations of the kind that Marx had in mind when writing *Capital*. As would be the case with all major postmodern theorists, Lyotard stressed the role of difference in our culture and argued strongly for this to be given its due and not suppressed in the name of a dominant ideology.

Lyotard's most famous work is *The Postmodern Condition,* in which he set forth a general argument against grand narratives, or metanarratives, arguing that these had lost their credibility by the later twentieth century and ought to be subjected to sustained challenge to undermine the power they wielded. What was wanted now, in his view, was an attitude of 'incredulity toward metanarratives' to be fostered.[17] The way forward was to be 'little narrative', which was not committed to any overall theory of everything, as in the manner of Marxism, and was instead, as Lyotard saw it, responsive to the uniqueness of 'events' as they unfolded in time.[18] Grand narratives tried to predetermine events and turn them to their own account, but for Lyotard this was impossible. Little narratives might be thought of as akin to pressure groups, assembled to counteract specific abuses of institutionalized power (as, for example, the Greens have set themselves to do with the world's major energy companies). The point was to end the particular abuse and then dissolve, so that the movement did not grow into a grand narrative in its turn and impose its will on others in the time-honoured fashion. Postmodernism is invariably suspicious of the creation of power blocs, seeing these as inimical to the expression of difference in our culture.

Grand narratives created imbalances of power where 'differends', or incommensurable world-views, occurred.[19] Those in power refused to acknowledge the validity of their opponents' outlook and settled all disputes on the basis of their own set of values. This was what little narratives were expected to correct, creating the space for dissenting voices to be heard and the dominant ideology to be called to account. The enemy as Lyotard saw it was the totalizing tendency of grand narratives, which sought to make everyone submit to their world-view. In consequence, Lyotard felt himself committed to 'wage a war on totality' as a concept.[20] That becomes a postmodern motif: the call to resist the actions of overbearing systems on behalf of the cause of difference. Systems are also to be resisted because of their delusive belief that they can control events as they arise, whereas Lyotard wants to emphasize the existentialist quality of events, their novelty, and unpredictability.

Postmodern theory owes a great deal to debates that took place in the architectural world. The architectural theorist Charles Jencks, for example, led a campaign against modernist architecture, the 'International Style' as it came to be known in its heyday in the mid-twentieth century, which he argued was being forced on an unwilling public who found its productions very alienating (hence the emergence of vandalism in so many high-rise tower block estates). Jencks argued that in order to overcome the public's dislike of the modernist style, architects should make some radical changes to their practice. He encouraged what he called 'double-coding', combining elements of both old and new building styles so that the general public was given something familiar from its everyday experience with which to identify.[21] This has since become fairly standard practice, and the notion of constructing a dialogue between the present and the past has become deeply entrenched within postmodern thought. The grand narrative of modernism, which found value only in originality and experimentation with form, dismissing older styles as outmoded and irrelevant to the modern lifestyle, was being rejected as authoritarian and totalitarian in ethos by Jencks and his peers.

The work of Gilles Deleuze and Felix Guattari provides yet another example of the deep dislike of authoritarianism amongst the postmodernist community. In their provocative two-volume study *Capitalism and Schizophrenia* (*Anti-Oedipus* and *A Thousand Plateaus*, respectively[22]) they picture a world in which individuals have been manoeuvred into a condition of subjugation by the ruling powers. Collectively, they describe this establishment project of keeping us all in line as 'Oedipus', and urge us to develop methods to counter its strictures, an 'Anti-Oedipus'. Oedipus postulates a standard mode of behaviour that punishes anyone who deviates from the norm. For the authors this represents an unjust restriction on the plurality inherent in personal identity (all of us having a range of 'selves'), and they recommend various stratagems to uphold this in the face of the onslaught of Oedipus – such as, most controversially, schizophrenia. Then in *A Thousand Plateaus* they put forward the concept of nomadism as a means of staying out of the reach of the ruling authorities. Nomadism becomes a model of how to maintain one's intellectual independence, nomads having no firm commitments (in Deleuze and Guattari's terminology they are 'deterritorialized') and being willing to change location at a moment's notice to protect their freedom. Not having a stake in the establishment's project, which involves controlling a particular stretch of territory where its writ runs, nomads become something of a rogue element within it, thus constituting a permanent threat to the rulers' exercise of power. To be nomadic is for Deleuze and Guattari to be outside the repressive mechanism in society, Oedipus, and to be able to plot one's own course of action free of constraint and the tyranny of received ideas. Lyotard has a similar notion that he commends us to adopt, svelteness, which translates as adaptability and flexibility of response on the part of the individual; the ability to change roles as circumstances require.[23]

Post-Marxism can also be considered part of the postmodern movement, in that it seeks to maintain the spirit of Marxism while divesting itself of its dogmatic aspects – classical Marxism in its communist guise being notoriously unable to countenance internal opposition or dissenting voices, insisting on adherence to the party line in all circumstances. Yet again, cultural difference is both acknowledged and encouraged. Thinkers like Ernesto Laclau and Chantal Mouffe turned their back on institutional Marxism and its ideals, criticizing it for resorting to the concept of hegemony to explain the failure of its historical predictions rather than facing up to the increasingly glaring deficiencies within the theory itself: 'The "evident truths" of the past'... have been seriously challenged by an avalanche of historical mutations which have riven the ground on which those truths were constituted.'[24] Marxism was no longer to be regarded by the radical left as the only possible solution to our socio-political problems, and we were urged to strive instead to create a 'radical democratic' political system where a multitude of voices, most of them hitherto marginalized or suppressed by systems such as communism, were to be given the opportunity to make their case. A whole new generation of protest movements had grown up around the globe (little narratives, in effect), and Marxism had nothing much of substance to offer them; in fact, Marxism could only treat them as a hindrance to the achievement of its ultimate goals. As with Lyotard, the imperative was to generate opposition within authoritarian systems of thought; to reclaim the notion of democracy from its hypocritical usage in the communist world (where it came to mean one-party rule), as well as the cosy consensus that existed in most liberal democracies.

Another post-Marxist thinker, Slavoj Žižek, had some thought-provoking ideas as to why Marxism could retain its hold over the masses in countries like the communist Yugoslavia he grew up in, arguing that to some extent the populace could be held responsible for the party's success in this regard; that there was a degree of complicity to be noted. He suggested that the populace bought into the ruling ideology enough to make it viable, even if it also recognized that the ideology was deeply flawed and not really delivering on its promises (despite publicly claiming to be). After decades of indoctrination communist ideology had become such a part of everyone's life that they came to feel they had a stake in it, supporting it while simultaneously, almost schizophrenically one could say, being very aware of its failings: 'they know that their idea of Freedom is masking a form of exploitation, but still they continue to follow this idea of Freedom'.[25] This was not just a case of being overawed by the ruling communist party's power, but a desire to assert oneself politically, even if it was largely delusional (Žižek dubbed the state of mind 'enlightened false consciousness'[26]), and certainly not in one's long-term interests. We can find such behaviour in any belief system, however, and not just the communist. Drawing on the work of the radical post-Freudian psychoanalyst Jacques Lacan, Žižek uses the term 'fetish' to describe what is going on psychologically in the state of knowing/not knowing, suggesting that it is our way of dealing with a situation we do not like or have little control over:

> a fetish can play a very constructive role in allowing us to cope with the harsh reality: fetishists are not dreamers lost in their private worlds, they are thorough 'realists,' able to accept the way things effectively are – since they have their fetish to which they can cling in order to cancel the full impact of reality.[27]

Individuals within organizations often act in the way Žižek identifies, and the coaching process would have to take account of that. Taking on the system can be psychologically very difficult, and we often opt to stay loyal to the *status quo* because of how much emotional energy we have invested in it over the years (anyone who has followed their local football team through thick and thin over the years will recognize the symptom). Whether allowing ourselves to be governed by a fetish is in the longer-term interest of either the individual or the organization, is something we shall be considering in more detail in Chapter 8. Suffice to say for the time being that it is easy to be so taken in by an organization's reputation that we can turn a blind eye to any difficulties it may be sliding into, choosing to go on believing its pronouncements to the contrary.

Feminism lies somewhat outside the general run of critical theories. While it can make use of Marxist, structuralist, poststructuralist, or postmodernist techniques on occasion, feminism has its own political agenda that drives it: a commitment to achieving equality in all spheres of life between men and women, and to ending discrimination on the basis of gender. This means that it cuts across theories like Marxism, having a very different long-term objective. While there has been a strand of Marxist feminism, it has always been an uneasy form of collaboration, with more radical feminists arguing that the two positions are fundamentally incompatible, Marxism having a strong patriarchal streak in its make-up. Feminism sets out to undermine the power of patriarchy, so there is a definite system-challenging aspect to its goals, and Marxism is one of the systems that increasingly came under challenge in the later twentieth century. The debate is captured in the book *The Unhappy Marriage of Marxism and Feminism*, with the theorist Heidi Hartmann being particularly forthright in her opinion: 'Recent attempts to integrate marxism and feminism are unsatisfactory to us as feminists because they subsume the feminist struggle into the "larger" struggle against capital. To continue our simile further, either we need a healthier marriage or we need a divorce.'[28]

Some feminists became disenchanted enough with patriarchy to advocate separatism, difference feminism being a case in point. Taking its cue from deconstruction, this kind of feminism emphasizes the difference between men and women, encouraging women to construct a world-view based on their own characteristics rather than one parasitic on the male outlook and uncritically accepting its objectives. Luce Irigaray, for example, speaks of the 'female imaginary', urging women 'to keep themselves apart from men long enough ... to forge for themselves a social status that compels recognition, to earn their living in order to escape from the condition of prostitute.'[29] Others have contested the separatist line, defining it as 'womanism' and thus guilty of a biological essentialism that is unhelpful to overcoming gender discrimination in the wider cultural arena.[30] This reaction harks back to Simone de Beauvoir's famous assertion that, '[o]ne is not born but rather becomes, a woman';[31] in other words, to the recognition that gender roles are constructed and can therefore be changed. The glass ceiling manifestly still exists within public life, and organizations need to be reminded of Beauvoir's insight on a regular basis. Equally, women need to be reminded that gender 'reality' is not fixed and can be reconstructed.

Feminism offers a particularly pointed challenge to the organizational ethos, and has the potential to effect quite wide-ranging change in this area. As noted earlier, it cuts across the concerns of most other critical theories, and certainly has much to offer in a coaching context, where received assumptions, particularly about the relationship between the individual and the overall ethos, are being put under scrutiny. Perhaps even difference feminism can be drawn on in this context since the intention is plainly to call into question the dominant ideology of our culture, with its deeply entrenched masculinist bias. There can be a tactical quality to the use of such provocative theories.

Postcolonialism represents yet another challenge to grand narrative, this time the grand narrative assuming the cultural superiority of Western society. Edward Said pointed out how this had led to a situation where Eastern (in the first instance, Middle Eastern) society came to be conceptualized as inferior to the West, as lacking its moral, political, and technological sophistication. 'Orientalism', as he called this attitude, became 'a Western style for dominating, restructuring, and having authority over the Orient', the outcome being that 'the Orient was not (and is not) a free subject of thought or action'.[32] It was a grand narrative which eventually came to be accepted by the non-Western world itself, and throwing off that colonial yoke has been a long and painful process; one which, as Said observes, is still not completed in many parts of the world. The grand narrative still exists within the system of globalization, which assumes a Western model (neoliberalism) of economic activity, and thus trading practices, that has left many ex-colonial countries in a very disadvantaged position – often as little better than neocolonial outposts of multinational empires, with little meaningful control over their economic destiny.

Psychoanalysis has also been an important source of inspiration for critical theory, giving us the means by which systems can be analyzed in terms of their hidden determinants; determinants that can shape how the power structures of systems operate and thus constrain us to go along with systems which may not be in our best interests overall. Freud theorized that our unconscious drives dictated much of our conscious activity. There was a 'sub-text' to our behaviour therefore, and the more we understood of that, the more we could understand why we acted the way we did (and presumably could alter our behaviour to our personal advantage). Although those drives could be kept in check, they tended to break through eventually in 'the return of the repressed', leaving us even less in control of ourselves. Whether we could posit an unconscious of organizations is an intriguing question, but individuals within an organization could certainly benefit from a greater knowledge of their own unconscious drives. As integral parts of the system, the hidden determinants of each individual's behaviour, as well as what they might be repressing, would have to affect the workings of the system overall: the return of the repressed could well be to the system's disadvantage. Perhaps whistleblowing constitutes the return of the repressed? (a topic we shall be picking up in more detail in Chapter 8).

Žižek, again drawing on the work of Lacan, adds an interesting twist to the debate in claiming that the individual may not want to be 'cured' of their repression, and may in fact prefer to have it as part of their life; that they may come to 'enjoy the symptom'.[33] As another commentator on Lacan, Bruce Fink, has remarked, it can be the case that 'the patient does not want to change! If symptoms have developed, if the patient engages in symptomatic behaviour, it is because a great deal of energy has become tied up in those symptoms.... At some level, the individual enjoys his or her symptoms.'[34] Again, we shall pick up on this in more detail in Chapter 8 when discussing how to integrate critical theory into the coaching process, but it is not hard to see how such behaviour can develop in an organizational context – nor how damaging it could be to the organization's prospects.

Complexity theory lends yet another interesting dimension to critical theory, particularly its concept of the 'edge of chaos'. Systems are seen to operate best when they are put under pressure and manage to keep themselves on the right side of chaos by their creative response to the pressure. When systems fail to develop in such a creative manner, when they become static, merely continuing on as always without engaging positively with the changing circumstances around them, then they run the risk of collapsing (one might conjecture that financial bubbles are an exemplification of this process). Complexity demands that we pay very close attention to the internal dynamics of systems, to the possibility that small changes in one area can create dramatically disproportionate changes at a macro level as the effects of the original action successively magnify (the 'butterfly effect' as it has been called, where '[w]ith some poetic licence, the beating of a butterfly's wings in Brazil could spark off a tornado in Texas'[35]). The larger an organization is, the more susceptible it is to such effects, since the internal dynamics of such a system are often very poorly understood by those managing it, being deemed to be linear, thus predictable, whereas they are in fact non-linear – and as the science writers Peter Coveney and Roger Highfield have emphasized, 'nonlinearity produces complex and frequently unexpected results'.[36] The more rigid the system, the less likely it will able to cope with the unexpected – as dogmatic management would find out to its cost.

Critical theory: Uses and abuses

Like any system of thought, critical theory can be used or abused, and we need to pay close attention to what kinds of abuse can arise before recommending its more systematic application in the coaching process. Its most positive quality is its ability to offer a challenge to power structures. Such structures only too easily overwhelm the individual, but critical theory provides the tools by which they can be held to account and their methods and ethos brought under review. Postmodern theory, as we shall go on to discuss in more detail below, is particularly adept in this regard, building on a generalized suspicion of institutional authority that has grown up in the West in recent decades. In the West at least, neither the political nor the managerial class are trusted to the extent that they used to be, especially when it comes to dealing with things like environmental abuse and financial crisis. Postmodernism is an attempt to theorize this generalized sense of discontent with the ruling authorities and their attendant power structures.

The more negative side of critical theory is that it can be a method of imposing values on systems which precludes the development of dissenting viewpoints. Some theories, such as Marxism, can be very authoritarian in style, refusing to accord any validity to opposing theories or outlooks – for all that it can be very effective in drawing attention to economically exploitative practices. Any theory carries a set of policies and attitudes with it, but when these harden into dogma they can be very harmful: communism's history as a political system manifestly did not lead to the liberation of the proletariat, and its demise has been mourned by few (even by the Chinese Communist Party which has now opted for a state-managed capitalism instead). Neither is this just a problem for the Marxist–socialist camp, as the example of neoliberalism makes abundantly clear. With its uncritical commitment to extreme *laissez faire* principles and belief that these constitute the only valid basis on which economic life can be conducted, neoliberalism has been a major cause of the current global financial crisis. It is largely because so few within the financial or corporate world were willing to contest the principles of neoliberalism that the credit crunch occurred. Neoliberalism was simply taken to be the natural order of things, the way the world was designed to work, and thus there was no effective check on the excesses that were perpetrated in its name: 'two decades of powerlessness', as the economic journalist Paul Mason remarked, 'have inculcated a profound lack of ambition upon capitalism's critics'.[37] Those who did try to challenge its principles were disregarded, even if they were important players within the global financial system, such as the highly successful hedge-fund operators George Soros or Warren Buffet.[38] If they could make little impact on the neoliberal consensus, then it is not surprizing that so little opposition came from those further down in the pecking order.

Postmodernism: The critique of authority and the defence of narrative

Postmodern thought has been critical of authority since its beginnings, and it has led the way in challenging the assumptions lying behind institutional power. Taking postmodernism in the broad-based sense outlined above, as a general cultural trend rather than a specific movement as such, we can see why it is worth fostering the attitudes it encourages us to adopt towards grand narratives. More scepticism in our public life would be a very positive development, and grand narratives certainly deserve to be viewed in a sceptical light. All organizations have their own grand narrative, implemented and defended by the higher management, and internal criticism of this is rarely welcomed – certainly not if it gets into any level of detail. The desire instead is to ensure compliance with its principles at the individual level, such that the organization's developmental trajectory is predictable. Conformity is seen as a virtue by those controlling the grand narrative, rather than a barrier to progress: organizations can be very one-dimensional in that respect.

Postmodernism recommends that we move away from such oppressive narratives to recognize that a plurality of narratives within systems is a far preferable state of affairs. Narrative itself, rather in the manner of its structuralist conception, is taken to be a universal phenomenon, intrinsic to human communication. Lyotard in particular emphasizes this, referring to 'the preeminence of the narrative form in the formulation of traditional knowledge.... Narration is the quintessential form of customary knowledge, in more ways than one'.[39] Where we go wrong, in Lyotard's opinion, is in allowing certain narratives to be considered authoritative, and to take precedence over others. Narrative itself is fairly neutral, and it legitimates itself without requiring reference to any outside body of principles where authority is deemed to lie:

> Narratives... determine criteria of competence and/or illustrate how they are to be applied. They thus define what has the right to be said and done in the culture in question, and since they are themselves a part of that culture, they are legitimated by the simple fact that they do what they do.[40]

We expect there to be narratives in our social existence; indeed, we are more or less programmed to operate that way. The problem that has arisen in Western society, however, is that narratives are now required to be legitimated by reference to some such outside authority, which means that only certain narratives are found to be acceptable. Lyotard argues for a far more pragmatic attitude to narrative, for any example to be judged on its social utility rather than its slavish adherence to a set of principles (Marxist, for example, or religious of pretty well any denomination). He also wants there to be a plurality of narratives in circulation, and for new, little, narratives constantly to be coming on stream to refresh debate and prevent stagnation of ideas. The narrative imperative is to be defended, but the grand narrative imperative resisted.

Such an approach also fits in with the demands of complexity theory, the assumption being that the more little narratives are created, the more likely we are as a society to regenerate ourselves and prevent any slippage into either stasis or chaos: plurality equals adaptability and regeneration from this perspective. Lyotard asserts that this is the state of play in science nowadays, claiming that it is in consequence progressively undermining our traditional view of knowledge, and thus the possibility of there ever being credible grand narratives and theories of everything:

> Postmodern science – by concerning itself with such things as undecidables, the limits of precise control, conflicts characterized by incomplete information, '*fracta*', catastrophes, and pragmatic paradoxes – is theorizing its own evolution as discontinuous, catastrophic, nonrectifiable, and paradoxical. It is changing the meaning of the word *knowledge*, while expressing how such a change can take place. It is producing not the known, but the unknown. And it suggests a model of legitimation that has nothing to do with maximized performance[.][41]

Maximizing performance, in this sense, means doing one's best to shore up the grand narrative, whatever that may be – precisely what most large organizations are trying to do most of the time with their employees, often through coaching programmes. (Thomas Kuhn had earlier postulated that this was a standard characteristic of scientific practice: the vigorous defence of existing paradigms, with practitioners striving to 'save the phenomena' involved in each case.[42] Žižek is making much the same point about political paradigms when he speaks of 'enlightened false consciousness'.) Postmodernism wants something much more tactical than this, however, with the dominant narrative in question being subjected to constant scrutiny to prevent it closing off debate – or more subtly perhaps, determining the terms of debate such that the outcomes are predictable and do not threaten its authority (Lyotard's differend in action).

Pick 'n mix theory

Nowadays it is increasingly the case that analysts put together their own synthesis, adapting aspects of a range of theories into a model that reflects their own clutch of interests. We might speak of this as a pick 'n mix approach, and it can be modified to fit circumstances as required. There is no need to feel a binding commitment towards any particular theory; the whole body of literature can be raided to give one a spectrum of methods to deploy in the sense-making process. Critical theory is rich in concepts which enable the user to gain a new perspective on their situation, to construct new narratives that serve to further the debate in their field. The more of these techniques that can be brought to bear on sense-making, the more options there will be for individuals to adopt, and that has to be a particular benefit to the practice of coaching. In effect, we are advocating pragmatism as the best policy.

We have broken down critical theory into two main groups: system-building and system-challenging, and suggested that the latter is currently the mode attracting most attention. But either approach can be used within the coaching process as a source of models, depending on the situation prevailing: change means that organizations need to be both challenged and reconfigured regularly, both in terms of their formal structure and the interpersonal relationships within that (to bring the sociological–formalist distinction into play again). There is still mileage to be had in working out the specific grammar of organizations, for example, and using this to construct new narrative lines that will express the organization's strengths to best advantage. The key is to make sure that no one particular system-building approach is regarded as definitive (a common failing in this area), and to be sceptical in general about the idea of a theory of everything. Theories of everything have a distinct tendency to become dogmatic over time, and to encourage followers to perpetuate the system in question rather than respond creatively to change: saving the phenomena is all too common a reaction to the emergence of the unknown. Hegemony was an example of that process within Marxism, and we have also seen how destructive dogmatism was in the case of neoliberal economics, pushing the financial system to the very brink of disaster with its one-dimensional ideology. Unless a critical mentality is fostered within organizations, we are in real danger of that situation recurring regularly, and that would hardly be in the wider public interest. Critical theory offers us a body of material and range of methods by which we can develop that mentality.

6
Scepticism in Public Life

Postmodern theorists have encouraged us to be highly sceptical of the motives of institutional authority, and the virtues of such an attitude in public life will now be considered. Scepticism is a long-running and well-respected part of the Western philosophical tradition, developed in the first instance in classical Greek culture, and it has functioned very effectively within that tradition over the years as a form of internal critique, checking the more outlandish claims made by the philosophical fraternity. To be sceptical is to be explicitly anti-authoritarian in outlook, and thus to foster radical, and ongoing, assessment of belief systems and received wisdom – in short, the dominant ideology of the time. The various areas of public life where such an exercise would be very valuable indeed in the current climate will now be explored, with reference to politics and the financial sector in particular. There is a general lack of sceptical attitudes in these areas, where a fundamentalist mind-set is so often in operation instead (reinforced by group-think), and their absence is to be deplored. All systems benefit from an internal critique, and where this is absent the system in question can all too easily close in on itself and lose touch with changes in the wider world, as well as with how it is perceived there, to its ultimate detriment: long-held beliefs harden into dogma and the system gradually loses its resilience. A coaching practice more geared to scepticism would be a significant step towards challenging the fundamentalism which has created so many problems in the business world in recent times, and after making the case for the public utility of scepticism that is what we shall be outlining in detail in Chapter 8. Before that, however, we shall briefly survey some of the key moments in the history of scepticism, going on to point out where we are most in want of its spirit in public life at present.

The roots of philosophical scepticism

Scepticism's roots lie in classical Greek thought (although as we shall go on to see later, sceptical traditions can be found in non-Western cultures too), such as the movement known as Pyrrhonism, which went on to influence thinkers well into the modern period. The supposed founder, Pyrrho of Elis, is an obscure figure who lived from 360 to 275 BC and about whom little is known, but the movement associated with his name developed over a period of centuries, to be codified in the form we know it now by the Alexandrian philosopher Sextus Empiricus in the second century AD. Pyrrhonism established some of the main principles by which scepticism has come to be known, such as that we have no foolproof criteria by which to judge the truth or falsity of statements:

> in order for the dispute that has arisen about standards to be decided, we must possess an agreed standard through which we can judge it; and in order for us to possess an agreed standard, the dispute about standards must already have been decided.[1]

It is an observation which has dogged philosophical discourse ever since, being notoriously difficult to refute (in technical terms it is known as 'antifoundationalism', since it is denying the existence of foundations, or grounds, to argument). Yet it has many benefits: it forces us to consider what we take for granted in our thought and argument, assumptions that may have no firm philosophical foundation at all, and that we should not be depending upon to back up our statements. In turn, that means we have to start looking for ways to overcome this hurdle to discourse, refining our analytical methods as we go in order to address any gaps and contradictions that are emerging in our defence of our beliefs – and sceptics will insist that we must keep on doing so, that this is a process which never really comes to an end. Sceptics are constitutionally unable to entertain the possibility of there being a theory of everything.

This is all to the good as far as philosophical discourse is concerned, as the ideal here is to be as logical as possible and to leave no loose ends in the composition of your arguments. The drawback is that such a line of reasoning can also lead to a disabling relativism that can make it pretty well impossible to prove anything at all: as Sextus put it, scepticism demands that 'we come ... to a suspension of judgement', and he finds this a highly desirable state to be in.[2] This is a situation, however, which effectively undermines discourse and debate in general (a point we shall return to later): in the words of the eminent historian of scepticism, Richard H. Popkin, Pyrrhonism turns into 'a purge that eliminates everything including itself'.[3]

Pyrrhonism is nevertheless a very powerful form of scepticism, and it continued to hold a fascination for successive generations of philosophers after Sextus (although Christian thought, no friend to scepticism, tended to hold the stage for several centuries in between throughout most of Europe). There was a notable revival of interest in Pyrrhonist philosophy in sixteenth century France, for example, with figures like Michel Montaigne absorbing its principles, and this formed the cultural background to the enquiries of such high-profile philosophical thinkers as René Descartes.

Scepticism in modern philosophy

Scepticism in its modern philosophical form is generally held to begin with Descartes, particularly in his *Meditations on First Philosophy*, one of the founding works of modern philosophy. In this, Descartes systematically deploys sceptical techniques in a bid to construct a robust theory of knowledge that we can rely on not to mislead us; although ultimately he is a far less sceptical thinker than he first presents himself to us, and was in fact a critic of Pyrrhonist thought and methods. Descartes' starting point is to call into doubt all his knowledge until he can find something self-evidently true and beyond all possible doubt on which to base it, describing himself as feeling taxed by 'the multitude of errors that I had accepted as true in my earliest years, and the dubiousness of the whole superstructure I had since then reared on them'.[4] He is aware that his senses sometimes deceive him (we can have hallucinations, for example), and concludes that these cannot constitute a trustworthy guide as to what is true or false; so knowledge will have to be based on something stronger than just our sense experience, as 'a wise man never entirely trusts those who have once cheated him.'[5] Descartes also speculates that we might actually be existing in a dream-like state, or even being tricked by an 'evil spirit' that there are such things as other human beings and an external world (scepticism does seem to promote such extreme speculation).[6] Absolutely everything in his experience is apparently up for the most rigorous scrutiny.

The solution that is posited to the problem is the proposition *cogito ergo sum* ('I think therefore I am'). That is, the one thing Descartes can never doubt is that he is thinking: 'I must at length conclude that this proposition "I am", "I exist", whenever I utter it or conceive it in my mind, is necessarily true.'[7] The *cogito* is self-evidently, indisputably, true and thus can form a solid ground for a theory of knowledge. Descartes immediately starts examining what else he has in his mind, and soon finds other ideas he is convinced have the same status as the *cogito*: most notably, and also notoriously, that God exists: 'from the mere fact that I exist, and have in me some idea of a most perfect being, that is, God, it is clearly demonstrated that God also exists'.[8] There does seem to be something of a leap taking place here, however, and it reveals the limits of Descartes' scepticism, which will stop short of casting any really serious doubt on God's existence.

Descartes' scepticism is often dismissed as half-hearted by more thoroughgoing philosophical sceptics, with one such accusing him of being 'indecently credulous' when it comes to the existence of God;[9] yet it still has something to teach us and can be called upon in the coaching process. Closely scrutinizing the basis of our beliefs is always a useful exercise, and it is to be expected that there will be some we shall not wish to jettison (the religious variety being amongst the most prominent, but everyone will have their own particular sticking points derived from their ideological outlook). As long as we are aware of this, and can keep a questioning mind about what underpins these particular beliefs, then the Cartesian approach still has much to commend it. At the very least, it spurs us to come up with some kind of justification for those most deeply held beliefs, consistent with a sceptical attitude towards received wisdom. And it is always possible that we might feel moved to go farther than Descartes actually did once we have started on that route ourselves; to be truly rigorous in investigating the superstructure we have created to make sense of our world.

The Enlightenment *philosophes* certainly showed themselves willing to go much further on religious matters than Descartes was prepared to, with Baron d'Holbach, for example, railing against 'those insupportable chains which tyrants [and] priests have forged for all nations', and claiming that Christianity was 'founded on imposture, ignorance, and credulity':[10] a line of attack which did much to encourage the development of atheism in the period. The *philosophes* provide an excellent example of how scepticism can be deployed successfully to challenge orthodoxy, with a carefully delineated target being taken to task for its overbearing manner and quest for universal domination. Religion is for such thinkers a grand narrative just asking to be brought down, and to raise doubts about its founding principles is a highly effective tactic to adopt.

Scepticism takes on a much harder edge in the work of the *philosophes*' contemporary David Hume, where it seems designed to confuse and even destabilize the reader. Hume applies scepticism to causality and personal identity, with a fairly devastating effect as far as our everyday beliefs about the world are concerned. Cause and effect, Hume argues, have no necessary connection between them; we assume the same effect will always happen from a given cause because that is what we have experienced in the past, but we cannot guarantee they will be so joined on the next occasion we encounter them. In Hume's view it is merely habit, or 'that propensity, which custom produces, to pass from an object to the idea of its usual attendant' as he describes it, that leads us to assume a necessary connection, but at any point we could be disabused of this by a contrary instance occurring – as from this perspective is entirely possible.[11] We want the connection to be there, it makes us feel more secure about our position in the world for that to apply; but in real terms it is not, just the psychological desire for it. There is, in other words, no knowledge of the future – such as our assumption that nature will continue to be as uniform than as it has been in the past. This is an important insight, if perhaps less dramatic in relevance than Hume believes – as we shall go on to see when we turn to the work of Immanuel Kant below.

When it comes to personal identity, Hume's ideas are particularly radical, and still much debated today in the philosophy world. As individuals, he argues, we are constantly being bombarded by sense impressions from the world around us, such that the contents of our mind are always in a state of restless transition: new sets of impressions are ceaselessly flooding in, and we have no choice but passively to endure this. In consequence, we cannot speak of there being any essential self within us, some defining core identity, as Hume is at pains to point out:

> For my part, when I enter most intimately into what I call *myself*, I always stumble on some particular perception or other, of heat or cold, light or shade, love or hatred, pain or pleasure. I never can catch *myself* at any time without a perception, and never can observe anything but the perception. . . . I may venture to affirm of the rest of mankind, that they are nothing but a bundle or collection of different perceptions, which succeed each other with an inconceivable rapidity, and are in a perpetual flux and movement. Our eyes cannot turn in their sockets without varying our perceptions. Our thought is still more variable than our sight; and all our other senses and faculties contribute to this change; nor is there any single power of the soul, which remains unalterably the same, perhaps for one moment.[12]

The notion of an essential self is therefore an illusion and there is no coherence over time to our personal identity, which runs counter to most people's vision of themselves, as well as the nature of the world around them. Such enquiries reveal just how disorienting really thoroughgoing scepticism can be, and Hume is no less thoroughgoing when it comes to religion, dismissively describing its doctrines as little better than 'sick men's dreams'.[13]

Hume's scepticism is intellectually admirable, but can be very negative in its impact. It seems to leave us in a condition of limbo, unable to proceed with any sense of confidence on any project at all. If personal identity really is as tenuous a concept as Hume is claiming, then it would be hard to put any trust in the words of other human beings, who would be just as little disposed to believe what we said back to them: each time around our mental picture would be completely different. It is one thing to acknowledge the possibility of multiple selves (something generally accepted nowadays, if only in the sense that it is recognized we play a range of roles in our lives and these require us to act differently according to the context we are in), another to have to accept that there is no continuity at all as to how these present themselves each time around. Neither could we have much confidence in a world where causality was apparently so contingent. Organizations could hardly function at all if the Humean perspective was correct; there could be little hope of there being commonly held objectives or any consistency of action on the part of the individuals involved.

Hume pictures a world that is potentially very chaotic; indeed, it is a source of some wonder how it has managed to hold up in apparently workable fashion for as long as it has if causality actually is as undependable as he claims. Even Hume himself is disturbed by the implications of his researches into such topics, conceding that they have to be put to one side periodically if he is to overcome the 'philosophical melancholy' they can induce in him, and thus enable him to 'act like other people in the common affairs of life'.[14] What is needed is a way of opening out that scepticism such that it can be seen to have clear relevance to 'the common affairs of life', and we shall be making several suggestions as to how this can be done later in the chapter, with coaching very much part of the plan.

It was over just such points that Kant felt obliged to provide an alternative model of the world and how we relate to it than that offered by Hume. Kant posits the presence of the same mental apparatus in each of us, which then guarantees a common understanding of the world. All of us process experience through mental categories (of quantity, quality, relation, and modality, along with their various sub-categories, respectively[15]), which determine the way the world appears to us: causes always precede effects, time flows forward such that the present always succeeds the past, etc. The world may well have a different character to the one we perceive (consisting of what Kant calls 'things in themselves', which are unknowable), but we can only perceive it as we are set up to do, through the mental categories that all of us possess: 'all objects are therefore mere appearances, and not given to us as things in themselves.'[16] In other words, we construct the world that we experience – a very powerful theory in helping to dispel some of scepticism's less palatable claims, which would render sense-making a very problematical exercise (a problem that recurs in postmodern thought, as we shall go on to see). Cause and effect patterns would remain the same in the future because we would continue to structure them that way, the only way our faculties could (even if that is not quite the same thing as claiming to have knowledge of the future).

Scepticism's star waxes and wanes in philosophical history, and although it has continued to play a significant role in the modern period, it has often been overshadowed by grandiose system-building exercises such as Hegelianism and Marxism, whose rationale and objectives were considered in Chapter 5. It starts to come into its own again, as we also discussed in Chapter 5, with the advent of poststructuralism and postmodernism, whose reaction against system-building has set the agenda for much philosophical discourse of late. We are in a system-challenging phase at present, and as we shall go on to argue, coaching can derive inspiration from this turn of events.

Jacques Derrida's work, for example, pictures a world in many ways like that of Hume, where it is all but impossible to construct a coherent worldview or sense of personal identity because of the lack of pattern in the world around us. For Derrida, the totalizing imperative that drives theories such as Marxism and structuralism runs against the grain of the way the world really is – incomplete, unpredictable, largely random, in a state of becoming rather than being (to invoke another long-running philosophical debate). Intellectual authority can only be a delusion from this perspective, although it is a delusion that has put down very deep roots in our culture and that we find exceedingly hard to give up, as Derrida consistently complains. Gilles Deleuze and Felix Guattari are similarly disposed to emphasize the absence of pattern, as well as the chaotic nature of personal identity, arguing that this undermines all notions of institutional authority as well: 'Oedipus', as they term it, urging us to reject its scheme for domination of our lives. Since there is no ground for establishing either intellectual or institutional authority we are under no obligation to allow either to exercise the control over us that they are wont to claim. Scepticism would seem to be the only sensible attitude to adopt under the circumstances, or even 'super-scepticism' as one of the authors here has elsewhere described this outlook, with its insistence that meaning is always in a state of flux (ceaselessly contaminated by traces of other contexts), that absolutes of any kind are impossible, and that identity is never quite there in its entirety.[17] As one of the leading commentators on deconstruction described

Derrida's conception of the 'various signs' (in the structuralist sense of the term) we encounter in the world:

> Such is the strange 'being' of the sign: half of it always 'not there' and the other half always 'not that.' The structure of the sign is determined by the trace or track of that other which is forever absent. This other is of course never to be found in its full being.[18]

Super-scepticism seems to imply that we can never initiate discourse at all. Everything we say, Derrida contends, is to be considered as 'under erasure' (*sous rature*), and its meaning can never be recaptured by us; there is no permanence to be found in the communicative process.[19] Not surprizingly, there are many in the philosophical establishment for whom this is an unacceptable conclusion to reach, running directly contrary to its commitment to debate and dialogue. Charges of nihilism are often made against poststructuralist thinkers like Derrida, and indeed are applicable more generally to the sceptical tradition, which does often appear to be more concerned with telling us what we can't do than what we can, with emphasizing the barriers to communication than trying to find ways round these. Super-scepticism may represent the farther shores of scepticism, but it is still consistent with the motivating impulse behind the tradition, and if it can appear nihilistic in manner then its success at calling the claims of authority into question do need to be highlighted. It is not the pointless exercise its detractors often damn it as, although it has to be conceded that it will be too radical a method of thought for most, and that it is probably best used sparingly.

Postmodernist thinkers like Lyotard tend to be sceptical not just about what we think we know, but about what we can ever hope to know. Lyotard felt that scientific enquiry now produced not knowledge but the unknown, continually coming across mysteries in the course of its enquiries that its theories could not resolve (physics has been particularly productive in this respect in recent years, landing us with such problems as what existed before the big bang, or generated it; as well as such counter-intuitive entities to ponder over as black holes, dark matter, and dark energy). As we discussed in Chapter 5, this meant that a theory of everything was to be considered an impossible dream; there were things we could never know, things that we simply did not have the ability to know. (It is instructive to note in this context that a Grand Unified Theory (GUT) remains frustratingly elusive to the scientific community, despite periodic claims for quite some time now that we are right on the verge of it. Many scientists are in fact beginning to backtrack on this and question whether such total understanding of the physical realm will ever be achievable, with John D. Barrow, as a case in point, asserting that we reach a stage with such a theory where 'it tells that there are things that it cannot tell us'.[20] Neither can Barrow see this state of affairs ever coming to an end.)

Lyotard was particularly exercised by the notion of the sublime, the concept for everything that lay beyond our understanding (in Barrow's terms, what theories could not tell us), regarding this as evidence of human limitations – unbreachable limitations that were built into us.[21] We could make no judgements about the sublime, because we could understand neither its workings nor its objectives, these were forever hidden from us. We had to accept that the sublime could never be brought under our control, nor in any way manipulated by us. What such a realization ought to do was give us a sense of proportion as to what we were capable of as human beings. As Barrow was later to describe it, we had to concede that there was a realm of the impossible as well as the possible (rather like the Kantian thing in itself).

Sceptics traditionally emphasize our inability to make judgments (or justify them anyway), and this does create considerable problems for them when it comes to legal or moral matters. How does one settle disputes if there is no possible ground for making judgments in the first place, no self-evidently true criterion by which to construct them or to compare them to afterwards? How does a society set up a legal code under those conditions? Or if it does, how can it persuade its citizens to abide by its rulings? Any such rulings would run the risk of being dubbed arbitrary, which is the last thing that is wanted in a legal system, undermining its whole purpose. Lyotard's answer is to turn to pragmatism, arguing that we should make such judgements on a 'case by case' basis, without feeling in any way bound by previous practice; his argument being that as we have 'no metalanguage' by which to 'ground political or ethical decisions' we have no choice but to proceed in this manner.[22] Pragmatic decisions are judged by their effects, or our intuitive sense of what is right or wrong (admittedly a very problematical criterion, especially given the extent of cultural difference present in a society like our own nowadays, plus postmodernism's insistence on the instability of our personal identity), rather than by their adherence to a set of rules. And indeed we make many such decisions over the course of our lives, without worrying too much about their lack of formal justification (outside the academy these tend to be negotiated on an ongoing basis). One might even venture to suggest that the majority of our everyday decisions are pragmatically arrived at. Postmodernism draws on the work of such radical thinkers as Friedrich Nietzsche when it comes to its bias towards pragmatism, Nietzsche famously arguing that there are no facts, 'only interpretations. We cannot establish any fact "in itself": perhaps it is folly to want to do such a thing' (the theory known as 'perspectivism').[23] Truth, for Nietzsche, is merely what we have come to find convenient to believe over time, so it must always be a candidate for reassessment.

Pragmatism does resolve the problem of how to proceed in such cases therefore, but at a cost. The dread problem of relativism raises its head yet again, meaning that there can be no guarantee of consistency or equality of treatment in the judgements that are made under this dispensation, since we have nothing to gauge them against. There is also the danger that personal factors might well intrude to an unfair degree to skew decisions. But the adoption of pragmatism does show that scepticism need not constitute a dead end as far as discourse is concerned (no matter how much super-scepticism may seem to be trying to engineer this), and as we shall go on to discuss below it is best treated as a tactical method of engaging in debates anyway – which makes it particularly appropriate when it comes to coaching, which certainly does have an inherently tactical aspect to it. Scepticism's drawbacks are easily identifiable, but it is nevertheless a strong method of argument that can be very effective when deployed against dogmatism – and dogmatism is something that the coaching process is designed to counter at all levels within organizations, where it is all too prevalent. Individuals can be stifled by dogmatism, thus inhibited from expressing their talents to the full, which is to society's loss no less than their own. Dogmatism is what prevents change and entrenches bad habits, and fostering the conditions for change has to be at the centre of the coaching process.

One of the great virtues of David Hume's work is that he makes us confront the phenomenon of dogmatism and admit to ourselves just how widespread it is amongst our peers:

> The greater part of mankind are naturally apt to be affirmative and dogmatical in their opinions; and while they see objects only on one side, and have no idea of any counterpoising argument, they throw themselves precipitately into the principles, to which they are inclined; nor have they any indulgence for those who entertain opposite sentiments.[24]

'Opposite sentiments' are surely what coaching ought actively to be encouraging, with the 'dogmatical' imperative to be regarded as counter-productive to success in this area: the antithesis of what any coach is trying to achieve in a structured coaching programme. In the recent credit crisis opposite sentiments were indeed not indulged by those in charge of the major financial corporations, with only too disastrous results for society at large that we are still trying to come to terms with. There was a desperate need for the belief system of finance to be challenged from within, to be made to justify its procedures and practices with a far greater sense of transparency than it was inclined to do. Sadly enough, the group-think that applies in such cases made sure that any such voices were either afraid to assert themselves with enough conviction to be taken seriously, or were marginalized to the point of being largely ignored. One insider even referred dismissively to such critics as 'dinosaurs', as if the entire concept of monitoring had been transcended in the new financial regime:[25] a classic example of dogmatism in action.

If there was a desperate need for sceptical analysis as the market heated up, then there is even more of a need for it now as the system struggles to reconstruct itself in the aftermath of its humiliating collapse and severe loss of public confidence. It would be a tragedy if the necessity for self-reflection was not one of the primary lessons to be learned from the sorry experience of financial collapse. The sector became impervious to criticism, and that is always a danger sign for any system: we *need* sceptical temperaments to be in attendance, voicing awkward opinions that unsettle us and make us think, otherwise we run the risk of further collapses of this kind.

It is worth noting that scepticism does put in an appearance in non-Western cultures, even those, like Islam, with a strong theocratic tradition, which is in general very hostile to the sceptical mindset. Al-Ghazali (1058–1111) is one such thinker in that tradition, and his scepticism was quite far-reaching for its time and cultural context. In his best-known work, *The Incoherence of the Philosophers*, he argues that the philosophical tradition which the Islamic world had inherited from the Greeks (Aristotle, for example, being a particularly influential source) was incompatible with the doctrines of the Koran.[26] He was later to apologize for his scepticism, and it has to be admitted that this method of thought remains fairly marginal to the Islamic tradition overall – tellingly enough, al-Ghazali was never sceptical about religious authority, only philosophical. But the emergence of any form of scepticism at all does indicate that even the most ostensibly authoritarian systems (and theocracies can be very rigid in this respect) can be called into question from within, and we can take heart from that.[27]

Scepticism as tactics

The critical point to make about scepticism is that to be at its most effective it has to be tactical in operation. Ultimately it is a technique which puts the onus on one's opponent to prove his or her point, and more particularly the logical basis for holding it, rather than establishing a fully worked-out alternative interpretation itself. The grounds of the opponent's position are called into question, and he is pushed into a defensive mode in reaction, which is to the sceptic's advantage, enabling him or her to keep raising objections as to the justifications being advanced. It is a negative form of thought therefore, concerned to undermine arguments rather than create them; but it is no less powerful for being so, especially when it comes to puncturing pretensions. As a modern commentator has put it, 'being an uncomfortable position, it is tolerable only if it can be employed to make self-important people still more uncomfortable'.[28] And there is no lack of self-important people in public life. Scepticism is a way of cross-examining received opinion and its goal is to put authority on the spot, demanding that it justify its claims, and in the process prevent it from acting 'precipitately' in the manner identified by Hume, thus closing down debate. When it achieves these objectives, scepticism's value is easy to appreciate, and it can be turned to advantage in coaching on that basis.

The point of such tactical manoeuvres is to sow doubt in the opponent's mind, to make him less sure of his beliefs, and to restrict the growth of dogmatism and fundamentalism. Any of us can become dogmatic about what we believe in, and scepticism offers a welcome corrective to this tendency. It is always worth remembering that for all its apparently nihilistic, even destructive, streak, deconstruction is at base a tactical exercise designed to make us aware of just how many questionable assumptions our discourse is riddled with, and how easily we fall into the trap of accepting these at face value. The sceptic will always be concerned to bring this to our attention, and is performing a public service in doing so. It is only when scepticism turns in on itself that it induces the 'philosophical melancholy' Hume complains about: when it is directed outwards at dogmatism it can be a very stimulating activity, and that is how we feel the sceptical enterprise should be perceived.

Applying scepticism in public life

There is a distinct tendency in public life for dogmatism to develop as power structures are created.[29] Power can be very seductive, wherever it is located, and few who gain it will give it up easily – a point made repeatedly by the critical theorist Michel Foucault throughout his writings, where power is seen to be the source of most of the evils that arise in our culture. This is so whether the context is political or organizational; the managerial ethos is generally to hang on to power and to resist any challenges made to it, whether coming from inside the organization or outside. Organizations outside the political sphere do not have the same oppositional tendency built into them as the political at least ostensibly have, and can be even more grudging about the need for change. The International Monetary Fund and the World Bank, for example, have persisted with policies which have been socially disastrous in a string of countries around the world (the developing world in particular) for several decades now, refusing to concede that neoliberalism and the unregulated market – plus a massive scale-down of the public sector – may not constitute the answer to every nation's economic problems. The policy has been to adopt a 'one size fits all' approach and to insist on compliance with this by any country that seeks out their aid.[30] Their collective attitude is an instructive example of the dogmatist mindset in operation, with market fundamentalism being assumed to be beyond criticism. The commitment to the private sector at the expense of the public has remained undimmed in these bodies, despite the adverse effects the implementation of their policies in large-scale recipients of their aid such as Argentina and the old Eastern bloc countries have had (Argentinian society being reduced to the use of barter for economic transactions at one stage in the 1990s). They are still giving out much the same message in the aftermath of the credit crunch, even though many major economists are arguing that neoliberalism will exacerbate the crisis and that a Keynesian approach, where public spending is instead boosted during economic downturns to encourage demand, is more likely to be effective. Such dogmatism is only too common in large organizations, which tend to become set in their ways over time and very reluctant to alter their basic ideology: tradition can set in very quickly and cover a multitude of sins.

Democracy ought to be the natural home of scepticism, since it enshrines the notion of opposition within the political system, requiring those in power to defend their policies on a regular basis from the criticism offered by their rivals. The adversarial system is supposed to guarantee that all policies are subjected to examination and not put into practice lightly: the opposition is always on hand to draw attention to any failures in this respect, and will use these to raise doubt in the public mind as to the competence of the party in power. Accountability will be insisted upon, in the public interest. That is to describe the system in its ideal state, however, and as we are all aware it does not always function in quite that fashion. All too often it is a case of one form of dogmatism confronting another, without either side really examining their own beliefs in any significant detail. Where this can be countered is through the informal political process that exists in any mature democracy, consisting of the media, and various special interest and pressure groups, as well as the commercial sector to some extent. All of these can mount campaigns against any abuse of power that occurs, as well as against the formal political system itself, which can easily become distanced from the general public and somewhat incestuous in its workings (hence expenses scandals such as the one the UK has just witnessed amongst its parliamentary representatives).

The informal political sector is inherently sceptical in attitude, wishing to call attention to the failings of those in power, often pushing this to the point of satire, and even outright ridicule. Suspicion of the motives of authority figures is cultivated by the media (whether right or left in political orientation), encouraging the public not to put blind trust in them and to be alert to the fact that power can be abused – with the general public invariably the loser when that happens. If this is overdone then it can, admittedly, create an attitude of cynicism about formal politics, but a certain degree of this can be justified as long as it stimulates interest in what is happening in the political process overall. It is not unreasonable to make those in power feel uncomfortable, and to know they will not automatically be given the benefit of the doubt, that in fact they must keep proving they deserve public support.

It is important to note that although it is helpful to understand at least something of the history of scepticism as a philosophical tradition, what inspired it, and continues to intrigue practitioners in the field, its use in public life need not be constrained by its professional concerns. Outside the academy scepticism can, and should, be looser in interpretation and more flexible in application, a tactical weapon to be accessed in order to stir up debate and reassessment of methods and objectives within institutional bodies and organizations. Neither is scepticism incompatible with holding strong beliefs of one's own (whether religious or political), which at first glance it would appear to discourage: it is a technique that one can move in and out of as circumstances dictate (as even Hume indicated he did), while remaining aware that scepticism can always be turned back against one's own position in due course. We can draw yet again on critical theory for conceptual reinforcement here: Lyotard's notion of 'svelteness', which for him represented the ability to change roles to fit the situation at hand, without feeling trapped in a particular kind of identity. What we should now seek to develop in our character was, Lyotard contended, 'flexibility, speed, metamorphic capacity', enabling us to stay in dialogue with the system rather than being overwhelmed by it and losing our individual voice.[31] The svelte individual is adaptability personified, shifting smoothly between roles and debates, maintaining an open and enquiring mind at all times, and being relatively unencumbered by ideological baggage: all the things that large organizations, especially those with long histories, find it so hard to be.

Ultimately, scepticism is a state of mind as much as anything: a determined refusal to lapse into a dogmatic stance when confronted by criticism or requests for clarification of one's beliefs, and a willingness both to ask and to respond positively to searching questions. Public life can only gain from there being much more of this in operation in daily affairs, with 'counterpoising arguments' being to the fore rather than 'affirmative and dogmatical opinions' which simply reinforce existing prejudices.

Uses and abuses of scepticism

Scepticism is a very powerful method of challenging received wisdom and our everyday beliefs, which, as Hume so tellingly pointed out, are very often based on nothing stronger than mere habit. If something works over time then we tend to assume it must be true and that we should continue on with it, but that does not mean it will always work in future, or that it is even the best way to proceed. All traditions find themselves superseded eventually and it is right to subject them regularly to a quizzical eye, to cast doubt on the superstructures they have built up over the years. Tradition, too, has its good points, and we do need to remain in touch with our past and have a sense of where we have come from historically; but it can easily ossify, coming to prize conformity with established practice above all else – which is generally to the advantage of those in power, for whom it means less chance of a threat arising to their authority. (A fictional example of what this might be like taken to its extreme can be found in Mervyn Peake's *Gormenghast* trilogy, where tradition has taken over public life to the extent that it consists of little else but slavishly following rituals whose original meaning has long since been forgotten. Yet any attempt to tamper with the system is regarded with horror.[32]) The philosopher C. H. Whiteley's observation that really serious scepticism 'is usually directed against some entrenched intellectual Establishment' is always worth bearing in mind as a guide.[33] Entrenched establishments can act as a barrier to needed change, and it is one of scepticism's strongest selling points that it is always willing to take these entities on and require them to account publicly for their practices. Establishments will always form in any organized society, and they can have their value (professional accreditation bodies which exist to maintain standards, for example), but they benefit from being kept under a certain degree of stress – one of the most important lessons that complexity theory holds for us is that systems must be kept on edge otherwise they will most likely lose their impetus. Seen from this perspective, scepticism is integral to any healthy system: questions always need to be asked, actions justified, policies debated, and scepticism expedites these activities very efficiently.

However, the drawbacks of scepticism have to be admitted as well. As an analytical method it is undeniably negative in intention, and it can be nitpicking in style. Sceptics can be very irritating to debate with, telling you what is questionable about your views and unsustainable in your assumptions, but not necessarily how to put these right (other than to 'suspend' them, which is not always an acceptable option), or offering much in the way of a viable alternative themselves. Like it or not, judgements do have to be made in any society, and we cannot avoid them just because they produce some philosophical paradoxes along the way: a society run entirely on Pyrrhonist lines would be very impractical – and probably would not survive for very long either, one suspects. Then there is the tricky issue of relativism, which will always make its appearance along with scepticism. Relativism is a self-defeating position to find oneself in because it undermines the sceptic's claims as much as it does those of her opponents. If there is no ground for truth, then sceptics can no more prove their claims than their opponents can – at which point we reach stasis in a philosophical context. Unless it is deployed tactically, as we have just recommended above, then scepticism can become a rather arid exercise. It can, and should, be used to inspire reform, but it always has to be remembered that it is a technique rather than an ideology or a belief-system in its own right – it needs a system to work within, something to work against.

The sceptical coach: The sceptical coachee

So where does this leave us with coaching? Why, and how, should we develop the notion of the sceptical coach and the sceptical coachee? As we insisted before, scepticism has a great deal of relevance to our daily affairs, both in and out of the workplace. The benefits of a sceptical attitude towards authority are many, especially if it is applied in a tactical manner, designed to achieve a particular goal, rather than just challenging authority for the pure sake of it (which one can sometimes feel is the case with Pyrrhonists, and their desire to suspend the act of judgement altogether). Making those who dispense managerial judgements feel 'uncomfortable' is all to the ultimate good of the organization (in whatever field), a critical element in ensuring its longer-term health. As we know from the credit crunch, it takes more than the implementation of formal monitoring and auditing procedures to ensure that systems remain ethical in their conduct: habit can enshrine a host of questionable practices. Coachees should be encouraged to develop a sceptical temperament, to keep both their own and the organization's beliefs and policies under scrutiny, and to be on the lookout for the emergence of a destructive dogmatism within these: the managerial superstructure, like Descartes' youthful beliefs before he discovered scepticism, may well be dubious and error-strewn.

If nothing else, coaching helps to keep us aware that other interpretations are always possible, and that we should not feel ourselves bound by what tradition or convention dictate. And of course that is what the coach too must be doing, continually testing her beliefs and practices within the coaching framework, continually making it clear that other interpretations can be developed, and that it is desirable to foster the conditions for this to happen (as Derrida rather more dramatically put it, '[t]he future can only be anticipated in the form of an absolute danger. It is that which breaks absolutely with constituted normality'[34]). How this can be done forms the subject of Chapter 8; but before tackling that let us consider just what went wrong to provoke the credit crisis, forcing us to reassess our relationship to authority in both the private and public spheres.

Part IV

Theory into Coaching

7
The Market Paradigm: What Went Wrong?

The credit crisis is still with us, and may be for quite some time yet as the shock to the system was deep and profound, going well past the point where it could bounce back rapidly as if from a temporary downturn of the kind that all economies expect to happen periodically. In this instance long-established practices and assumptions have been thrown into disarray, especially since these were based on a belief in the self-correcting power of the market. Markets, it was believed almost universally within the financial community, would always tend towards equilibrium if allowed to go about their business without outside interference (hence the concerted opposition to any significant government role in their running): investors were rational beings and therefore would always act in such a way as to protect their self-interest. Plainly, that did not occur in this case, any more than it did in the Wall Street Crash of 1929, the only other truly comparable financial crisis of modern times in terms of global damage. Investors can in fact be extremely irrational, and bubbles can, and do, arise, often with catastrophic consequences for the national economies involved.[1] We have the dubious distinction of having added one of the most damaging bubbles ever to the historical canon, one that future generations will no doubt study with considerable fascination, wondering why we did not heed the plentiful warnings of trouble ahead and take suitably evasive action while we still stood the chance.

The financial community's ability to forget the lessons offered by the experience of bubbles is, however, legendary. They are invariably regarded as phenomena belonging to economically less sophisticated ages than our own, lacking our scientific expertise. We, on the other hand, picture ourselves as not so naive as to allow booms to get out of hand in the manner that our forebears did, and in effect to have tamed the market to do our bidding. A genuinely free market is seen to be the key to maintaining growth: the bull market so beloved of traders and economic analysts. So the entire trend of financial life for the last few decades has been to move steadily away from regulation towards an open global market where restrictions on the movement of capital or goods would be minimal (ideally there would be none at all if the more fanatical of the market fundamentalists had their way, and they have been campaigning tirelessly to that end over the last few decades). In terms of market behaviour, in the West particularly, what this has meant has been easier credit and more speculation, generating a financial boom that even showed itself impervious to such periodic blips as the dot.com debacle of the early 1990s, which the system managed to absorb fairly comfortably despite some heavy losses being sustained on some highly speculative ventures (boo.com, for example, being a $135 million failure). We now know that this boom was built on a culture of risk-taking so excessive that it was just asking for trouble: a 'house of cards', as one commentator aptly has described it, that was bound to topple eventually, more self-destruct than self-correct.[2] At some point something just had to give way in a market structured on an ever-increasing debt mountain.

The upshot of the credit crisis has been that a system which has exhibited little but disdain for government involvement in the market now finds itself, with the deepest of ironies, surviving only through the agency of repeated government intervention and massive injections of public money. A paradigm has been breached, and that creates an opportunity for a new look at the ideology of the marketplace, and how this has taken over our lives in the name of a rampant consumerism that is beginning to worry many socially conscious commentators quite considerably.[3] In one particularly trenchant reading of the crisis and its cultural context, we have surrendered not just to the consumerist but to the corporate ethic, with Douglas Rushkoff arguing that '[w]e behaved like corporations ourselves, extracting the asset value of our homes and moving on with our families, going into more debt and assuming we'd have the chance to do it again.'[4] Here again, belief in the self-correct mechanism has been punctured, and a host of individuals have found to their dismay that they cannot necessarily rely on such chances always appearing for their benefit.

The unlikely role of hormones and emotions

Organizations and systems have their own particular house metanarratives and these dictate a certain conformity of behaviour that, to put it gently, discourages the emergence of adversary voices within the corporate structure (and in a culture which is often still defiantly masculinist in character, 'adversary' can also come to mean female, especially those who raise objections to the existence of a 'glass ceiling' blocking their progress). One of the more interesting theories in support of a challenge to the adversarial approach associated with a masculinist character is the role that emotions play in financial decision-making, embracing both greed and fear. Financial theory has been dominated by a central premise which claims that markets are efficient. The result is that traditional finance has evolved normatively by developing rational financial tools and ideas of how traders should behave, therefore ignoring actual behaviour. Challenging the rational model, critics of the Efficient Markets Hypothesis have argued that investors express possible ruinous biases attributed to emotional responses such as fear and greed. Sébastien Michenaud and Bruno Solnik suggest that regret is another emotion traders experience which leads to pain and anger when they take a bad decision.[5] Regret, as a powerful negative emotion, may lead individuals to make apparently sub-optimal, non-rational decisions to counteract the outcome of bad decisions and according to Michenaud and Solnik it is an important psychological trait in investment choices. It follows that regret aversion will influence future decision-making.[6]

Research also demonstrates that overconfidence leads to poor performance and that overconfidence is more likely to be found amongst male traders than female: such overconfidence is pervasive and leads to the inevitable ego trap. The result is that overconfidence leads to higher levels of trading and risk-taking. A significant psychological fact which accompanies overconfidence is the illusion of control, with many people believing they are able to control and predict the unpredictable: the 'master of the universe' syndrome so scathingly portrayed in Tom Wolfe's novel *The Bonfire of the Vanities*.[7] As recent history has testified, such overconfidence, coupled with emotions and other psychological biases, not only leads to trading losses but if unchecked leads to the destruction of an industry as well. Kent H. Baker and John R. Nofsinger argue that most people are worse decision-makers than their self-perception might indicate.[8] Furthermore, people seek information and confirmation to affirm their beliefs. Such self-deception, as we have seen, can lead to disastrous consequences.

According to media reports the stock market displays many human behavioural traits such as sadness, optimism, pessimism, and moodiness. Two Cambridge neurologists, John M. Coates and Joseph Herbert, have discovered a significant link between the behaviour exhibited by traders and their levels of hormones, such as testosterone, and which is linked with emotion.[9] This is in direct contrast with the external image of investor decisions being driven by rational analysis after obtaining all available information; an assumption increasingly being abandoned by economists. Hence Richard Bronk's call for a turn to 'romantic economics', where imagination takes precedence over a narrow-minded rationalism espoused by the majority of the profession.[10] Research would suggest that high-performing traders do in fact rely heavily on their emotions and hunches – if not perhaps in the artistic manner that Bronk is seeking. It would appear that a high level of testosterone acts as the elixir of male aggressiveness, otherwise labelled as competitiveness, leading to greed and more greed and the eventual overconfidence that undoubtedly contributed to the economic crisis. The converse applies when cortisol is produced during uncertainty and volatility leading to fear, which also prevents clear, analytical thinking. The role of emotion and hormones provides a different perspective to the causes of boom and bust. One recommendation by Dr. Coates to balance the excessive levels of testosterone and cortisol is to increase the number of women and older men on the trading floors; a change which would no doubt be considered controversial by some in what prides itself as being a supercharged activity.

The group-think route to financial crisis

In retrospect it is relatively easy to identify questionable practices, rogue corporations and individuals, and systematic regulatory failures, and to lay the blame on these for the crisis that resulted.

A steady stream of books since the crisis broke has done just that, and there is general agreement amongst the authors that far-reaching change has to come about, and fairly urgently too, if we are to resurrect the financial system in any viable form that still serves a recognizable social purpose.[11] Credit derivatives have been vilified, as have a portfolio of barely understood financial products that were unleashed on the market and traded in with more enthusiasm than forethought; the bonus system attacked; corporate greed and social irresponsibility drawn attention to; government naivety highlighted. Add these all together and they suggest that there is something very wrong indeed within the belief system underpinning the financial sector. The literature is all suitably apocalyptic in tone, speaking of gods that have failed, meltdown, catastrophe, ruin, and the like. None of the authors seems in any doubt that we have gone through a culturally defining moment that should make us take stock of where we are and what we are trying to achieve. But will we?

The market paradigm, and its effect on corporate and investor behaviour, needs to be broken down and analysed to determine why and how it managed to generate a crisis on the scale that it did. What were the beliefs involved which could allow things to drift so far out of control that the entire world financial order was threatened with collapse? (One financier, drawing on species history, was even moved to wonder if we were witnessing an 'extinction event' as banks and hedge funds started to go under.[12]) What was the psychology of the participants that left them unable to acknowledge the dangers they were running? The next step will be to consider whether it is possible to build in some safeguards to the system to prevent the mistakes from being repeated. Coaching, and the encouragement of a sceptical temperament that asks awkward questions, will be allotted a key role in the process. The contention will be that scepticism can and should be taught, that it can and should be fostered, and all to both the corporate and the public good. First, however, just what did go awry within the belief system to cause it to malfunction quite so spectacularly as it did in 2008–9?

One obvious answer to that last question is: the ubiquity of group-think within the commercial sector. A hugely underestimated factor in understanding psychological biases and emotional influences is the role of social influences on investors. Peer groups tend to develop shared norms and beliefs and a desire to live similar lifestyles: conformity creeps in here too. Beliefs about the practice of trading and investing are also part of the group norms and to act otherwise would be to contradict them. Managements rarely like to be challenged too strenuously on their decisions or strategies, and expect – one might even go so far as to say, demand – assent rather than dissent. Team-building exercises, that training standby of the corporate world, are all about serving the same cause, working towards a common objective, and sublimating individual personality to that effect. Liberal democracy may claim that it is based on a commitment to individualism and that individual initiative drives it in the commercial domain (the entrepreneurial ethic we are always being asked to admire as the basis for our economic well-being), but the reality is that anyone working in an organization is soon schooled into the practice of group-think – and again, this is almost always heavily masculinist in its bias, requiring considerable contortions on the part of the female employees if they are to survive. One might well be ambitious and do one's utmost to further one's career within the organizational set-up, but the likelihood is that this objective will be conducted within the parameters of a tightly defined corporate vision, which expects, and generally rewards, loyalty.

What has further emerged from the post-mortem is the collusion that so many in the financial sector have been party to. The concept of group-think is not a new phenomenon, first being mooted by Janis in 1972, and it can contribute to putting an entire organization at risk.[13] One of the major symptoms of group-think is collusion and the lengths individuals and groups will go to in order to protect the ideology of the group. Group-think may also lead to an elitism that isolates a small section from the rest of the group or organization creating a sense of separateness and possibly an overstated sense of self-worth; the 'untouchables', as they want to picture themselves. The result is a lack of self-censoring critical thinking, with the insulation of the group and its shared belief of psychological safety acting as a barrier against the need for change. Whilst the group is producing results, they are more or less left alone to self-correct any possible anomalies. There is also the sense of invulnerability that permeates the group, organization, or industry.

A lesson to be learned from group-think is that leaders have to be trained in and rewarded for creating and sustaining critical thinking.[14] The result of group-think confirms research by Carmeli, which suggests that although managers recognize that they are at risk of failure, instead of guarding against it or facing it when it happens and learning from it, there is the tendency for them to ignore it[15] – fetishization in action again. The deficiencies in decision-making within a group-think scenario are the result of distorted thinking which includes the emotional states referred to above, such as fear and elation. Janis believes that the blind spots encountered in group-think have their roots in our social prejudices and within organizations, in inadequacies in information-processing.[16] These inadequacies prevent understanding of the complex, and in this case, catastrophic consequences of flawed decision-making which is compounded over a period of time. It is therefore mooted that organizations fail to learn from the error of their ways. Janis quotes Nietzsche, who said that madness is the exception in individuals but the rule in groups.[17] This is self-evident when we observe group behaviour such as scapegoating, mindless conformity, and the collective misjudgement and denial which could only be described as madness. It is evident that even the most senior group of leaders in so-called respected industries are not immune to such forms of group derangement.

A motivation for group-think is group cohesiveness, as it engenders a sense of solidarity and positive feelings amongst the group members. However, the dark side harbours the tendency to fall victim to gross errors which lead to shared misjudgements. The tendency is then to manipulate and suppress information and voices of dissent attempting to present evidence to the contrary. Subtle constraints are imposed on group members, preventing individuals from exercising their critical powers and engaging in open expression of their doubts. At first the critical member becomes the focus of persuasion by other group members in order to persuade that individual to revise his or her dissident ideas. If that fails, the deviant is increasingly isolated and ostracized by the group. Taken to the extreme the individual will be labelled as a whistleblower, which often has negative results for individuals and their careers (the argument for whistleblowing is put forward in Chapter 9). Research has shown that the more cohesive the group becomes, the greater the likelihood is of it rejecting any nonconformists that emerge. In parallel is the rejection and isolation from outside critics who threaten to disrupt the *status quo* or any serious questioning of group norms.

The consequences of group-think are evidence of the inability of organizations and industries to self-regulate and to challenge their own norms and values. As we have seen in worst-case scenarios, such as the meltdown of the banking sector, this leads to flawed decision-making of incomprehensible proportions and is akin to mass suicide. From his observations, Janis concludes that 'any social group subconsciously establishes a hidden agenda which sets out to maintain and protect group cohesion and intragroup relations.'[18] He goes on to assert that, '[g]roupthink refers to a deterioration of mental efficiency, reality testing, and moral judgment that results from in-group pressures.'[19] The banking industry is the result of the stark reality which results in the rejection of critical voices attempting to rein in overconfident and deluded group-think.

An outcome of pervasive group-think over time is the emergence of an illusion of invulnerability and pervasive group euphoria which results in the signs of danger going unheeded; the banking sector being a textbook case of this phenomenon. With hindsight the buoyant optimism within the industry created a shared belief that the good times would continue indefinitely, blanking out any signs to the contrary. Coupled with the sense of invulnerability is the emergence of elitism, clearly the case among the testosterone-driven alpha males who traded their way to near extinction in the frantic bid to outstrip their peers. As we have noted, consensual validation prevents critical thinking and reality testing, and there is also evidence of collusion within and without the industry with the illusion of elitism. These entrenched beliefs and associated behaviours pervading the City leads to the avoidance of tackling the root causes of the crises, such as the eye-watering bonuses which continue to be paid to traders despite apparent attempts at challenging these practices (governments being at best half-hearted at taking on the financial sector). This may be the result of self-appointed mindguards often associated with group dynamics, who take it upon themselves to protect the group from deviants who seek to alter the group norms. Group pressures which maintain such illusion are often the result of leadership practices. The banking industry would benefit from critical soul searching of a style of leadership which allowed the destructive practices to continue up to and beyond the brink of disaster – and coaching offers a ready means to put the process into motion.

In an attempt to understand and thereby avoid the occurrence of group-think, it is to be noted that it is found within groups seeking to maintain self-esteem especially when their decisions may lead to social and self-disapproval. As Janis contends, the illusion of invulnerability and shared rationalizations helps to counteract any sense of inadequacy and pessimism associated with the inability at finding solutions during a crisis.[20] The same applies during times of great gains to the group and acts as a cover-up for a risky course of action which may result in being found out – as was manifestly the case within the finance sector. Through the pooling of intellectual resources and rationalizations the group is able to bolster individual confidence and the ability to take risks. When things do go awry, the tendency of the group is to attribute the blame elsewhere in order to maintain their perceived innocence and to protect the *status quo* at any cost. Such behaviour also serves as a mechanism to reduce anxiety and guilt.

The learning process suggests that reflective learning (that is, critical thinking) involving healthy scepticism is the most appropriate way to ensure that an open mind is exercised and assumptions challenged and scrutinized; this is also referred to as double-loop learning. What is clear from the post-mortem is that group-think extends beyond a team, department, or organization to a whole industry. Trading and investment requires credibility and trust amongst partners in the face of an unpredictable future. As Jocelyn Pixley argues, the trust-inducing assessments that organizations carry out as part of the process to build trust between organizations are incapable of providing certainty in a volatile and unpredictable environment.[21] In addition, the guardians of such trust are human and therefore susceptible to failings such as corruption, conflict of interest, and other emotional weaknesses and psychological biases. Such trust, as has been apparent, is also susceptible to group-think, which has permeated the industry as a whole. Through a perverse logic one could understand why hardly anyone would give credence to voices of dissent while the going was good and rewards high.

Social constructionism offers one theory by way of explanation for the phenomenon of group-think. The relatedness referred to between individuals within teams, departments, organizations and between organizations within an industry is fundamental to constructionism. The central premise of social constructionism is that knowledge is a product of this relatedness and constructed between individuals. Social constructionists, such as Gergen, view the reality we experience not as a map reflecting what is out there, but the product of a communal interchange.[22] Furthermore, the socially constructed reality shared within a group results in related actions and as their view of circumstances change, so do their corresponding actions. Social constructionism claims that the beliefs and norms of a group are the result of active interchange between people engaged in reciprocal relationships, and as Gergen notes, this emphasizes a 'communal interdependence'.[23] The negative outcome of group-think is that reality becomes objectified, leading to closure of arguments, options are dismissed, relationships are frozen, and voices of difference go unheard.[24] Peter L. Berger and Thomas Luckmann point out that irrespective of how powerful and large organizations may appear, they are the result of human construction.[25] Gergen goes further to say that, '[t]hey are lived fictions in a world where there is no living beyond fiction.'[26] All institutions, including organizations, are objectified human activities. Organizations are dynamic and reality is continually being redefined and renegotiated within them. According to a constructivist perspective, the ills that trouble an organization are directly a result of the negotiated reality.

Coaching, on the other hand, is very much concerned with developing the individual (notably his or her faculty of self-awareness), thus placing it in opposition to the group-think mode. Coaching may also be one of the few powerful interventions that could successfully bring about a challenge to the group norms and reality constructed within an organization or industry. We would argue that this is one of its strongest selling points as an activity, and one that should be accentuated: women in particular have much to gain from this. The more pluralist that organizations proceed to become, the more they are designed to promote genuinely adversarial voices internally, the less likely we are to run headlong into crisis in the manner that we have done recently – the collective does not always know best, nor must its will always be obeyed.

The argument for introducing gender balance

In a foreword to the book by Avivah Wittenberg-Cox and Sarah Maitland, *Why Women Mean Business*, Niall FitzGerald KBE, Deputy

Chairman of Thomson Reuters, questions the boardroom behaviours that have resulted in the near destruction of the financial giants worldwide.[27] He goes on to suggest that a gender balance on the boards would provide a diversity which would deliver a more stable and balanced approach to corporate performance. Gender diversity may well act as a check against the group-think phenomenon discussed above. The crisis in the banking sector certainly once again raises questions of the male-dominated model of leadership and its rules and regulations that continue to shape institutions. Wittenberg-Cox and Maitland argue that the meltdown of the finance industry has revealed the rot within the system and challenge the assumption that says it could possibly be 'business as usual' from now on.[28] They go on to assert that it will only be through leadership composed of a partnership between men and women that a saner and therefore safer model of capitalism can be built. In 2010, women continue to experience the same barriers of the last century which prevent them from realizing their full potential, and the low representation of women in leadership positions, in particular, remains unchanged. Organizational practices contribute significantly to encourage the imbalance between male and female. Women are, for example, consistently placed in support roles due to an erroneous assumption that they have a lower level of ambition than that of men.

There is significant evidence that women continue to be disadvantaged through financial rewards that remain higher for men than for women. As the corporate world often considers compensation as a major indicator of a successful career, this puts women in a weaker position than that of their male colleagues. Research also indicates that self-promoting and confident women are more likely to be rejected as they are seen to be a threat to men. Women find themselves in a no-win situation: confidence poses a threat and modesty reinforces the male view of women as being weak and less competent than men. It is only in recent years that the dominance of a masculine model has come under much scrutiny. Up until then it had gone largely unchallenged, being seen as a taken-for-granted reality. The dominance of men in leadership positions was perceived as the norm and, on the contrary, the appearance and presence of women regarded as being out of place and therefore troubling. Masculine qualities have been the yardstick by which leadership has been judged and measured and these deeply ingrained views will naturally dismiss feminine behaviour as powerless and ineffective. What we have observed from group-think and the beliefs that underpin its practices proves that we have some way to go yet for those beliefs to be recognized and for the exclusion of difference, such as a female perspective to leadership, to be brought to conscious attention and positively acted upon.

Following the meltdown of the financial sector, newspaper headlines commenting on the absence of women at the top of organizations were commonplace. Debates ensued in various quarters as to whether the crisis would have been averted if there had been better balance of leadership in the industry. The risk awareness expressed by women is often misinterpreted as risk aversion and from what we have seen above, confidence and risk-taking are synonymous with successful traders. However, the definition of what constitutes 'success' will surely come under scrutiny and be subject to redefinition. It would be erroneous solely to blame men for the financial crisis and it is evident that the system colluded in failing to confront the group-think of the sector. These include the regulators, the bosses of the banks who did not understand the new financial vehicles, the governments encouraging light regulation, not to mention the bonus culture which remains a sacred cow. It would, however, be interesting to know the ratio of men and women in the aforementioned institutions.

An interesting study conducted by Michel Ferrary, Professor at CERAM Business School in France, calls for management to be 'feminized', on the grounds that an improved gender balance could play a significant role in tempering the culture of risk-taking that has dominated the financial sector hitherto and which has gone unchecked.[29] His study also reveals that banks with a more equal gender balance have been better equipped to deal with the economic crisis than banks with the more usual male-dominated hierarchy. As the credit crisis drags on, are we possibly seeing the rumblings of a gender revolution in the industry or will the alpha male norms continue to dominate and maintain the *status quo*?[30]

Cautionary voices of reason

There were some adversary voices making themselves heard as the credit bubble grew, however, and in some cases these were very eminent figures in the world of finance. Warren Buffet and George Soros consistently showed themselves to be very uneasy about developments in the sector, with the latter being particularly voluble on the topic; the Nobel Prize-winning economist Paul Krugman was expressing grave doubts about the economic models being used in the boom as far back as the 1990s, warning in his book *The Return of Depression Economics* that these might even spark off a new depression.[31] (Revising the work in 2008, Krugman struck an even more worried note. He had suggested the first time around that if we were not careful the economic problems then arising might well spread like the plague, but in the interim caution had not been exercised and, in his somewhat apocalyptic assessment, we find that 'now the plague is upon us'.[32]) But the group-think ethic could discount these voices as being eccentric as long as the boom rolled on, which of course it did for several years, providing all the evidence that the advocates of neoliberal economics felt they needed to vindicate their practices. Products such as credit derivatives, credit default swaps, and so on were thought to remove most of the risk factor from speculation, so speculation grew all the wilder, widening the network of those involved very considerably.[33] In consequence, there are few financial institutions that have not been left with a sizeable amount of toxic debts on their books after the mad round of 'pass the parcel' (in one commentator's dismissive phrase[34]) that ensued.

The opposition to regulation grew too, with even governments coming to regard this as a hindrance to economic expansion, leading them to adopt progressively more market fundamentalist-friendly policies – the 'light touch' approach favoured by such as New Labour in the UK and the Republican Party in the US (although most Western governments relaxed their regulation of business to a very significant degree compared to previous practice). Critical reflection on the economic metanarrative was signally missing, with the true believers seeing no need for it. Now, however, we can realize just how tragic a mistake that was – and not just for those in the finance industry either, no one being completely immune from the effects of economic collapse. Anyone with a bank account will have had cause to worry (they still do), as will anyone with a company pension – indeed, anyone at all with a job, and their dependents, anywhere in the world, no matter how well- or poorly paid they may be.

Overall, the credit crisis has proved to be a particularly instructive example of what can go wrong when one interpretation is allowed to dominate to the extent of becoming authoritarian and totalitarian: a case study that will repay close attention for some time to come in this respect. Assumptions which should have been subjected to constant scrutiny were simply being taken as gospel instead, and many banks and financial houses ended up in a position where they were unable to cover their outlay unless the system kept on expanding remorselessly – which most of them quite literally proceeded to put their money on (or their clients' money, to be more precise). The system began to resemble a gigantic pyramid scheme and as such was instrinsically unstable. It was a situation exacerbated by the fact that the division between the speculating and savings functions of banks had been largely removed, thus enabling banks to risk their capital to a far greater degree than had been the norm in the post–Second World War world (the Glass-Steagall Act in the USA, which was passed during the Depression years to guarantee this separation, was superseded by far less restrictive legislation in 1999). Banks in the USA, for example, are permitted to have as much as 40 times their assets out on loan at any one time; which is fine as long as there is a boom going on, but a crisis in waiting if this suddenly goes into reverse. Although noises have been made by governments such as the British and American to reconsider this arrangement (in effect, turning banks into pluralist organizations in a business sense), nothing very concrete has emerged as yet. The banks themselves, not surprizingly, are anything but keen at the prospect either, since it would significantly curb the volume of their operations in the market and thus reduce the bonuses of their higher management personnel. One could say that most of the sector is effectively in denial as to what precipitated the crisis. Whether in this area or elsewhere, coaching is a way of addressing corporate denial, so all the more reason to call for its sceptical side to be emphasized.

The Northern Rock fiasco, however, demonstrated what could happen once this instability became apparent to both the financial authorities and then the general public (media reportage of the long queues of angry customers, urgently seeking withdrawals of their savings, outside the company's offices, brought home the reality of the looming crisis to the British public as nothing else had succeeded in doing up to that point).[35] As a company, Northern Rock was notorious for having a gung-ho higher management which brooked no opposition to its expansionary policies, with the result that even its directors kept quiet about any unease they may have felt as to possible dangers. For companies in that mode, internal scepticism is about as welcome as an instance of treason would be in governmental circles; at the very least an expression of bad faith that should be excised as quickly as possible, on the grounds that it harms the company's image. The fact that, right up to the last moment, Northern Rock was being feted as a model of business success by both the finance industry and the British government, proudly promoting itself as one of the fastest-growing banks in the UK (most notably in the area of mortgage lending), is an indication of just how deeply embedded the market fundamentalist belief system had become. Almost no one in a responsible position was willing to question the practices to which this system had given rise, or to counsel restraint. The bubble was simply allowed to grow ever larger, on the assumption that the debt-mountain was a sign of success and that we had the necessary skill to manage it.

Northern Rock provided the UK's worst-case scenario in the developing crisis, Lehman Brothers America's, with doomsday headlines being the order of the day. One was rescued, the other was allowed to collapse; but there were dozens of similar cases to note in those countries as well as around the rest of the world. Trust in the system simply evaporated and politicians were forced into some very hurried, and very desperate, decisions they were ill-equipped to make, products as they were as individuals of economic good times rather than bad. Nationalized banks had not been on the agenda. Pretty well all the world's major banks and finance houses found themselves caught up in the crisis, with toxic debts being distributed across the system in an almost viral fashion, the outbreak of plague that Krugman had feared we were setting ourselves up for. No one thought they would become toxic when the trading mania in the new financial products was raging of course, and despite a woeful lack of understanding as to what the products actually included, or entailed, the major players in the industry decided that they had no option but to join in or run the risk of falling behind their competitors (and with bonuses being contingent on trading turnover that was a condition strenuously to be avoided). The attitude seemed to be that if others were doing it then it must be alright: the system was trusted – or being more critical, one could say that it was blindly followed with a herd-like mentality that showed the culture of group-think at its worst. In fact, group-think was paving the way to crisis.

Subprime virus: Credit derivative plague

What brought the crisis to a head was the collapse of the American subprime mortgage market, which future social and economic historians will no doubt find a rich source of material on how a metanarrative (especially one fuelled by greed) can lead us drastically astray. The expansionary imperative behind the credit boom meant that new markets had to keep being found and exploited as thoroughly and quickly as possible, and this eventually led to areas being explored that were traditionally thought to be problematical. On the back of an unprecedented boom in the housing market throughout the West, mortgage conditions had become less and less stringent in the closing decades of the twentieth century and then into the early years of the twenty-first. Mortgage brokers were increasingly willing to loan over 100% of the purchase price of houses to get people onto their books, and increasingly willing, too, to lend to those in lower-income brackets who would not normally be considered acceptable as clients – the subprime section of the credit-rated world. It was felt that the risk of default in the latter group was absorbable in the overall picture, and that the lender could always sell the properties on if repossession ever had to be instigated. The assumption was that the stock market would keep on climbing and share prices rising – as seemed to be the case, with most analysts predicting a very bright future on the economic front (most of us conveniently forgetting how unreliable futurology tends to be). Assets on the books were what counted, and these were remorselessly piled up, with all those involved in the transaction on the lending side pocketing handsome commissions for their efforts as they went – which only made them all the more committed to prolonging the enterprise in any way they could. This hitherto largely untapped market grew very rapidly, and lenders began to look for ways of minimizing the risk of default to themselves, which is where credit derivatives came onto the scene.

Credit derivatives were widely thought to have the capacity to bring about a revolution in the world of lending and financial speculation, enabling companies to spread risk on their loans and thus cut their liabilities in the cases where anything did go wrong. They were not as such a new idea, but they were subjected to a great deal of fine-tuning as a financial product in the later twentieth century, and the industry felt this had made them much more attractive as trading entities. Once they took off as a product there were substantial profits to be made by those astute enough to know how best to sell them on to other buyers and keep the market buoyant. The preferred practice was to bundle up various levels of risk in packages (graded accordingly by ratings agencies like Standard and Poor's) such that the high-risk entities were offset by the low, the principle being that everything averaged out in the longer term. In theory this seems a sound procedure, but over time the slicing up of the various risks, and then their re-combination with a bewildering variety of others of varying degrees of creditworthiness, became so complicated that it was hard to tell what a given package was actually worth. Eventually, many financial institutions had to admit that they could no longer make such assessments, that the averaging out process no longer seemed to be working as expected. So began a painful process of writing off large amounts of assets they held on their books: a process which, once started (as with the French bank BNP Paribas's well-publicized problems[36]), spread very rapidly. Again, the viral analogy is an apt one: no institution seemed able to develop an immunity to the condition, and suddenly everyone seemed dangerously vulnerable, fearful that they would be next in line for the plague to strike.

There proved to be precious little in the way of contingency plans for such an event, because the metanarrative was not supposed to fail: everyone was playing the game they had all been assured was the only one that was sensible to play in the current climate, based on the premise that bull markets were in the ascendancy (again the lesson has to be, best beware futurology). The only thing that prevented the global financial system from imploding altogether was government intervention on the grand scale, with billions of dollars, pounds, euros, and so on being pumped into ailing institutions and markets by politicians scared that they were facing the economic abyss and potentially the collapse of an entire way of life. Expediency took precedence over any argument for ideological purity in this instance, even in the USA. For market fundamentalists that represented a massive blow to their belief system; the exact antithesis of how they thought the world should be operating. There was genuine shock within the industry at this dramatic turn of events, as the financial journalist Gillian Tett reported: ' "We are moving into a world of socialist banking, where the government can meddle wherever it wants," lamented one senior European bank executive. A new era of finance had dawned – albeit not one that most bankers had ever expected, far less wanted, to see.'[37] The limitations of group-think had been brutally exposed.

Countering group-think

The belief system behind the credit bubble, neoliberal economics, acted to quash debate therefore, when what was really required was a constant round of this to identify the system's weak points and thus head off trouble. Anyone with a sceptical turn of mind would have been able to see these readily enough, and it would have been to the system's advantage if this had happened on a regular basis, if individuals had been given the encouragement to express dissenting views (including feminist ones) and know that these would be listened to with respect and taken seriously. Northern Rock needed it, Lehman Brothers needed it, but their commitment to group-think militated against such a development. Group-think could turn a blind eye to the essential volatility of markets; sceptics, with their ingrained tendency to ask awkward questions and remain suspicious of received wisdom, could not. Unless such independent attitudes are allowed to emerge within the financial sector, we shall almost undoubtedly end up with yet more crises – and how many more such shocks the system could take is debatable. At some point, government intervention will cease to be enough to resolve the problem, and in point of fact we still do not know if it has even succeeded in doing so in this current case. The system is still beset with instabilities and insecurities; still in need of periodic injections of public money ('quantitative easing', as it is somewhat euphemistically referred to now); full recovery is still being pushed into the indefinite future by many commentators wary, rightly enough, of the validity of claims from the political class to be able to detect green shoots of recovery springing up all around in the economy. Optimism and realism do not always match up, and it is one of the sceptic's tasks to make those instances widely known, to refuse to toe the party line for reasons of mere political expediency – in effect, to stop us from taking refuge in fetishization.

The virtues of a critical outlook are only too obvious in this sector therefore, although the signs that this is developing in the aftermath of the crisis are not particularly encouraging to date, with the banking industry doing its best to go on as before now that it has been rescued by the public purse. Apart from anything else, the notorious bonus system has made a strong comeback in the UK and USA, and although this has generated a certain amount of debate in political circles, it has tended to be fairly low-key, with governments being notably hesitant to come into open confrontation with any of the major players in the financial sector. Unless there is much more of a public outcry than there has been so far, one suspects this will become standard practice again. And it has to be noted that the bonus culture thrives on risk, on 'chasing alpha', as Philip Augar has described it: 'alpha' being the City's term for 'supercharged profit'.[38] For supercharged profit one can also, however, read supercharged risk.

How can we set about mitigating the effects of group-think? All organizations are prone to this and will most likely see it as evidence of efficiency and common purpose on their part, rather than a potential weakness urgently needing to be addressed through methods such as, for example, a more vigorous form of coaching designed to promote greater individualism and intellectual independence within the corporate hierarchy. What we are recommending is that coaching should be more geared towards developing that trait in coachees, making it clear that the current organizational metanarrative they are operating under is just one among many that could be constructed, and that it needs to be kept under constant review to prevent it from ossifying. Organizational (and political) narratives ought to be kept as fluid as possible, and they will not be so unless there is genuine questioning going on about them within the systems in question. That could even mean, as we shall go on to discuss in more detail in Chapter 9, that the coachee could feel justified in developing a whistleblowing mentality to draw attention to the shortcomings of group-think and how these were serving to generate crisis (although we concede that would be an extreme implication of radical coaching that calls for very careful handling). The financial sector bought into the narrative of neoliberalism with unabashed enthusiasm, its practitioners convincing themselves that they had discovered the perfect system to overturn the 'boom and bust' cycle that had bedevilled global economic life throughout modern history. They hadn't, and there is a very important lesson to be learned from their presumption: that group-think distorts reality and can seriously undermine organizational health.

There are clear opportunities for coaching to make a significant contribution to overcoming the situation we find ourselves stuck in. The need for critical coaching is even more apparent having considered the psychological dimension to the market paradigm, and how this has served to reinforce the group-think ethic – particularly its masculinist dimension. A feminist reading of the credit crisis is well overdue, and its findings could certainly inform the coaching process to good effect. Gender, as we have signalled, is another area that deserves to come under the microscope in the aftermath of the crisis. One major caveat to this suggestion is how willing would the industry be to expose their weaknesses to the scrutiny of a critical coach? How we might tackle that reluctance by demonstrating the benefits of a more radical approach to coaching forms the topic of our next chapter.

8
A New Dawn: Applying Critical Theory to Coaching

We can now consider how to go about integrating a range of critical theories into coaching, such that the coachee will have a wider intellectual repertoire to call on in charting the course of her career. This means extracting from each particular theory what will be most useful in a workplace environment, the objective being to enable the coachee to see their organizational situation from a variety of viewpoints – perhaps even, as we shall go on to discuss in detail in Chapter 9, that of whistleblowing, with all the delicate issues that raises for the coaching profession.

What would it mean then, as a case in point, to work out your organization's grammar, and how would this help you to negotiate your way within the organization? From a structuralist point of view, the operation of all systems falls into distinctive recurrent patterns, and identifying those patterns enables you to make more effective interventions. How does one part of the organization relate to another? How does one part of the organization communicate with another? What hierarchies are in place and how do these maintain themselves? How is policy decided upon, and how is it implemented? We tend to take those patterns for granted, and in a smoothly running organization they will hardly be noticed on a daily basis, but instinctively we follow their dictates, so it can only be to our advantage to make these explicit so that we can gauge whether they are serving the organization to the best advantage: communication between different parts of an organization can almost always be improved, hierarchies can become oppressive and authoritarian, the rationale behind policy can be misinformed or its implementation be counter-productive to the effect sought. Habit and routine, so simple for all of us to fall into, can blind us to faults and flaws that could be corrected if we reflected upon them, and coaches will always be keen for us to reflect on our environment and our contribution towards its make-up.

The key thing to remember about the grammar of any system is that it can be changed. This does not mean that the grammar is to be regarded as arbitrary or anarchic, as any change that is put forward has to be accepted by all participants as the new way of proceeding from some specified point onwards. What it tells us instead is that grammar is made up of a series of conventions, and that conventions need not be considered to bind us, that they are open to alteration as long as agreement can be reached. Grammar in a general sense is merely what has come to be accepted on a consensus basis; it does not have the force of natural law. To adopt a structuralist perspective is to be attentive to a system's grammar rather than being a captive to it. It is also to recognize that no one can exercise complete control over the narratives constructed from that grammar; that 'death of the author' applies once a narrative is released into general circulation. Policy 'narratives' will be interpreted by their 'readers' in ways that their 'authors' might never have intended. Even the most authoritarian-minded management does not have quite the power it thinks it has in this respect, and it can be illuminating to trace the various ways that organizational narratives are appropriated by their recipients such that the signs can come to mean subtly different things. Attentiveness to the complexities of this process can certainly enhance the coachee's understanding of how the organization functions, and that can be personally advantageous in constructing a career pathway: the more inside information, the better when it comes to plotting one's moves through the organizational set-up.

It can be instructive as well to take a poststructuralist line to one's organizational grammar and the narratives constructed from it, and see where these might be making unwarranted assumptions. Again, one does not need a specific commitment to the entire poststructuralist ethos: its techniques are there to be used to discover what they can yield that can give us a new perspective on our position within the organization. Ideas can be appropriated however we choose to, and put to whatever purpose we deem useful for us. Pragmatism is very much the name of the game in this regard – and it does help to think of theories as games we can move in and out of, each with their own rules and objectives that we can sign up to for as long as we want or find helpful. It is by no means necessary to be a card-carrying poststructuralist to deploy poststructuralist techniques. If nothing else, poststructuralism should teach us to be wary of overly neat methods of analysis: systems are far less predictable in their operation than we are prone to think.

The poststructuralist and postmodernist obsession with difference may seem a rather internal philosophical concern, a desire as much as anything to challenge the structuralist insistence on emphasizing common features across systems, and thus of only peripheral interest at best in the workplace, but it does have some practical implications which are worth drawing attention to in a coaching context. All organizations have a house style which can infiltrate even the most mundane aspects of employees' behaviour: there is a well-attested human tendency to want to blend in with one's surroundings, to fit into the house style as it were, especially in the early stages of one's career when one is trying to make the right impression. Conformity can have a deadening effect, however, closing off the possibility of new ideas that would refresh and reinvigorate the organizational outlook. Women in particular are only too well aware of how difficult it can be to challenge the masculinist ethos that is so prevalent in organizational life and that insists on certain codes of behaviour and methods being followed: if they want to progress they generally have to mimic these as best they can. The public relations machine of many businesses, especially the multinationals and global institutions, endeavours to persuade us that diversity matters and that it is wholeheartedly embraced within their organizations. However, much of this is mere window dressing and paying lip service to pressures being exerted by legislation and political correctness. It is painfully obvious that business remains largely the playground of men, designed by men for men, particularly at the senior levels of organizations. It is a statistical fact that diversity stops at the boardroom. We just have to observe the senior population of most businesses to see that they are mainly comprised of pinstripe-suited white males. Women still make up less than 10% of the senior management population.[1]

The stories which dominate organizations and their practices reflect predominantly male values therefore, with the result that women continue to find themselves in support roles due to erroneous assumptions regarding women and their level of ambition as it compares to that of men. Persistent stereotyping and fear of what is different plays a significant role in maintaining the lack of diversity at the senior end of organizations. The consequence is that the hierarchy is perceived as the domain of men and masculine values are given higher status than that of feminine. A further stumbling block preventing women from fulfilling their potential is their collusion with the myth that women are inferior to men. Women are socialized to be 'nice girls' and to be compliant rather than competitive; men, on the other hand, are encouraged to be brash and demanding. This does help men to develop a healthier self-belief later in life. Organizations continue to reinforce a culture whereby corporate masculinity is a requirement of senior management, whether you are male or female. Equality has led to the erroneous belief that the only way women can compete with men is to emulate them.

Coaching is particularly powerful in assisting the individual to tackle both the external barriers and, more importantly, the powerful internal barriers that exist in organizations. The reason coaching is such a valuable tool is due to the fact that it addresses the values and beliefs we all hold about the world, ourselves, and our place in that world. Coaching provides the mechanism through which individuals and organizations are able to challenge the stories and narratives which dominate the organization and therefore the behavioural patterns of those within it. Through narratives and the relating of stories, members of an organization are able to communicate abstract ideas which allows for the creation of shared expectations and interpretations, establishing the rules of behaviour (or 'grammar', as we have earlier described it). Storytelling can also be used, however, to exert power, manipulate, distort, and suppress the diversity of alternative stories; so it is important to ensure that there is always scope for developing new ones, and not to become stuck in a rut with a dominant one.

The success of organizations within a global marketplace will depend largely on their recognition and inclusion of diversity. Those who represent diversity need to take responsibility for the role they play in creating organizations that truly reflect the societies in which we live and operate. Cultivating difference and diversity can make an organization more flexible (more in line with the make-up of the general population for a start), so coachees can usefully analyze the attitudes taken to difference and diversity in their own workplace to consider whether there is the chance to broaden the house style in that sphere. Once one strips away the jargon involved in much post-structuralist writing on this subject, this is essentially what is being said there: that it is always a bad sign culturally when difference and diversity are marginalized or suppressed in the name of an overall metanarrative, that someone is bound to be losing out when that happens. It is no mere esoteric philosophical issue therefore, but of direct relevance to our everyday affairs, and worthy of inclusion in a coaching programme on those grounds.

What would it involve to develop a sceptical attitude within an organizational framework, and how might coaching facilitate this? The coach is able to draw on a rich tradition of thought in this area, running as we have seen from classical Greek philosophy through to contemporary postmodernism, all of it committed to holding authority up to thoroughgoing scrutiny and questioning its terms of reference, its assumptions, and its methods. In the first instance, the coachee can be encouraged to examine her beliefs to see what lies behind them, whether they can be justified by anything other than tradition or habit. The same thing goes with company policy of course, that too can be examined to see whether its underlying justification is intrinsically sound or not. As David Hume pointed out, it is all too often habit that underpins our beliefs, and it is always a salutary exercise to explore these in some detail to see if this is so in our own particular case: habit, after all, can very easily harden into dogmatism, as well as blinding us to emerging problems. Scepticism means requiring solid reasons for actions, and if these are not forthcoming (other than citing habit or tradition), then it is an indication of a structural weakness in the belief system that could turn out to have adverse effects eventually. Organizations which operate in this way, trusting to the past, will find themselves in difficulty if they have to respond to any sudden social, political, or technological shift – and as we know from recent history, these can be on a scale radical enough to alter the entire business landscape, effectively rendering traditional methods and assumptions obsolete almost at a stroke. Asking awkward questions about the grounds for organizational policy – precisely the kind of thing that scepticism teaches us to do – can therefore pay dividends in the longer term. Scepticism can seem negative in its approach, and can meet resistance on that score, but its saving grace is that it leads us firmly away from uncritical belief and unthinking acceptance of the *status quo*, fostering an enquiring mind at all times.

Deleuze and Guattari's notion of nomadism can also be drawn upon by coachees as a model for how to keep themselves flexible and open-minded within a framework, which as we have seen standardly promotes conformity in the name of company policy. Nomads feel no need to defend territory for its own sake, being unwilling to submit themselves totally to the demands of the controlling power, which much prefers a settled way of life it can keep under close supervision. There is an important assertion of individuality to be noted here, as well as of pragmatism towards the positions that one holds (intellectually as well as territorially): sometimes one just has to move on – to pick up on a point we made earlier, to try a different game to see where that might lead us. Lyotard's svelteness fulfils a similar function, helping individuals to conceive of themselves as something more than just a mere cog in a machine, as someone who has real options available to her and the strength of will to access them when required. The goal in each case is to keep oneself adaptable, to be able to respond to changing circumstances without being held back by dogmatic beliefs, to be willing to explore new avenues and ways of doing things. To be nomadic or svelte is to set oneself firmly against the culture of group-think.

If we go back to the roots of coaching in competitive sports, we find that such adaptability is one of the most highly prized qualities an individual participant can have: the ability to change tactics if a game-plan is not yielding the expected results. Sportsmen and sportswomen nowadays are generally very heavily coached, rarely going out to compete – whether in an individual or a team sport – without a detailed game-plan, often drawn up by a veritable committee of coaches. The positive side of this practice is that it means they are not just relying on chance or luck, merely hoping for the best as it were, but trying to shape circumstances to their goals; but the negative side is that it can be very difficult to move away from the game-plan even if it is patently not working out. Players or teams can become trapped in the plan, unable to envisage other methods of proceeding, mechanically following the script they were given despite its obvious lack of impact: a case of what one sportswriter has wittily dubbed 'paralysis by analysis'.[2] When that happens it usually leads to defeat. Similar things can happen in war (the charge of the Light Brigade would be a classic example, as would the stalemate caused by trench warfare in the First World War); the point has often been made by historians that military general staffs tend to fight each war on the basis of the tactics from the last, frequently with disastrous results. Tactical flexibility within organizations is surely highly desirable, and critical theory offers us a range of ways through which to develop that mindset.

Postmodern theory lays great stress on the role of narrative in our lives; in particular on our ability to construct narratives to help us achieve specific objectives that we have set ourselves. Narrative is for a theorist like Lyotard one of our most basic tools in making sense of the world: 'the quintessential form of customary knowledge', as he refers to it in *The Postmodern Condition*. So natural is our disposition towards narrative that it needs no external justification for its use: 'narrative knowledge does not give priority to the question of its own legitimation[.] ... [I]t certifies itself in the pragmatics of its own transmission without having recourse to argumentation and proof.'[3] Which is to say that we should not feel beholden to any outside authority when concocting narratives to help us make sense of our personal circumstances (in a work environment, say), and that our narrative should be judged by the effect it has rather than on its adherence to rules laid down beforehand by others. In consequence, there is a multitude of narratives that can be created in any situation: 'there is no alternative' is never part of the postmodernist's outlook, we can always add a new perspective. The metanarrative need not be thought to limit one's horizons: other narratives can be brought into dialogue with it at any point – and, we would argue, should be. Given Lyotard's emphasis on being responsive to the event, with its existentialist overtones, the importance of being able to narrativize our personal situation as it changes becomes very evident.

The use of narrative and storytelling has grown significantly as a body of theory in the research of organizational discourse. David Boje, an eminent authority on the subject, demonstrates through his writing how the multiplicity of stories we can select from in this context will depend on the history, meaning of events, the locality, prior sequence of the stories, as well as the transformation of the characters within organizations as they enact these. He contends that, 'narrative-control and story-diffusion are the force and counter-force of self-organizing'.[4] Boje argues that organizational storytelling has the capacity of acting as a force for diversity and disorder. In essence, storytelling is a vehicle through which characters within organizations can make sense of their individual and collective world. Coaching intervention allows the individual as well as the organization to understand the stories they have told retrospectively and provides a mechanism through which to challenge and revise the stories or even to tell a different, more up-to-date story.

The critical point that Lyotard is making is that the future is open, and that we need not feel constrained by the metanarratives that have been set up in our culture to keep us in line. This is also the essence of a constructionist perspective, which suggests that we have the choice and power to create a different story, should we choose to do so. The capacity to put together new 'little' narratives to contest the power of the metanarratives we have to contend with in our daily life is permanently there, and in fact any metanarrative can only work if people allow it to do so. If, on the other hand, as Lyotard puts it, 'incredulity' becomes widespread, then metanarratives will find it difficult to thrive, or even survive at all: when enough of us cease to 'have recourse' to them, when complicity is withdrawn, then metanarratives just wither away.[5] This is a trait which coachees can be encouraged to develop, especially if they are unhappy with the organizational metanarrative they are working within. Postmodernism's insistence that there are always other narratives which can be constructed in any social or political situation should be borne in mind: again, it is a case of making sure that we do not become trapped within a particular narrative (and that includes game-plans). Organizations that do become so trapped rarely prosper – and neither do their employees of course. Being open to new narratives is to everyone's benefit; a sign of confidence within an organization. An organization which is not open in this way, not willing to keep exploring options in both good times and bad but relying on group-think instead, has to raise serious doubts as to its longer-term viability.

It is also worthwhile encouraging the coachee to think through Žižek's point about our practised ability to deceive ourselves concerning the reality of the situation we are in as regards the systems of our culture – our skill at fetishization, as he conceived of it. Metanarratives can become such an integral part of our lives that we can hardly imagine our existence without them. We become so used to making sense of the world through the doctrines of the dominant metanarrative in play, generally having been born into it and indoctrinated in its values from then onwards, that we feel constrained to go along with it and accept its reading of events, even if it is manifestly not achieving its goals – as Žižek saw to be the case in the communist regimes of Eastern Europe, such as the Yugoslavia that he grew up in. Citizens of those countries could be said to have been in a condition of both knowing and not knowing the true state of affairs, socially and politically, and of developing the fetish as a way of coping with an unpalatable situation: in other words, of being overly willing to give the metanarrative the benefit of the doubt, and of developing a mass group-think attitude towards it and its functionaries. Coachees can use this insight to consider whether a similar state might apply within their own institution; whether they are going along with policies and procedures even though they can see that they are not working out as claimed by the management, and perhaps using the fetish to avoid addressing the problem, or even blanking it out altogether. Either can happen, as Žižek warns, since the 'fetish can function in two opposite ways: either its role remains unconscious...or you think that the fetish is that which really matters.'[6]

Breaking out of the cycle of fetishization would be very beneficial to the organization, enabling it to shed unwanted ideological baggage that is more than likely holding up its progress (exactly what nomadism and svelteness are trying to stay away from). Even at their worst, organizations in the West do not wield anything like the same degree of power over their employees as a totalitarian state does over its citizens, and we have to keep reminding ourselves that their policies can be challenged from within (although we are not denying this can be a tricky and even painful process for any individual to put into practice, particularly if it takes her into the domain of whistleblowing). Recognizing our own ability to fetishize our behaviour, in either of the two ways identified by Žižek, can come to be an important part of starting to exercise more control over our career development – something any coachee would surely agree is a positive step.

The banking sector certainly managed to deceive itself in this manner, quite comprehensively so, and it has suffered accordingly, requiring a massive injection of taxpayers' money to stave off collapse in a whole host of cases and losing a great deal of credibility as a result. Yet most of the industry is still proceeding as if the policies that were in place at the time of the recent crash are the right ones; another classic example of becoming trapped within a narrative or game-plan – or in Žižekian terms, of staying under the power of one's fetish. Once again the value of a sceptical outlook becomes plain: it demands that one moves past fetishes to the real state of affairs. With banking that would mean amongst other things admitting that playing 'pass the parcel' with credit derivatives was bound to fall apart as a policy at some point (there could not be an infinite number of recipients after all), and also that being dependent on a constantly expanding stock market to shore up ever-increasing, to the point of truly alarming, levels of debt was to leave oneself unable to cope with any significant economic downturn. The assumption instead was that an upward trajectory would be the norm for the indefinite future, and that if any downturns ever did occur they would be more in the nature of minor blips, to be rapidly overcome. Neoliberal economics offers a fertile field of enquiry as to the dangers of fetishization, with more blocking out of reality going on amongst its adherents than one would ever want in such a critical part of our culture, on which everyone's living standards depends.

It could well be that fetishization represents a barrier to the achievement of CSR, since the latter is in many ways an acknowledgment that organizations do not in the main act with the full public interest in mind. Corporate Social Responsibility requires a very different mindset that owns up to the past failings of the business sector, and that can pose considerable problems for an organization's employees. The private sector's real concern is profit and it would generally prefer to be given a free hand to pursue this, however it sees fit; that is what neoliberal economics campaigns for, calling on governments to reduce regulation on business to the barest minimum such that business can just get on with it. The theory is that this system generates more wealth that steadily will trickle down to the general public (the monetarist line of argument, as propagated by such high-profile economists as Milton Freedman), thus improving everyone's economic situation. Anything that restricts the process is therefore to society's disadvantage, and to be avoided. Corporate Social Responsibility is likely to be restrictive in just this way, however, as it assumes the implementation of voluntary curbs on business practice in order to comply with ethical standards drawn up to protect the public. This can set up a conflict of interest that organizations and their employees can find difficult to resolve, and fetishization can well come into play as a coping mechanism: those involved both know and don't know how they should behave to be more ethically responsible, both know and don't know where their organization is falling short of the CSR ideal. To embrace CSR enthusiastically would be to admit that sometimes there are more important things than profit, or shareholders' interests (or perhaps that these are best served in the long run by deferred gratification), but that is at odds with the general business ethic we have developed in modern Western society. The secret that lies at the heart of that ethic, and capitalism in general, that someone has to lose out in such a competitive game, is kept at bay, and everyone continues on as if the business ethic really was in the public interest and that there was very little risk involved overall.

Žižek's point is that appearance and reality can differ markedly when it comes to ideology, and this has implications for all large organizations. The parallel with his observations about life under communism would be that organizations can claim to be operating according to the dictates of CSR while their actions, or the outcomes of their actions at any rate, indicate otherwise. Employees within the organization can become adept at convincing themselves that the appearance of CSR is the reality of CSR, because that is the official organizational ideology, while simultaneously recognizing that the reality is in breach of CSR principles. Organizational policy towards the environment is an interesting test case in this regard. Almost all large organizations claim to be pro-green these days, even if a close examination of their policies reveals otherwise – the phenomenon known as 'greenwash', which amounts to a confidence trick being played on the general public. Greenwash on a cynical enough scale is precisely the kind of thing that raises the issue of whistleblowing, which is a clear case of individuals moving beyond fetishization. Indeed, we would want to claim that CSR demands that fetishization should be addressed, and that discrepancies between appearance and reality must be faced up to honestly by all concerned. The benefits of such a policy are only too obvious when it comes to the environment.

We can also see how 'enjoying one's symptom' can come to play a critical role in this process of fetishization (even if it is a much more 'knowing' mental state than the fetish itself[7]), with individuals being encouraged to recognize that they can indeed become resistant to change as a group, even if they can appreciate somewhere in their mind that it could be disastrous for all of them if they don't. A certain fatalism can take effect in organizations which run into severe difficulties, and that can turn into a self-fulfilling prophecy, with a horrified fascination developing within everyone involved at what it might feel like to experience the worst-case scenario – such as financial collapse (dystopian visions can exercise a powerful appeal, as many an author has understood over the years). In such cases it can be very hard to implement evasive action, and one wonders if such an attitude perhaps played a part in the banking crisis, preventing the sector from pulling itself back from the abyss. It is certainly worthwhile asking coachees to reflect on theories like this, and to be on their guard against the development of such symptoms. In this case, psychoanalytic theory can have a very practical application – for all the often esoteric quality of its source.

Without wishing to turn the coach into a psychoanalyst, there is at the very least an interesting basis for dialogue in Bruce Fink's observation that individuals may succeed in getting themselves into a position where, psychologically speaking, they do not really want to change, having become so attached to their symptoms that they can hardly bear to let them go. Coaching is above all committed to change as a positive personal development, and whatever it is that is standing in the way of the coachee being able to reach that state, whether internal or external in nature, is surely worth exploring. While we might come to understand the psychology behind enjoying the prospect of dystopia at a personal level, the reality of this on the economic front would be highly unlikely to be enjoyable for society at large. It would be an entirely reasonable objective of coaching to make us realize this and to think about what would constitute appropriate preventative action.

Another area in which fetishization clearly is very active indeed is that of gender. Rather in the way that all organizations now claim to be green, they also claim to be against sexism and discrimination on the grounds of gender; apart from anything else, there are now laws against this in most Western countries and general public support for these. Yet again, however, as discussed elsewhere, the reality does not always match the claims, and few organizations in the West can be said to have completely abolished the glass ceiling. Both male and female coachees can benefit from exposure to feminist theory, and there is no lack of statistics and data to draw on to back up the contention that we are still a long way from gender equality in the workplace. In Žižek's terms of reference this is both known and not known in higher management circles, who can find it very difficult to conceive of business on anything other than the old, highly competitive masculinist model. Unless voices for feminism are heard more frequently within the organizational world this will not change very substantially, so introducing feminist narratives into coaching would seem to be justified. The point needs to be made that a restructuring of organizational life on feminist lines would be advantageous to all, encouraging a more cooperative spirit internally to temper the ultra-competitive ethos that tends to prevail at present – and that generates socio-political disasters like the credit crisis when taken to extremes. The chances are that would also mean a greater receptivity to CSR and a more ethically conscious business outlook overall, a prospect that the general public could only welcome after the drama of recent upheavals.

Turning to science, chaos and complexity theories have also begun to make an impact on organizational theory, and it would be helpful to identify where they overlap with the theories we have been working our way through in this chapter. Complexity theory emphasizes the value of existing at the edge of chaos, as well as the principle of self-organization. The edge of chaos is a condition that stimulates invention and ingenuity in order to keep positioned there, and it is the optimum state for systems to be in as far as accessing and processing information goes. The edge of chaos is not seen as an abyss, rather that state or condition which holds the potential for innovation and change. Change and transformation are associated with such non-equilibrium conditions. However, the detailed form of such emergent structures or change cannot be predicted. Instead, what is required for any human organization to function coherently is a shared understanding of purpose, a clearly communicated and constantly reinforced set of values. Such values will govern behaviour and incentives sufficiently to convince its members that their own best interest is served by orienting their behaviour towards the purpose of the organization. Evolution, co-evolution, and punctuated equilibrium mean the company's world is not fixed, but constantly changing. The science of complexity therefore reinforces the constructionist perspective of reality creation which we have argued for throughout, namely that organizational reality is the result of the interaction between individual members within the organization. Although individuals are free to choose their response to the interactions and to change the rules and scripts that govern their behaviour, such freedom, as suggested by Žižek, is often traded for the collusion to maintain the *status quo*.

Svelteness would be a desirable trait to cultivate under such circumstances, whereas it is unlikely that an authoritarian metanarrative would cope very well with the demands that would be made on it for constant reinvention. Little narratives are more likely to be conducive to self-organization as well, since they create new lines of enquiry and new perspectives (not to mention new identities), with metanarratives being more concerned with maintaining the *status quo* to preserve their power base. Little narratives are in fact actively seeking the kind of radical change that self-organization triggers, forcing the metanarrative to keep processing new streams of information and thus not to rest on its accomplishments. The tension that such radicalism might create between individual and organization forms the topic of our next chapter.

9
Coaching and the Whistleblowing Dilemma

Critical theory in general has the capacity to generate a range of new perspectives about both the organization and her place within it for the coachee, becoming a means by which she can maximize the opportunities open to her for personal development. It expands the coachee's intellectual resources and gives her a greater depth of understanding as to the operation, both formal and informal, of her organization. But what if that understanding suggests that whistleblowing is in order? We conceded in Chapter 6 that whistleblowing might be an extreme implication of the radical coaching process, in that the coachee, having been imbued with a sceptical outlook (thus significantly reconstructing her professional identity), might feel justified in resorting to this tactic in certain circumstances. Radical coaching aims to counter the effect of group-think, which at its worst can lead organizations into the abyss – as patently happened in the case of the banks and finance houses in the recent international credit crisis, where, as we noted in Chapter 6, any opposition to neoliberal economic practices tended either to be suppressed or just simply ignored altogether by the management class. It would seem defensible for an individual to want to draw attention to such a problem and try to prevent it, both for the organization's and the public's good. But it is one thing to foster an adversarial mentality in coachees that sees them developing an independent voice within their organization, something altogether more contentious to promote whistleblowing, which few organizations will ever look kindly upon. As Wim Vandekerckhove has observed in his recent study of the phenomenon, the general organizational response is 'that whistleblowing is contrasted to company loyalty, and is seen as a breach of that loyalty'.[1]

We need to consider whether such an effect of coaching can in truth be defended, or whether it goes beyond what the process, even in its most radical form, should be involved in doing. In other words, is the encouragement, whether tacit or not, of whistleblowing a legitimate part of the coaching repertoire, or should it be regarded as overstepping the mark? Is it posing a dilemma, or presenting an opportunity? The first point to make is that organizations would almost undoubtedly shy away from any coaching programme with an explicit commitment to the development of a whistleblowing mentality. They would perceive that as going well beyond coaching's remit, which as far as most organizations are concerned is mainly to improve the efficiency of their employees rather than to turn them into potential rogue elements within the corporate structure; the organization's preference being for the training rather than the self-developmental aspect to be emphasized in such exercises. From an organizational perspective, whistleblowing is an act of bad faith that cannot easily be condoned, and the tendency is to close ranks against the whistleblower and deny whatever accusations have been made against it. Putting the organization in a bad light will always irritate its higher echelons, for whom it can only represent a threat to their reputation and credibility – and most likely, profit margins too. Yet might organizations be made to appreciate the benefits of whistleblowing nevertheless? It is to their advantage, one would think, to possess internal safeguards against stumbling into anti-social or illicit activities. To indulge in that kind of behaviour, and to insist on employee compliance with it (let us say in cases of environmental abuse, a not uncommon occurrence these days), is to give up all pretence to CSR, thus running the risk of a backlash from the public which could also trigger unwelcome political attention in its turn.[2] Whistleblowing puts the public interest before the corporate, so it could be argued that the individuals involved are acting in the best spirit of CSR (at least officially, America tends to interpret it in that positive way and has a Whistleblower Protection Act (1989) on its books, although the federal government has rather cynically managed to find some loopholes in it when cases have been brought against it by its own employees in recent years[3]).

Whistleblowing is the action which follows the belief or interpretation of an individual or small group to what they perceive as being unethical or immoral behaviour on the part of members of a group such as an organization or institution. As Jesica R. Mesmer-Magnus and Chockalingam Viswesvaran put it: 'Employees have three options to address an unsatisfactory situation faced within an organization: (1) To exit the organization, (2) voice discontent (i.e. blow the whistle), or (3) remain silent.'[4] As in the case of global warming, voices of dissent are not only aimed at institutions such as governments, but society as a whole. From a coaching perspective, the action would be the product of a sceptical mindset, rather than ideological indoctrination by the coach, so it could be interpreted as laudable. It is surely far better for such things to be brought out into the open than for abuse or injustice to continue because of corporate negligence or outright lawbreaking. Sceptics do not consider it their duty to defend a metanarrative to the death (they are constitutionally nomadic in this respect), but to face up to its flaws and contradictions and to make these known as widely as possible. That certainly squares with whistleblowing when undertaken for ethical reasons. Lars Lindblom identifies the moral dilemma of whistleblowing as follows: 'The ethical debate on whistleblowing concerns centrally the conflict between the right to political free speech and the duty of loyalty to the organization where one works.'[5]

Most of the public would probably agree with such sentiments when it involved issues like environmental abuse, but what if it was something more locally specific such as company profitability, or even company survival, that was at stake? Would this too merit a move into whistleblowing? One could argue, 'Yes if it were a question of protecting the public well-being', which was certainly true in the case of the financial sector and what have turned out to be its ruinous trading practices of the last decade or two. If more people had broken ranks to express open opposition to the policies being pursued so aggressively by the banks (the mad round of trading in credit derivatives, for example), and the authoritarian group-think lying behind them, then it could have sparked more public debate about how the sector was being run, as well as raising awareness of the lack of social responsibility being shown in the unseemly scramble for 'supercharged profit'. 'Were the bankers mad?' Gillian Tett has mused, 'Blind? Evil. Or were they simply grotesquely greedy?';[6] whichever description you think applies best, someone should have been asking such questions, from the inside, and forcefully too, before the system went into meltdown. There is evidence to suggest that acceptance of bad practices is more likely if it accumulates over a period of time; the frog in boiling water syndrome. As discussed earlier, the psychological biases and blind spots to which we are prone make it difficult for individuals to contemplate and accept that their behaviour may be unethical or that they may be colluding with the malpractices of others. They may therefore initially engage in persuasive self-talk to justify their own as well as the actions and behaviour of others – fetishization, as we can now recognize it. To resort to becoming a whistleblower is an act of tremendous courage on behalf of an individual who finds herself in a situation she is incapable of condoning, despite the likely adverse consequences in career terms of speaking out.

We would argue that, assuming a self-developmental agenda, scepticism should arise naturally out of the coaching project and that it is an integral part of developing an independence of spirit in the coachee, who is to be encouraged to see beyond the metanarrative and the restrictive ethic of group-think. To be a whistleblower is to be a prime example of the little narrative in action, taking a principled stand against any abuse of power or narrowness of social vision that is putting the public interest at risk. Postmodernism provides the theoretical tools by which to construct this position, which ultimately is a campaign for more transparency within the organizational world such that abuse is not allowed to occur, and little narratives given the opportunity to flourish. A whistleblower is announcing a counter-narrative, and that is what postmodernism wants to see emerging on a regular basis in dialectical progression.

Feminism can very usefully be drawn on in this context. It almost automatically generates a sceptical mindset in its followers since it considers the masculinist metanarrative which has traditionally underpinned our culture to be based on false premises, rejecting its claims as to gender attributes and the social roles postulated to follow on from these. To be a feminist is to insist that there should be other narratives in play than the one that is, for example, dominant in the corporate world, constructed as it is largely on male character traits. Research also suggests that women are more likely than men to blow the whistle.[7] One could say that feminists are in a permanently whistleblowing relationship with patriarchy, and that they perform a valuable public service by being so; another reason to support the campaign for a greater gender balance at senior levels. Without their efforts it is unlikely that we would have achieved the necessary change of consciousness to make the workplace a more equal environment than it hitherto has been (an ongoing project, as we know). Steven Kaplan et al. introduce research which indicates that women are more ethical than men, but unfortunately, research further suggests that women are more likely to be polite and accommodating when dealing with differences of opinions.[8]

Daniel Goleman, well-known for his books on emotional intelligence, responded in an interview for the journal *In View* on the role of whistleblowing and rocking the boat in the circumstances leading to the banking crisis that whistleblowers are individuals who hold values of the highest level.[9] He goes on to argue that organizations should 'treasure' these individuals for the role they play in the protection of the mission of the organization instead of the punitive response which is more normally the response to whistleblowing. A healthy system that is self-correcting requires it to be completely transparent so that problems can be addressed as and when they arise – ideally, as soon as possible. The role of the whistleblower is to alert the system that a problem is emerging that needs correcting. In a book defending whistleblowing, Goleman strongly challenges the self-deception we engage in within groups, whether that is found in organizations or society – and Žižek has made it clear just how widespread this phenomenon can be in our lives. Goleman's interpretations of the self-deception we create within a group resonate with the ideas of group-think discussed in Chapter 7. He goes one step further, namely to challenge the practices that suppress the voices of dissent and often the witch-hunt against the perceived traitors which ensues. Goleman proposes that it is only the courage of the whistleblowers that will 'save us from the narcotic of self-deception'.[10] Unlike the majority within the group, whistleblowers do not succumb to the powerful antidote of denial as a psychological tactic in dealing with the knowledge that something is amiss in the system: in other words, they resist the temptation to fetishize, and they should be given credit for this.

There is an assumption that the bottom-line will act as a safeguard against the dangerous pathology of group-think within organizations. Surely, success and failure act as a reality check which theoretically should be immune to even the most vigorous form of group-think? One can only hope that recent events will have put paid to any such assumptions from reoccurring in future. Furthermore, evidence suggests that individuals with a strong motivation for power will not do things in line with standards of excellence, especially if these hold back a personal driver such as power. Equally, high-powered leaders are unlikely to tolerate challenges to their decisions and would expect loyalty without question. The valuable role of the deviant or whistleblower is to act as the voice of conscience in order to save the group from themselves. In the absence of an internal critical voice, the coach is ideally placed as a non-member of the group and therefore less prone to sharing the blind spots of the group. The coach is also less likely to have a personal agenda for keeping and protecting the *status quo* or the fear of criticizing the group reality.

We have already alluded to the role that emotions, such as fear and greed, play in influencing the behaviour of traders. Fear is a strong deterrent in organizations against voices of dissent and in most cases ensures employee silence. A combination of these powerful emotions will often result in a sense of helplessness on the part of the individual and is likely to prevent the person from speaking out against dubious business practices. The fears associated with loss of employment, social status, financial gain, reputation are all strong motivators for not breaking ranks in this way. Despite legislation to protect a whistleblower, the reality is that most whistleblowers will find it untenable to remain with an employer after they have been party to disclosing malpractices within the organization. It might even be that they will not find employment elsewhere within that sector should they leave. This begs the question as to how voices of dissent are perceived within organizations. Are they welcomed and seen to provide a service to the organization or are they to be silenced or even removed altogether? Furthermore, the reluctance to challenge authority is ingrained within the fibre of society, and, one could argue, has contributed to sustaining hierarchies and the protection of privileges even if these were gained at the expense of others. Associated with authority is the compliance with decisions and actions of those in power. Apart from innate fears, there are also the learned fears we develop through direct or indirect experiences within certain circumstances. From a very early age we are socialized into the rules of society and the consequences of violating those rules. Obedience to authority thus continues throughout our lives and is associated with most of the institutions that play a role there, from religion through to government and both public- and private-sector organizations. Power associated with formal authority puts pressure on individuals to behave in ways which they might otherwise not do. The collective wrongdoing within the banking sector permeated the whole sector after all, as well as its individual institutions.

Changes in the psychological contract between organizations and employees in recent years have meant that the longer term and possible employment for life contracts have become much rarer, and employees have had to assume more responsibility for their own careers. The result is that the loyalty organizations once expected from their employees is no longer so freely forthcoming. This notion is supported by Joyce Rothschild: 'Finally, I would argue that individuals' fundamental relationship with their employers has changed markedly over the last couple of decades.'[11] This may also contribute to individuals being more willing to act upon perceived malpractices within the organization. It is true that although individuals may observe immoral or illegal practices being carried out by some in the organization, they are not necessarily always willing to act on that information and may choose to turn a blind eye instead. Eva E. Tsahuridu and Wim Vandekerckhove believe that whistleblowers are moral agents who perceive a duty beyond that of the organization to include an obligation to society.[12] It could be said that the changes in the psychological contract have led to the demise of the 'one-dimensional' organizational man and instead employees perceive their moral duty to extend beyond the organization and to include a duty to society and the environment. For such individuals the boundaries between organizations and society have become blurred and they would possibly answer the question as to whose benefit the organizations exist for, with an answer that would include service to society and the environment as well as to the shareholders of the company. Rothschild makes an interesting observation in relation to whistleblowers:

> The whistleblowing event, not so much the original disclosure as the escalation of reprisals, that come in its wake, constitute so profound an experience for many of these people that it reshapes how they see themselves and their place in the world. Many of these

> people now see their experience as having been a 'whistleblower' as a central piece of their identity.[13]

In order for organizations to function, they require a certain amount of compliance and employees gladly offer this in return for the organization meeting their personal needs – however, the question is just how far should that compliance stretch?

Organizational practices contribute to secrecy within organizations. The specialization of certain roles, and the creation of a cadre of specialists due to their superior knowledge of the subject or activity, mean that they may operate with little external control. This has certainly been the case with the traders in the investment banks as it has become apparent that they have operated more or less independently with very few checks, as not many understand the complexities of their roles (often including their superiors, worryingly enough for the rest of us). One could draw the conclusion that organizational wrongdoing has increased in recent years, starting with the Enron scandal which appeared to have opened the floodgates to numerous other unethical corporate practices. Are organizations behaving more unethically and illegally or are more people concerned with holding organizations accountable to their duty towards society? Harold Hassink et al. argue that, '[a]lthough many companies have a code of conduct, many of them are merely paying lip service to the notion of encouraging ethical behaviour.'[14] Mesmer-Magnus and Viswesvaran's research reveals that most whistleblowers attempt to address concerns through internal channels first before going public.[15] The concerns raised by whistleblowers are rarely welcomed and are often ignored or marginalized. It is only when they fail to be heard internally that they would resort to blowing the whistle outside their own organization. As Lindblom postulates, the ethical dilemma of whistleblowing is the tension between an individual's right to free speech versus the loyalty and duty an employee should express towards their organization as part of their contract of employment.[16] He proceeds to put forward an interesting point, namely that it should be the right of the individual to blow the whistle, but it does not imply that it is the duty of the individual to do so. Individuals therefore also have the right not to blow the whistle, should they so choose. This debate highlights the notion that whistleblowing and loyalty are in the minds of many seen as incommensurable.

Lindblom also points out that loyalty is more complex than it appears as there is a loyalty towards fellow employees and loyalty to the organization. Loyalty towards co-workers is akin to the loyalty one has for one's friends and family and the latter is associated with one's duties and responsibilities towards the organization which pays your salary. Jukka Varelius challenges the notion that whistleblowing contradicts loyalty to the organization: 'This is because blowing the whistle about one's employer's wrongdoing and being loyal to them serves the same goal, the moral good of the employer.'[17]

A case can therefore be made for whistleblowing, but does that mean that it should be a specific objective of a coaching programme within an institutional framework? Rather, what the coach is doing there is facilitating the development of self-reflection and an open enquiring mind in coachees. We would like to hope that if there were more of these characteristics on display within organizations then disasters such as the credit crunch could be averted; that group-think would become less influential and independence of spirit more valued, and even fostered, within the organizational set-up. One of the objectives of coaching is to develop a greater sense of self-awareness within the individual, which includes a clear awareness of the values the individual holds and therefore of the drivers of their actions. Such recognition may very well lead to acknowledgement that the values of the individual are incongruent with that of the organization. Should reconciliation of individual values not be possible with those of the organization, then the individual may very well terminate her employment. Severing the relationship with the organization is not necessarily part of the coaching contract and should be regarded instead as an outcome of the process. It does raise an ethical dilemma, and as discussed in Chapter 2 coaching as a profession is not yet regulated and debates as to the role, responsibilities, and legal obligations of the coach have not yet been clarified in relation to the ownership for concerns of possible organizational malpractice. If the coaching practice is true to critical principles such concerns would be addressed rather than skirted around or ignored.

Whistleblowing is also a matter of conscience, and although that is not a direct concern of coaching either, it is a trait likely to develop as a by-product of the process and its concentration on the development of self-reflection and analytical skills. Both coaches and coachees need to be aware of this implication of the process, and it could be argued that it is a highly desirable outcome in the longer term. Perhaps the onus ought to be on the organization not to stray so far from the requirements of CSR that employees are faced with the dilemma of whether or not to resort to whistleblowing? Or not to become so wrapped up in group-think that they cannot recognize when they are heading for disaster and thus manufacturing such opportunities? If whistleblowing does occur, then it is a clear signal of system malfunction, and it takes a significant breakdown in employee–management relations to prompt such a dramatic response. It does not seem so radical to provide coachees with the skills – drawn from critical theory – to deal with such an episode if and when it arises in the course of their career.

10
Conclusion: Radical Coaching and Business as Usual

Only time will determine whether we learn from our mistakes to update our beliefs and ideologies, resulting in a foresight which would temper our collective behaviour and investment practices. It would have to be said that the response so far has been somewhat disappointing. There is disturbing evidence to suggest that we have not in fact learnt very much at all from past experience and indeed that hindsight appears to be reinforcing confidence in the old ways and the emergence of 'business as usual'. As Karl-Erik Wärneryd counsels, '[h]indsight depends on memory and memory is fallible'.[1] Memory is also notoriously selective, and it is interesting to note in this respect that attention is currently fixed on the national debt as the problem that we must face up to politically, rather than what caused it to mushroom in size so suddenly. Dealing with the symptoms only is unlikely to effect a cure for our ideological ills however, and looks suspiciously like yet another instance of Žižekian fetishization in action.

Nevertheless, the witch-hunt of investors that has ensued following the meltdown of the banking industry may be seen as rather unfair, since society as a whole needs to reflect and engage in some serious soul searching to determine the role we have played in bringing about the worst economic climate since the Great Depression of the 1930s – even if only unwittingly in most of our cases. Our impatience to consume what we desire in the present, as opposed to a future time when we can properly afford it, has fuelled the credit boom and therefore assigns a portion of the guilt involved to the consumer. As John Naish has argued in a provocative recent book, '[w]e need to develop a sense of *enough*.... We have created a culture that has one overriding message – we do not yet have all we need to be satisfied. The answer, we are told, is to have, see, be and do even more. Always more.'[2] If we are to evade another credit crunch then there simply cannot be 'always more' for us to claim; logic alone would argue that this has to come to an end somewhere, and that we are being foolish to pretend otherwise. It is on precisely such an issue that our ideology calls for updating; at some point we just have to recognize that 'business as usual' is the problem not the solution.

Of equal importance in rebuilding the public's confidence in the market is corporate social responsibility. As we noted earlier, headlines of corporate scandals have become all too commonplace in recent years with the collapse of high-profile companies such as Enron and Worldcom. One could argue that the corruption so exposed within the corporate world was merely the tip of the iceberg and little did we know that these events would herald even greater scandals to come. A much stronger version of CSR (Corporate Social Responsibility), one to which the business world feels a real and enduring commitment, and provides hard evidence of this, is sorely wanted. But this is a debate which is only just beginning to develop, and which will no doubt meet spirited resistance from the ranks of the 'business as usual' advocates, who have apparently already managed to forget such traumatic events as the fall of Lehman Brothers and the forced nationalization of Northern Rock (not to mention the collapse of the mortgage market in both the UK and the US). Nevertheless, we shall be making our case for a much more robust CSR later on in this chapter.

Following the near demise of the banking industry we have also experienced the scandal of greedy politicians in the UK, with parliamentary expenses being systematically and shamelessly abused by a significant percentage of MPs. Not surprizingly this has led to a widespread disenchantment with politics and a significant decline in trust of politicians on the part of the general public. We might well wonder what other monolithic institution that we as a society have placed our trust in could turn out to have feet of clay. We predict that the next scandal may very well come from the educational sector which has through its group-think practices in recent years allowed greed to overpower the erstwhile jealously guarded standards of learning and education in countries like the UK, especially within the realms of further and higher education. On an even wider scale, the group-think that pervades society and maintains destructive beliefs and practices which continue to fuel global warming, may yet prove irreversible. If we are to overhaul the complex policy-making machines which drive institutions such as government and industry we need to establish a new intervention strategy, identified as long ago as 1972 by Irving L. Janis.[3] His suggestions in counteracting group-think included extensive use of critical evaluators in policy-forming groups. Translated into contemporary parlance, this would mean assigning a critical coach to each member of such groups. As we have argued throughout the book, critical coaching may very well be a highly appropriate strategy to apply in such contexts, provided the policy makers are willing to open their inner chambers to detailed scrutiny and a challenge of their assumptions and beliefs. Furthermore, as will be apparent from our arguments, there needs to be a concerted effort made to reintroduce and protect the role of critical thinking to encourage healthy debate and scepticism within the organizational world. Group-think must not be allowed to go unopposed, but instead be kept under constant observation and required to justify its policies on a regular basis as a matter of course.

It is clear from the evidence that it is near impossible for group members to query their own group norms themselves. Instead it requires an external source such as the critical coach to provide the impetus for this to occur. Numerous studies have revealed that the psychological power of conformity engendered by group norms and the group authority figures will lead individual members to abide by these norms, even if it necessitates inflicting pain on someone else.[4] As we have seen with the banking sector, group norms exert tremendous pressure on individuals to the point that the drive for consensus seriously impairs the ability of rational decision-making, closing off the exploration of alternatives within a group. As Janis remarks, silence is often interpreted as consensus with the group decisions. We can observe one of the key symptoms of group-think as outlined by Janis in the behaviour of the traders who have contributed to the banking crisis, namely an illusion of invulnerability which fuelled arrogant behaviour and a denial of the danger signals which were all too apparent for those willing to see. We argued in earlier chapters that there is an urgent need for a balance of genders on the boards of organizations, as the presence of women would act to temper the male disposition towards competition and risk-taking by adding voices of reason. This is borne out by the hard-hitting Commons Treasury Committee Report released for publication in March 2010 which suggests that the lack of female directors in the City of London has been a critical factor in the financial crisis.[5] The report also argues that for the financial sector to prosper once again, it needs to attract the best available talent, which includes the currently wasted talent available amongst women. It further advocates that the finance sector needs to strengthen its corporate governance, a conclusion we would strongly support. It is an irony, however, that the committee laying down the law to the City to get their house in order has only one woman on it. Are they best placed to cast the first stone?

There is an ostensibly positive aspect to group-think which suggests that it stimulates a group to make riskier decisions than more conservative decisions would be if taken independently. A group should also, in theory, temper the overly ambitious and also possibly destructive behaviour of individual mavericks. There are times and circumstances in organizations when the ability to take risks may lead to tremendous gain. However, it is a double-edged sword scenario and the banking industry crossed the boundary into the destructive realm of group-think, where insiders lose the ability to recognize that they are making mistakes – often very big mistakes. Janis concedes that on rare occasions group-think may lead to a positive outcome; however, he concludes that, '[t]he positive effects are generally outweighed by the poor quality of the group's decision making. My assumption is that the more frequently a group displays the symptoms the worse will be the quality of its decisions, on average.'[6] Recent history seems to prove him right. In the earlier chapters we noted the growth of an internal coaching capacity within organizations. The phenomenon of group-think raises a serious question as to the possibility of internal coaching and whether it has the ability to challenge internal norms and paradigms. Is it merely reinforcing the group norms thereby stifling any voices of dissent or debate?

Rethinking Corporate Social Responsibility

However, it would appear that in some quarters there is still the perception of business as usual. As we write, it is all but incomprehensible to observe the reappearance of the eye-watering bonuses being proposed in the financial sector on the grounds that this is the only way to motivate their employees, and that if one group does it then all must follow suit – whether their annual results warrant it or not, it would seem. As Chris Roebuck of London's Cass Business School told the BBC in a questions and answers debate, the only reason that banks pay such big bonuses is because all other banks are doing the same. He then goes on to suggest that '[i]f all the banks paid a much lower rate then that would be the level bankers would accept – the market rate.'[7] The bonus system has to be an example of group-think at its worst; the industry is in meltdown, but its major players persist in clinging to the wreckage of what once was. It is a moot point whether the sector has been at all chastened by the experience that brought it to the very brink of extinction, to be saved by, as we must keep reminding ourselves, the general taxpayer, thus massively increasing the national debt and mortgaging our economic future. It is a moot point, too, whether the sector has any conception at all of CSR: social conscience seems to be in very short supply amongst the financial community.

However, as Lisa Matthewman et al. point out, '[r]epeatedly when organizations behave unethically there has been a prevailing culture tacitly supporting unethical behaviour'.[8] The demise of Enron in 2001 led to a landslide of some of the largest corporate bankruptcies in American history, all involving unethical business practices. The greed of the executives was directly responsible for the disappearance of these organizations, and the same greed clearly permeated the banking sector and other parts of society too. The catalogue of organizational destruction unleashed through greed sends a fundamental shockwave throughout organizations and institutions that CSR ought to be a priority of all responsible leaders. It is based on a principle that organizations and their leaders should take full responsibility for their behaviour, which affects society, communities, and the planet. Furthermore, not only should they be responsible for their behaviour, but they should be held accountable for it.

The concepts and theories of CSR have featured in organizational literature for many years, but with the exception of some early factory owners such as Cadbury and Rowntree, Lever Brothers, and a few recent organizations such as The Body Shop, one could argue that it has merely served as public relations rhetoric. Matthewman et al. remind us that '[m]any of these early progressive employers were influenced by their Quaker beliefs';[9] but that kind of strong-minded moral commitment is vanishingly rare in today's ruthlessly neoliberal economic climate – a climate that is the very epitome of the one-dimensionality that Marcuse had warned us was destroying the richness of our cultural heritage. Corporate Social Responsibility is based on the principles of stakeholder theory which states that the purpose of organizations is not merely to serve the interests of the shareholders and maximize their return, but also to take into account the needs of other stakeholders such as the employees, local community, suppliers, and customers, to name a few of those affected. However, the start of this century has witnessed some of the most catastrophic examples of corporate social *irresponsibility*, which market fundamentalism has done much to generate. A key principle of CSR is that organizations will pursue their objective for economic growth within a legal and regulatory framework. From the examples quoted, it is evident that this principle has been seriously violated and that society has been left to pay the price, in the form of massive budget deficits and all the cuts in public services they have brought in their wake.

Higher education and group-think

The university sector in many ways constitutes a model of how organizations ought to operate, and of where coaching could be used to maximum effect in terms of both personnel and the organizational mission. All the more worrying, therefore, that the sector in the UK is increasingly finding itself being pressured into adopting a hard-edged business profile based on market principles that often conflict seriously with its underlying rationale of public service. As governments intervene more and more frequently, and public funding systematically declines, university managements are being pushed into the group-think mode in order to compete on the open market. But before dealing with this issue, let us consider first what the strengths and weaknesses of the university are as an organizational model.

University lecturers have traditionally enjoyed a fairly high degree of autonomy in the performance of their job, being managed in the main at departmental or faculty level, where they can have a real input into policy decisions. This can, of course, vary a great deal in practice, but there is undoubtedly far more scope for individual initiative and self-expression in this context than there is in the vast majority of organizational settings, where top-down management is more the rule. The content of what lecturers do in lectures and seminars, for example, as long as it is broadly addressing the topic of the course being studied, is left largely up to them and their professional judgement on such matters is respected. Self-development is not just expected by the system it is also actively desired by the individual, and it is generally rewarded – even if this is only at the level of increased professional status (more of a motivating factor in this area of employment than in most others, it should be noted). Departments and faculties are judged on the basis of the reputations built up by their individual members, so there is every incentive to give lecturers the opportunity to build up their skills in their chosen areas of intellectual interest and to strive for excellence amongst their peers. No one would embark on this particular career path unless that interest was there in the first place (rather as no one would go into professional sports without a similar desire); so there would seem to be a fruitfully symbiotic relationship between individual and organization of the kind that rarely applies in the standard business world, where employment is in general entered into for far more pragmatic reasons.

The organization is a site for individuals to achieve their chosen goals in the case of higher education therefore, rather than an entity which has already set the goals and requires the individual to conform to these. This tends to argue against the deployment of a top-down management model, with its preference for exercising control at all stages of the organization's processes. As in sport, coaching would seem to be a natural complement to this project: apart from anything else, scepticism is built into the academic psyche, and most members of the profession will take readily to adopting such an attitude to their institutional setting. Loyalty to the institution will in the main take second place to loyalty to one's subject and its intellectual concerns (also promoted by a range of professional associations). Whistleblowing probably comes more naturally to academics than it does to most other professions.

There has been a clear political trend in recent years in both the UK and Western Europe, however, to demand that the higher education sector becomes progressively more market oriented. Knowledge is increasingly seen as a product, with the student the buyer – utilizing a combination of self- and state-funding in the 'transaction' that is assumed to be taking place. It is an approach that has been openly welcomed in the business world, which has long campaigned for a greater commercialization of the public sector, and is prone to complaining that entrepreneurial skills are not widely enough taught in our educational system. The consequence is that universities are being forced to regard themselves as factories turning out graduates, and the more graduates they can turn out, the more buoyant they will be financially. Failing students attract fines, or even withdrawal of public funds (success rates being rigorously monitored by a range of auditing bodies these days), and it is no surprize that this has led to a great deal of anxiety in universities about both teaching methods and curriculum provision. Departments and faculties can find themselves under intense pressure to improve their success rate, while at the same time also being expected to keep increasing their income – which is not exactly an atmosphere conducive to intellectual experimentation and risk-taking. Research is now seen predominantly in financial terms by the average university, for example, and this does constrain what is done, with research-derived income coming to stand as an index of value. If external funding is received for a project, then the managerial attitude is that it must be worthwhile; if not, then it cannot be. It is the most reductive of arguments, and intellectually unsustainable: unfortunately it is also becoming the norm, and academics are having to adapt to its strictures whether they like it or not. In this increasingly competitive environment, top-down management is beginning to assert itself on the grounds that this is the only way to deliver organizational efficiency.

Students, too, as fee-paying 'consumers', have become more demanding (appeals against essay and examination grades are far more common than they used to be, for example), and there is a general fear in the sector that standards are beginning to slip, with grade inflation turning into a significant worry. In a sense, lecturing staff stand in a coaching relationship to students, facilitating their intellectual development through the teaching process, but this relationship is in danger of being eroded by the changing funding arrangements. Teaching a student and teaching a consumer are not quite the same thing.

Universities are also actively encouraged to move into the lucrative market for foreign students (who pay much higher fees than EU nationals), often with very unhappy results for those involved in what is essentially a profit-led exercise. The growth of foreign students outside of the EU has more than doubled over the last 10 years and is now a greater source of income than the grants being provided by government. The measurement of success of universities is now dominated by criteria identified with organizational success such as high numbers and income derived from such numbers. The British Council cautions universities not to perceive international students as 'cash cows' in an attempt to fill the budget holes left by Government cuts in funding, suggesting that to do so could undermine the reputation of British universities.[10]

There is a growing belief amongst academics that they are under increasing pressure to award higher marks. Furthermore, there is a widespread concern over the rise of plagiarism in universities. This has led to a belief in the academic community that universities are turning a blind eye to cheating and poor standards in order to improve results in the league tables that are becoming so popular in political circles as a method of judging the performance of the public sector. Academics are also finding themselves under considerable pressure to be lenient to international students for fear of stemming their flow and with it the much-needed financial income they bring. This generates a battle between the academics on the one side, attempting to maintain quality and control over their programmes, and managers on the other hand who, as stated by the British Council, regard students primarily as cash cows. The measurement of success is therefore not the quality of the work that students produce, but the numbers of students recruited and the income they proceed to provide. And true to the symptoms of group-think, the voices of opposition to this new order are being marginalized and silenced.

Group-think tends to thrive under circumstances like these, and that poses a real threat to the concept of academic autonomy: university managements are far more concerned with numbers nowadays than what is actually being taught, and throughput of students takes precedence over academic freedom. Whatever draws students in is good, whatever doesn't is considered bad for the institution's image. Smaller subjects are systematically being closed down throughout the sector in consequence, and universities in general have less range of coverage than they did in previous generations. This is a trend that will be very hard indeed to arrest as long as the business model dominates educational thinking, and it has to be said that the portents do not look particularly hopeful at present – even with the evidence in front of us of the dangers inherent in an overtly neoliberal approach in other walks of life like the financial industry. Universities too run the risk of becoming one-dimensional.

The imposition of a range of auditing procedures on the university sector has served to reinforce the shift to a business ethic: in fact, they represent the progressive 'Taylorisation' of the system. These demand that academics meet a range of targets decided upon by their managements in order to present the best possible picture to a government and general public that have become fixated by league tables (and mass media only too happy to feed that obsession by sensationalist headlines about 'failing' public institutions, 'incompetent' teachers, etc.). Academic work does not fit neatly into such schemes, which have a distinctly quantitative rather than qualitative bias that is alien to the highly speculative, and initially rarely goal-directed, nature of intellectual activity. Academics are only too aware of the distortions necessary to make their work fit into the auditing system, which ultimately amounts to a triumph of group-think over the individual. Auditing allows little room for dissent, maverick attitudes, or unconventional thinking, being designed above all to promote conformity of behaviour across sectors. This raises the spectre of coaching within the educational system degenerating into an exercise in helping individuals meet management-set performance targets rather than in developing their inner talents and abilities. If that happens, then we shall have training not coaching. As long as education is considered merely a 'product', something to be bought and sold on the open market in competition with other providers, then group-think will continue to exercise control over universities, reproducing some of the worst aspects of business practice in the process.

Group-think in society

As stated earlier, it could be argued that the unethical, and in some cases, illegal behaviour by corporate businesses and the banking sector took place within a prevailing social culture which tacitly supported such behaviour. As a society we have increasingly become hedonistic, expecting instant gratification of our needs and wants without due consideration of the consequences. There appears to be an imbalance between the rights and responsibilities of individuals with the emphasis of late being mainly on our rights. This notion is upheld by the Education Secretary at the time of writing, Alan Johnson, who told the annual conference of the NASUWT teachers' union in Belfast in 2007 that '[w]e must develop a new three Rs: rules, responsibility and respect.'[11] Lack of respect within schools continues with a lack of respect within society, and numerous communities are blighted by anti-social behaviour, living in fear of crime and disorder. As a society we urgently need to address the visible symptoms of the deeply rooted problems which have led to such behaviour, challenging the group-think which pervades our collective mindset, and critical coaching to underpin such a social movement may be one approach in achieving a more responsible society.

Collectively society is behaving increasingly in the manner one would expect of a petulant child – but who will be the responsible adult to show us the error of our ways? We believe that critical coaching as outlined in the preceding chapters provides the mechanism through which we can challenge the values and beliefs of the institutions which govern and determine the society we all inhabit. Such institutions include not only businesses or governments, but also the institution of the family. Critical coaching brings realization and recognition that each member of society contributes to creating the world they inhabit, and if we are experiencing a broken society then each and every one of us has made a contribution to that reality. However, critical coaching also offers the vehicle through which we could construct a different society. If society is viewed in its totality, this can appear an impossible task; yet if each individual and members of institutions make a change within their immediate environment, the ripples of change will spread. In Chapter 3, we gave an example of one innovative unit of Local Authority consisting of only a dozen or so individuals who are making a difference to individuals and families that have been ostracized by society. They are achieving this by using the tools of critical coaching to break the cycle of helplessness and to demonstrate alternative realities. In time these changes will affect the whole community.

There is one caveat worth reintroducing. We again refer to the potential danger of a metanarrative of coaching by drawing a parallel with the criticism Gergen levies against the mental health profession and the dangers of institutionalizing and technologizing the terminology and techniques of coaching. The result is that its use becomes the ownership of the profession who in turn assume the role of arbiter of how coaching is defined and practised, determining who the practitioners are, and how they will go about their practice.

Coaching in prisons

There are many different institutions in society which could benefit from critical coaching and nowhere is there an institution more in need of reform than that of the judicial system. The punishment imposed on offenders may ensure a sense of accountability for their crimes, but does it necessarily leave them with a clear sense of ownership and responsibility for their actions? It would appear not. If the purpose of prisons and rehabilitation centres is to ensure offenders change their behaviour and become responsible members of society, then the level of re-offending amongst prisoners would suggest that it falls far short of this objective. It is clear that the philosophy of punishment first and foremost does not have the desired effect of engendering remorse in hardened criminals, who find themselves locked into the reinforcing cycle of offence and punishment instead. It may be that critical coaching as outlined in previous chapters is the mirror which could force prisoners to come face-to-face with a responsibility for their actions and the consequences thereof. Punishment alone does not seem to achieve the desired outcome. Critical coaching, as we have argued throughout this study, provides the tools through which our ideologies and beliefs are challenged for the purpose of making more enabling choices, and its greater use within the prison system could well deliver substantial social dividends.

Radical coaching versus business as usual

As we have stated above, we do not believe that business as usual is really an option in the current economic climate, and that coaching should step into the breach to ensure that this does not become the default position. Radical coaching based on sceptical principles offers the opportunity at the individual level to make a break from corporate group-think and all the dubious practices that it has led to in recent history across the business sector – but particularly in banking and finance. Ideally, this will inspire a keener sense of social responsibility in coachees, who will gain the confidence to question their organizational policies, acting as the ongoing internal critique that all organizations need if they are to steer clear of a stultifying dogmatism. The cultivation of 'opposite sentiments' that Hume was so keen to promote has much to commend it in this context. Going on as before, business as usual, represents an evasion of CSR that runs counter to the public interest, and unless there is a change of consciousness within organizations that recognizes that wider picture, we are simply inviting yet more trouble on the economic front.

Ultimately, that is the main thrust of our argument, that there has to be a significant change of consciousness: a new Corporate Social Consciousness, as we might call it, genuinely committed to demonstrating Corporate Social Responsibility in all organizational dealings. We see this as most likely to come from the development of individuals within organizations, a bottom-up rather than top-down movement that will spread in viral fashion to refashion the organizational ethos, and a more radical form of coaching can be instrumental in generating this state of affairs. The aim has to be, as we noted earlier, sustainable change, rather than the all too prevalent notion within management circles that there can be some quick fix based on whatever the latest fad is in management theory that claims to be able to resolve any current problem – a fix that will sanction a return to business as usual and with that a loss of interest in such factors as social responsibility. It could be objected that business as usual merely sets the scene for crisis as usual. Individuals have to come to recognize that they constitute the conscience of their organization, and that puts a premium on the emergence of self-coaching. It could be argued that this is the primary objective of coaching, the only real way to institute sustainable change – to facilitate self-coaching. The more challenging the coaching process is, the more it draws on the rich and varied history of critical theory as we have recommended throughout this book, then the more likely we are to establish the basis for a Corporate Social Conscience – surely a goal well worth pursuing for all our sakes. We really do need to rethink the relationship between organizations and the public interest, and radical coaching ought to be in the vanguard of that enterprise.

Notes

1 Rethinking Coaching

1. Jean-François Lyotard, *The Postmodern Condition: A Report on Knowledge*, trans. Geoff Bennington and Brian Massumi, Manchester: Manchester University Press, 1984.
2. See, for example, Robert Bryce, *Pipe Dreams: Ego, Greed, and the Death of Enron*, New York: PublicAffairs, 2002, p. 5.
3. See, for example, Philip Augar, *The Greed Merchants: How the Investment Banks Played the Free Market Game*, London: Penguin, 2006 and Paul Mason, *Meltdown: the End of the Age of Greed*, London and New York: Verso, 2009.
4. House of Commons Treasury Committee Report, 'Women in the city', 3 April 2010, <www.parliament.uk> (accessed 5 May 2010).
5. Tracy McVeigh, 'The party's over for Iceland, the island that tried to buy the world', *The Observer*, 5 October 2008, <http://www.guardian.co.uk/world/2008/oct/05/iceland.creditcrunch> (accessed 1 August 2009).

2 Coaching as Theory and Practice

1. Dianne R. Stober, 'Coaching from a humanistic perspective', in Dianne R. Stober and Anthony M. Grant, eds, *Evidence Based Coaching Handbook: Putting Best Practices to Work for Your Clients*, Hoboken, NJ: John Wiley, 2006, pp. 17–50.
2. See Angelique du Toit, 'Making sense through coaching', *The Journal of Management Development*, 26:3 (2007), pp. 282–91.
3. Stober, 'Coaching from', p. 17; Anthony M. Grant, 'Past, present and future: the evolution of professional coaching and coaching psychology', in Stephen Palmer and Alison Whybrow, eds, *Handbook of Coaching Psychology: A Guide for Practitioners*, Hove: Routledge, 2007, pp. 23–39.
4. Anne Brockbank and Ian McGill, *Facilitating Reflective Learning in Higher Education*, Buckingham: SAGE and Open University Press, 2006.
5. Lorna J. Stewart, Siobhain O'Riordan, and Stephen Palmer, 'Before we know how we've done, we need to know what we're doing: operationalising coaching to provide a foundation for coaching evaluation', *The Coaching Psychologist*, 4:3 (2008), pp. 127–33.
6. Bob Garvey, Paul Stokes, and David Megginson, *Coaching and Mentoring: Theory and Practice*, London: SAGE, 2009.
7. Grant, 'Past, present and future', p. 25.
8. Miles Downey, *Effective Coaching: Lessons from the Coach's Coach*, 2nd edition, New York: Texere, 2003.

9. Grant, 'Past, present and future', p. 25.
10. Stober, 'Coaching from', p. 18.
11. Elaine Cox, Tatiana Bachkirova, and David Clutterbuck, eds, *The Complete Handbook of Coaching*, London: SAGE, 2010, p. 6.
12. Garvey et al., *Coaching and Mentoring*.
13. Vincent Lenhardt, *Coaching for Meaning*, Basingstoke: Palgrave Macmillan, 2004.
14. Tony Chapman, Bill Best, and Paul Van Casteren, *Executive Coaching: Exploding the Myths*, Basingstoke: Palgrave Macmillan, 2003.
15. See, for example, Manfred F. R. Kets de Vries, 'Leaders who self-destruct: the causes and cures', *Organizational Dynamics*, 17 (1989), pp. 5–17.
16. The sociologist Les Back puts forward a persuasive argument that cultural theory in general can benefit from its practitioners being more attentive to the stories of others, in *The Art of Listening*, Oxford and New York: Berg, 2007.
17. Carl R. Rogers, *A Way of Being*, New York: Mariner Books, 1980.
18. Carol Wilson, *Best Practice in Performance Coaching: A Handbook for Leaders, Coaching, HR Professionals and Organizations*, London: Kogan Page, 2007.
19. Peter Bluckert, 'Critical factors in executive coaching – the coaching relationship', *Industrial and Commercial Training*, 37:7 (2005), pp. 336–40.
20. Laura Whitworth, Henry Kimsey-House, and Phil Sandahl, *Co-Active Coaching: New Skills for Coaching People Toward Success in Work and Life*, Palo Alto, CA: Davies-Black, 1998; Mick Cope, *The Seven Cs of Coaching: The Definitive Guide to Collaborative Coaching*, Harlow: Pearson Education, 2004.
21. Tatiana Bachkirova, 'The cognitive-developmental approach to coaching', in Cox et al., *Complete Handbook*, pp. 132–45 (p. 141).
22. Seth Allcorn, 'Psychoanalytically informed executive coaching', in Stober and Grant, *Evidence Based Coaching*, pp. 129–49 (p. 129).
23. Carl R. Rogers, *On Becoming a Person*, London: Constable, 1967.
24. Ernesto Spinelli and Caroline Horner, 'An existential approach to coaching psychology', in Palmer and Whybrow, *Handbook*, pp. 118–32.
25. Mary B. O'Neill, *Executive Coaching with Backbone and Heart: A Systems Approach to Engaging Leaders with their Challenges*, San Francisco, CA: Jossey-Bass, 2000; Brockbank and McGill, *Facilitating Reflective Learning*; Alison Whybrow, 'Coaching psychology: coming of age?', *International Psychology Review*, 3:3 (2008), pp. 219–26; Carol Kauffman, 'The evolution of coaching: an interview with Sir John Whitmore', *Coaching: An International Journal of Theory, Research and Practice*, 1:1 (2008), pp. 11–15.
26. David Silsbee, *Presence-Based Coaching: Cultivating Self-Generative Leaders Through Mind, Body and Heart*, San Francisco, CA: Jossey-Bass, 2008, p. 21.
27. Mihaly Csikszentmihalyi, *Flow*, London: Rider, 2002.
28. Rogers, *Way of Being*.

29. Graham Lee, 'The psychodynamic approach to coaching', in Cox et al., *Complete Handbook*, pp. 23–36 (p. 25).
30. Daniel N. Stern, *The Present Moment in Psychotherapy and Everyday Life*, New York: W. W. Norton, 2004.
31. Gunnar Carlberg, 'Laughter opens the door: turning points in child psychotherapy', *Journal of Child Psychotherapy*, 23:3 (1997), pp. 331–49 (p. 335).
32. Tatiana Bachkirova, 'Role of coaching psychology in defining boundaries between counseling and coaching', in Palmer and Whybrow, *Handbook*, pp. 351–66.
33. Jack Mezirow, 'A critical theory of adult learning and education', *Adult Education Quarterly*, 31 (1981), pp. 3–24.
34. Graham Jones and Kirsty Spooner, 'Coaching high achievers', *Consulting Psychology Journal: Practice and Research*, 58:1 (2006), pp. 40–50; Whybrow, 'Coaching pyschology'; Rogers, *On Becoming*.
35. Whitworth et al., *Co-Active Coaching*.
36. Stober and Grant, *Evidence Based Coaching*, p. 1.
37. Wilson, *Best Practice*.
38. Ibid.
39. James C. Quick and Marilyn Macik-Frey, 'Behind the mask: coaching through deep interpersonal communication', *Consulting Psychology Journal: Practice and Research*, 56:2 (2004), pp. 67–74.
40. James T. Richard, 'Ideas on fostering creative problem solving in executive coaching', *Consulting Psychology Journal: Practice and Research*, 55:4 (2003), pp. 249–56.
41. John Whitmore, *Coaching for Performance: Growing People, Performance and Purpose*, 2nd edition, London: Nicholas Brealey, 1996.
42. See, for example, Travis J. Kemp, 'Searching for the elusive model of coaching: could the "holy grail" be right in front of us?', *International Psychology Review*, 3:3 (2008), pp. 219–26.
43. Cope, *Seven Cs*.
44. Erik de Haan and Yvonne Burger, *Coaching with Colleagues: An Action Guide for One-to-One Learning*, Basingstoke: Palgrave Macmillan, 2005.
45. Gibson Burrell and Gareth Morgan, *Sociological Paradigms and Organizational Analysis*, London: Ashgate, 1979; Brockbank and McGill, *Facilitating Reflective Learning*.
46. See, for example, Keith S. Dobson and David J. Dozois, 'Historical and philosophical bases of the cognitive-behavioural therapies', in Keith. S. Dobson, ed., *Handbook of Cognitive-Behavioural Therapies*, 2nd edition, New York: Guildford Press, 2001, pp. 3–39.
47. Whybrow, 'Coaching psychology'; P. Alex Linley and Susan Harrington, 'Integrating positive psychology and coaching psychology: shared assumptions and aspirations?', in Palmer and Whybrow, *Handbook*, pp. 40–56.
48. Allcorn, 'Psychoanalytically informed', p. 129.
49. Elizabeth C. Thach, 'The impact of executive coaching and 360 feedback on leadership effectiveness', *Leadership & Organization Development Journal*, 23:4 (2002), pp. 205–14.

50. See, for example, Vicki Hart, John Blattner, and Staci Leipsic, 'Coaching versus therapy', *Consulting Psychology Journal: Practice and Research*, 53:4 (2001), pp. 229–37.
51. Whybrow, 'Coaching psychology'.
52. Ernesto Spinelli, 'Coaching and therapy: similarities and divergences', *International Psychology Review*, 3:3 (2008), pp. 219–26.
53. Stephen Joseph and Richard Bryant-Jefferies, 'Person-centred coaching psychology', in Palmer and Whybrow, *Handbook*, pp. 211–28.
54. De Haan and Burger, *Coaching with Colleagues*.
55. Anthony M. Grant and Stephen Palmer, 'Coaching psychology workshop', Annual Conference of the Division of Counselling Psychology, British Psychological Society, Torquay, UK, 18 May 2002; Grant, 'Past, present and future'.
56. See, for example, Manfred F. R. Kets de Vries, Konstantin Korotov, and Elizabeth Florent-Treacy, *Coach and Couch: The Psychology of Making Better Leaders*, Basingstoke: Palgrave Macmillan, 2007.
57. Whybrow, 'Coaching psychology'.
58. Jonathan Passmore, 'Behavioural coaching', in Palmer and Whybrow, *Handbook*, pp. 73–85.
59. Stephen Palmer and Kasia Szymanska, 'Cognitive behavioural coaching: an integrative approach', in Palmer and Whybrow, *Handbook*, pp. 86–117.
60. Karl E. Weick, *The Social Psychology of Organizing*, New York: McGraw-Hill, 1979; Ernesto Spinelli and Caroline Horner, 'An existential approach to coaching psychology', in Palmer and Whybrow, *Handbook*, pp. 118–32.
61. Reinhard Stelter, 'Coaching: a process of personal and social meaning making', *International Coaching Psychology Review*, 2:2 (2007), pp. 191–201.
62. Spinelli and Horner, 'An existential approach'.
63. Ernesto Spinelli, 'Existential coaching', in Cox et al., *Complete Handbook*, pp. 94–106 (p. 101).
64. See, for example, Stewart et al., 'Before we know'.
65. Elaine Cox, 'An adult learning approach to coaching', in Stober and Grant, *Evidence Based Coaching*, pp. 193–218 (p. 194).
66. Kenneth J. Gergen, *Towards Transformation in Social Knowledge*, 2nd edition, London: SAGE, 1994.
67. Cope, *Seven Cs*.
68. Jeffrey E. Auerbach, 'Cognitive coaching', in Stober and Grant, *Evidence Based Coaching*, p. 113.
69. Halina Brunning, ed., *Executive Coaching: Systems-Psychodynamic Perspective*, London: H. Karnac, 2006.
70. See, for example, Sheila Kampa-Kokesch and Mary Z. Anderson, 'Executive coaching: a comprehensive review of the literature', *Consulting Psychology Journal: Practice and Research*, 53:4 (2001), pp. 205–28; Spinelli, 'Coaching and therapy'.

71. David Clutterbuck and Gill Lane, *The Situational Mentor: An International Review of Competences and Capabilities in Mentoring,* Aldershot: Gower, 2004.
72. Stephen Gibb, *Human Resource Development: Process, Practices and Perspectives,* 2nd edition, Basingstoke: Palgrave Macmillan, 2008.
73. Ibid., p. 173.
74. O'Neill, *Executive Coaching.*
75. Alison Whybrow and Vic Henderson, 'Concepts to support the integration and sustainability of coaching initiatives within organizations', in Palmer and Whybrow, *Handbook,* pp. 407–30.
76. Dianne R. Stober, 'Making it stick: coaching as a tool for organizational change', *Coaching: An International Journal of Theory, Research and Practice,* 1:1 (2008), pp. 71–80.
77. See, for example, Annette Fillery-Travis and David Lane, 'Research: does coaching work?', in Palmer and Whybrow, *Handbook,* pp. 57–70; Kauffman, 'Evolution of coaching'.
78. Auerbach, 'Cognitive coaching', p. 103.
79. Karol M. Wasylyshyn, 'Executive coaching: an outcome study', *Consulting Psychology Journal: Practice and Research,* 55:2 (2003), pp. 94–106.
80. Stephen Neale, Lisa Spencer-Arnell, and Liz Wilson, *Emotional Intelligence Coaching: Improving Performance for Leaders, Coaches and the Individual,* London: Kogan Page, 2009.
81. De Vries, 'Leaders'.
82. Wasylyshyn, 'Executive coaching'.
83. De Vries, 'Leaders'.
84. Quick and Macik-Frey, 'Behind the mask'.
85. Passmore, 'Behavioural coaching'.
86. De Vries, 'Leaders'.
87. Neale et al., *Emotional Intelligence.*
88. Quick and Macik-Frey, 'Behind the mask'.
89. Leo Giglio and Julie M. Urban, 'Coaching a leader: leveraging change at the top', *Journal of Management Development,* 17:2 (1998), pp. 93–105.
90. Steve O'Shaughnessy, 'Executive coaching: the route to business stardom', *Industrial and Commercial Training,* 33:6 (2001), pp. 194–7.
91. David Day, 'Leadership development: a review in context', *The Leadership Quarterly,* 11:4 (2000), pp. 581–613.
92. Stern, *Present Moment.*
93. David Clutterbuck and David Megginson, *Making Coaching Work: Creating a Coaching Culture,* London: Chartered Institute of Personnel and Development, 2005, p. 19.
94. Jennifer Joy-Matthews, David Megginson, and Mark Surtees, *Human Resource Development,* 3rd edition, London: Kogan Page, 2004, p. 104.
95. Downey, *Effective Coaching;* Timothy Gallwey, *The Inner Game of Tennis: The Classic Guide to the Mental Side of Peak Performance,* New York: Random House, 1974.
96. See, for example, David. E. Gray, 'Executive coaching: towards a dynamic alliance of psychotherapy and transformational learning processes', *Management Learning,* 37:4 (2006), pp. 475–97.

97. Stober and Grant, Introduction, *Evidence Based Coaching*, p. 4.
98. Cox, 'Adult learning approach', p. 194.
99. Jack Mezirow, *Transformative Dimensions of Adult Learning*, San Francisco, CA: Jossey-Bass, 1991.
100. Knud Illeris, 'A model for learning in working life', *The Journal of Workplace Learning*, 16:8 (2004), pp. 431–41.
101. Vivien Burr, *An Introduction to Social Constructionism*, London: Routledge, 1995; and Kenneth J. Gergen, 'The social constructionist movement in modern psychology', *American Psychologist*, 40:3 (1985), pp. 266–75, *The Saturated Self: Dilemmas of Identity in Contemporary Life*, New York: Basic Books, 1991, and *Toward Transformation*, 2nd edition, London: SAGE, 1994.
102. Malcolm S. Knowles, *The Modern Practice of Adult Education: From Pedagogy to Andragogy*, Englewood Cliffs, NJ: Prentice Hall, 1980, p. 43.
103. De Haan and Burger, *Coaching with Colleagues*.
104. De Vries, 'Leaders'.
105. Gray, 'Executive coaching'.
106. Wilson, *Best Practice*.
107. Brockbank and McGill, *Facilitating Reflective Learning*, p. 9.
108. De Haan and Burger, *Coaching with Colleagues*.
109. Garvey et al., *Coaching and Mentoring*.
110. Anne Deering and Anne Murphy, *The Difference Engine: Achieving Powerful and Sustainable Partnering*, Aldershot: Gower, 1998.
111. David Bohm and Lee Nichol, eds, *On Dialogue*, London: Routledge, 1996.
112. Peter Senge, *The Fifth Discipline: The Art and Practice of Learning Organization*, London: Routledge, 1990.
113. Bohm and Lee, *On Dialogue*.
114. Jennifer Garvey Berger, 'Adult development theory and executive coaching practice', in Stober and Grant, *Evidence Based Coaching*, pp. 77–102 (p. 77).
115. Bohm and Lee, *On Dialogue*, p. 6.
116. Cox, 'Adult learning approach', p. 199.
117. Whitworth et al., *Co-Active Coaching*.
118. Stephen Gibb and Peter Hill, 'From trail-blazing individualism to a social construction community: modeling knowledge construction in coaching', *The International Journal of Mentoring & Coaching*, IV:2 (2006), pp. 58–77.

3 Who Benefits from Coaching?: Case Studies

1. See Chartered Institute of Personnel Development, <http://www.cipd.co.uk/helpingpeoplelearn/_cchng.htm> (accessed 5 May 2010).
2. David Clutterbuck and David Megginson, *Making Coaching Work: Creating a Coaching Culture*, London: Chartered Institute of Personnel and Development, 2005, p. 30.

3. Sir Peter Gershon, 'Releasing resources to the front line: Independent Review of Public Sector Efficiency', July 2004, <www.hm-treasury.gov.uk> (accessed 1 May 2010).
4. See Chartered Institute of Personnel Development, 'Coaching at the BBC', <http://www.cipd.co.uk/helpingpeoplelearn/_bbcchg.htm> (accessed 5 May 2010).
5. Michael Cavanagh, 'Coaching from a systemic perspective: a complex adaptive conversation', in Dianne R. Stober and Anthony M. Grant, eds, *Evidence Based Coaching Handbook: Putting Best Practices to Work for Your Clients*, Hoboken, NJ: John Wiley, 2006, p. 325.

4 The Limitations of Coaching

1. John O. Ogbor, 'Critical theory and the hegemony of corporate culture', *Journal of Organizational Change*, 14:6 (2001), pp. 590–608 (p. 591).
2. Vega Zagier Roberts and Michael Jarrett, 'What is the difference and what makes the difference? A comparative study of psychodynamic and non-psychodynamic approaches to executive coaching', in Halina Brunning, ed., *Executive Coaching: Systems-Psychodynamic Perspective*, London: H. Karnac, 2006, pp. 3–40 (p. 29).
3. Manfred F. R. Kets de Vries, Konstantin Korotov, and Elizabeth Florent-Treacy, *Coach and Couch: The Psychology of Making Better Leaders*, Basingstoke: Palgrave Macmillan, 2007, p. xlii.
4. David Clutterbuck, 'Coaching reflection: the liberated coach', *Coaching: An International Journal of Theory, Research and Practice*, 3:1 (2010), pp. 73–81 (p. 73).
5. Anne Brockbank and Ian McGill, *Facilitating Reflective Learning in Higher Education*, Buckingham: SAGE and Open University Press, 2006, p. 9.
6. John Whitmore, *Coaching for Performance: Growing People, Performance and Purpose*, 2nd edition, London: Nicholas Brealey, 1996; Clutterbuck, 'Coaching reflection', p. 73.
7. See Tatiana Bachkirova, 'Role of coaching psychology in defining boundaries between counselling and coaching', in Stephen Palmer and Alison Whybrow, eds, *Handbook of Coaching Psychology: A Guide for Practitioners*, Hove: Routledge, 2007, pp. 351–66; Annette Fillery-Travis and David Lane, 'Research: does coaching work?', in Palmer and Whybrow, *Handbook*, pp. 57–70.
8. See Stephen Joseph and Richard Bryant-Jefferies, 'Person-centred coaching psychology', in Palmer and Whybrow, *Handbook*, pp. 211–28; Carol Wilson, *Best Practice in Performance Coaching: A Handbook for Leaders, Coaching, HR Professionals and Organizations*, London: Kogan Page, 2007.
9. Travis. J. Kemp, 'Searching for the elusive model of coaching: could the "holy grail" be right in front of us?', *International Psychology Review*, 3:3 (2008), pp. 219–26.
10. Bob Garvey, Paul Stokes, and David Megginson, *Coaching and Mentoring: Theory and Practice*, London: SAGE, 2009.

11. David Clutterbuck and David Megginson, *Making Coaching Work: Creating a Coaching Culture*, London: Chartered Institute of Personnel and Development, 2005, p. 2.
12. Garvey et al., *Coaching and Mentoring*, pp. 86–7.
13. Elouise Leonard-Cross, 'Developmental coaching: business benefit – fact or fad? An evaluative study to explore the impact of coaching in the workplace', *International Coaching Psychology Review*, 5:1 (2010), pp. 36–47 (p. 38).
14. Clutterbuck and Megginson, *Making Coaching Work*, p. 2.
15. Maj Karin Askeland, 'A reflexive inquiry into the ideologies and theoretical assumptions of coaching', *Coaching: An International Journal of Theory, Research and Practice*, 2:1 (2009), pp. 65–7 (p. 65).
16. Ibid.
17. Bruce Peltier, *The Psychology of Executive Coaching: Theory and Application*, 2nd edition, London: Routledge, 2010, p. xxiii.
18. Brockbank and McGill, *Facilitating Reflective Learning*, p. 265.
19. David B. Peterson, 'People are complex and the world is messy: a behavior-based approach to executive coaching', in Dianne R. Stober and Anthony M. Grant, eds, *Evidence Based Coaching: Putting Best Practices to Work for Your Clients*, Hoboken, NJ: John Wiley, 2006, pp. 51–76 (p. 51); Garvey et al., *Coaching and Mentoring*, p. 5.
20. Peterson, 'People are complex'.
21. John Price, 'The coaching/therapy boundary in organizational coaching', *Coaching: An International Journal of Theory, Research and Practice*, 2:1 (2009), pp. 65–75.
22. Kenneth J. Gergen, *Toward Transformation in Social Knowledge*, 2nd edition, London: SAGE, 1994; Michel Foucault, *Madness and Civilization: A History of Insanity in the Age of Reason* [1964], trans. Richard Howard, London: Tavistock, 1971.
23. Gergen, *Toward Transformation*, p. 158.
24. Peter Welman and Tatiana Bachkirova, 'The issue of power in the coaching relationship', in Stephen Palmer and Almuth McDowall, eds, *The Coaching Relationship: Putting People First*, London: Routledge, 2009, pp. 139–58.
25. See, for example, Michel Foucault, *Power/Knowledge: Selected Interviews and Other Writings 1972–1977*, in Colin Gordon, ed., Brighton: Harvester, 1980.
26. Garvey et al., *Coaching and Mentoring*, pp. 111–24.
27. John Rowan, 'The transpersonal approach to coaching', in Elaine Cox, Tatiana Bachkirova and David Clutterbuck, eds, *The Complete Handbook of Coaching*, London: SAGE, 2010, pp. 146–57 (p. 152).
28. See Aristotle, *De Anima (On the Soul)*, trans. Hugh-Lawson Tancred, London: Penguin, 2004.
29. See, for example, Carl G. Jung, *Symbols of Transformation*, vol. 6 of *The Collected Works*, in Gerhard Adler, Michael Fordham, and Sir Herbert Read, eds, trans. R. F. C. Hull, London: Routledge and Kegan Paul, 1956.
30. See Carl R. Rogers, *On Becoming a Person*, London: Constable, 1967.

31. See, for example, Abraham Maslow, *Motivation and Personality*, 2nd edition, New York: Harper and Row, 1970.
32. Carol Kaufman, 'Positive psychology: the science at the heart of coaching', in Stober and Grant, *Evidence Based Coaching*, pp. 219–54 (p. 219).
33. That attitude, whereby anything, even serious illness, is supposed to be regarded as a positive development in one's life, is sharply criticized by Barbara Ehrenreich in *Smile or Die: How Positive Thinking Fooled America and the World*, London: Granta, 2010.
34. Tatiana Bachkirova and Carol Kauffman, 'Editorial', *Coaching: An International Journal of Theory, Research and Practice*, 2:2 (2009), pp. 96–105 (p. 101).
35. Jonathan Passmore, 'Behavioural coaching', in Palmer and Whybrow, *Handbook*, pp. 73–85.
36. Brockbank and McGill, *Facilitating Reflective Learning*, p. 238.
37. Clutterbuck, 'Coaching reflection', p. 74.
38. Anthony M. Grant, 'Past, present and future: the evolution of professional coaching and coaching psychology', in Palmer and Whybrow, *Handbook*, pp. 23–39.
39. Lorna J. Stewart, Siobhain O'Riordan and Stephen Palmer, 'Before we know how we've done, we need to know what we're doing: operationalising coaching to provide a foundation for coaching evaluation', *The Coaching Psychologist*, 4:3 (2008), pp. 127–33.
40. Miles Downey, *Effective Coaching: Lessons from the Coach's Coach*, 2nd edition, New York: Texere, 2003.
41. Ibid.
42. See Dianne. R. Stober, 'Making it stick: coaching as a tool for organizational change', *Coaching: An International Journal of Theory, Research and Practice*, 1:1 (2008), pp. 71–80; Robert Witherspoon and Randall P. White, *Four Essential Ways that Coaching Can Help Executives*, Greensboro, NC: CCL Press, 1997.
43. Grant, 'Past, present and future'.
44. Kemp, 'Searching for the elusive model'.
45. David Silsbee, *Presence-Based Coaching: Cultivating Self-Generative Leaders Through Mind, Body and Heart*, San Francisco, CA: Jossey-Bass, 2008.
46. Ibid.
47. Anne Brockbank, 'Is the coaching fit for purpose?: a typology of coaching and learning approaches', *Coaching: An International Journal of Theory, Research and Practice*, 1:2 (2008), pp. 132–44 (p. 132).
48. Gibson Burrell and Gareth Morgan, *Sociological Paradigms and Organizational Analysis*, London: Ashgate, 1979; Brockbank, 'Is the coaching fit for purpose?'.
49. Garvey et al., *Coaching and Mentoring*, p. 53.
50. Kemp, 'Searching for the elusive model', p. 219.

5 The Rise of Critical Theory

1. See G. W. F. Hegel, *The Phenomenology of Spirit* [1807], trans. A. V. Miller, Oxford: Oxford University Press, 1977.

2. Karl Marx, *The Communist Manifesto* [1848], ed. Frederic L. Bender, New York and London: W. W. Norton, 1988.
3. Karl Marx, *Theses on Feuerbach*, XI, in Frederick Engels, *Ludwig Feuerbach and the End of Classical German Philosophy*, Peking: Foreign Languages Press, 1976, pp. 61–5 (p. 65).
4. Georg Lukács, *History and Class Consciousness: Studies in Marxist Dialectics* [1923], trans. Rodney Livingstone, London: Merlin Press, 1971.
5. See Theodor W. Adorno and Max Horkheimer, *Dialectic of Enlightenment* [1944], trans. John Cumming, London and New York: Verso, 1979.
6. See Herbert Marcuse, *One-Dimensional Man: Studies in the Ideology of an Advanced Capitalist Society*, London: Routledge and Kegan Paul, 1964.
7. See Ferdinand de Saussure, *Course in General Linguistics*, eds Charles Bally, Albert Sechehaye and Albert Reidlinger, trans. Wade Baskin, London: Peter Owen, 1960.
8. Roland Barthes, *Image Music, Text*, ed. and trans. Stephen Heath, London: Fontana, 1977, p. 79.
9. See the essay 'The Death of the Author', in ibid., pp. 142–8.
10. See Jacques Derrida, *Of Grammatology* [1967], trans. Gayatri Chakravorty Spivak, Baltimore, MD and London: Johns Hopkins University Press, 1974.
11. See Michel Foucault, *The History of Sexuality*, I–III: *The History of Sexuality: An Introduction* [1976], trans. Robert Hurley, Harmondsworth: Penguin, 1979; *The Use of Pleasure* [1984], trans. Robert Hurley, London: Penguin, 1987; *The Care of the Self* [1984], trans. Robert Hurley, London: Penguin, 1988.
12. See, for example, the work of Judith Butler, Eve Kosofsky Sedgwick, or D. A. Miller.
13. See Michel Foucault, *Madness and Civilization: A History of Insanity in the Age of Reason* [1964], trans. Richard Howard, London: Tavistock, 1971.
14. See Michel Foucault, *The Birth of the Clinic: An Archaeology of Medical Perception* [1963], trans. A. M. Sheridan-Smith, New York: Vintage, 1973, and *Discipline and Punish: The Birth of the Prison* [1975], trans. Alan Sheridan, New York: Pantheon, 1977.
15. See Jacques Derrida, *Margins of Philosophy* [1972], trans. Alan Bass, Hemel Hempstead: Harvester Wheatsheaf, 1982.
16. Jean-François Lyotard, *Political Writings*, trans. Bill Readings and Kevin Paul Geiman, London: UCL Press, 1993, p. 210.
17. Jean-François Lyotard, *The Postmodern Condition: A Report on Knowledge* [1979], trans. Geoff Bennington and Brian Massumi, Manchester: Manchester University Press, 1984, p. xxiv.
18. 'One could call an event the impact, on the system, of floods of energy such that the system does not manage to bind and channel this energy; the event would the traumatic encounter of energy with the regulating institution' (Lyotard, *Political Writings*, p. 64).
19. See Jean-François Lyotard, *The Differend: Phrases in Dispute* [1983], trans. Georges Van Den Abbeele, Manchester: Manchester University Press, 1988.

20. Lyotard, *Postmodern Condition*, p. 82.
21. Charles Jencks, *The Language of Post-Modern Architecture*, 6th edition, London: Academy Editions, 1991, p. 12.
22. Gilles Deleuze and Felix Guatarri, *Anti-Oedipus: Capitalism and Schizophrenia* [1972], trans. Robert Hurley, Mark Seem, and Helen R. Lane, London: Athlone Press, 1983, and *A Thousand Plateaus: Capitalism and Schizophrenia* [1980], trans. Brian Massumi, London: Athlone Press, 1988.
23. See Lyotard, 'A Svelte Appendix to the Postmodern Question', in *Political Writings*, pp. 25–9.
24. Ernesto Laclau and Chantal Mouffe, *Hegemony and Socialist Strategy: Towards a Radical Democratic Politics*, London: Verso, 1985, p. 1.
25. Slavoj Žižek, *The Sublime Object of Ideology*, London and New York: Verso, 1989, p. 33.
26. Ibid., p. 29.
27. Slavoj Žižek, *On Belief*, London and New York: Routledge, 2001, p. 14.
28. Heidi Hartmann, 'The unhappy marriage of marxism and feminism: towards a more progressive union', in Lydia Sargent, ed., *The Unhappy Marriage of Marxism and Feminism: A Debate on Class and Patriarchy*, London: Pluto Press, 1981, pp. 1–42 (p. 2).
29. Luce Irigaray, *This Sex Which Is Not One* [1977], trans. Catherine Porter, with Carolyn Burke, Ithaca, NY: Cornell University Press, 1985, p. 33.
30. See Rosalind Coward, *Sacred Cows: Is Feminism Relevant to the New Millennium?*, London: HarperCollins, 1999.
31. Simone de Beauvoir, *The Second Sex* [1949], trans. and ed. M. H. Pashley, Harmondsworth: Penguin, 1972, p. 295.
32. Edward Said, *Orientalism: Western Conceptions of the Orient*, 2nd edition, Harmondsworth: Penguin, 1995, p. 3.
33. See Slavoj Žižek, *Enjoy Your Symptom! Jacques Lacan in Hollywood and Out*, 2nd edition, London and New York: Routledge, 2008.
34. Bruce Fink, *A Clinical Introduction to Lacanian Psychoanalysis: Theory and Technique*, Cambridge, MA: Harvard University Press, 1997, p. 3.
35. Peter Coveney and Roger Highfield, *Frontiers of Complexity: The Search for Order in a Chaotic World*, London: Faber and Faber, 1995, p. 170.
36. Ibid., p. 9.
37. Paul Mason, *Meltdown: The End of the Age of Greed*, London and New York: Verso, 2009, p. 141.
38. For Soros's assessment of the credit crunch, see his *The Crash of 2008 and What it Means: The New Paradigm for Financial Markets*, New York: PublicAffairs, 2009. Warren Buffet even described the new range of financial products being developed (credit derivatives, for example) as 'weapons of mass destruction' – not so far off the mark in terms of what subsequently happened in the world's financial markets (quoted in Philip Augar, *Chasing Alpha: How Reckless Growth and Unchecked Ambition Ruined the City's Golden Decade*, London: Bodley Head, 2009, p. 14).
39. Lyotard, *Postmodern Condition*, p. 19.
40. Ibid., p. 23.
41. Ibid., p. 60.
42. See Thomas Kuhn, *The Structure of Scientific Revolutions*, 2nd edition, Chicago, IL, and London: University of Chicago Press, 1970.

6 Scepticism in Public Life

1. Sextus Empiricus, *Outlines of Scepticism*, trans. Julia Annas and Jonathan Barnes, Cambridge: Cambridge University Press, 1994, p. 72.
2. Ibid., p. 4.
3. Richard H. Popkin, *The History of Scepticism from Erasmus to Spinoza*, Berkeley, Los Angeles, and London: University of California Press, 1979, p. xi.
4. René Descartes, *Meditations on First Philosophy*, in *Philosophical Writings*, trans. and ed. Elizabeth Anscombe and Peter Thomas Geach, London: Thomas Nelson, 1970, p. 61.
5. Ibid., p. 62.
6. Ibid., p. 65.
7. Ibid., p. 67.
8. Ibid., p. 90.
9. C. H. Whiteley, 'Epistemological strategies', *Mind*, 78 (1969), pp. 25–34 (p. 26).
10. Baron d'Holbach, *The System of Nature*, I [1770], trans. H. D. Robinson and Alastair Jackson, Manchester: Clinamen Press, 1999, p. 4; and *Christianity Unveiled: Being an Examination of the Principles and Effects of the Christian Religion* [1761], trans. William Martin Johnson in *The Deist, or Moral Philosopher*, vol. II, London: R. Carlile, 1819, pp. 16–125 (p. 17).
11. David Hume, *A Treatise of Human Nature* [1739], ed. D. G. C. Macnabb, Glasgow: Fontana/Collins, 1962, p. 216.
12. Ibid., pp. 301–2.
13. David Hume, *Dialogues and Natural History of Religion* [1779, 1757], ed. J. C. A. Gaskin, Oxford: Oxford University Press, 1993, p. 184.
14. Hume, *Treatise*, p. 318.
15. Immanuel Kant, *Critique of Pure Reason* [1781], trans. Norman Kemp Smith, 2nd edition, London and Basingstoke: Macmillan, 1933, p. 113.
16. Ibid., p. 86.
17. Stuart Sim, *Contemporary Continental Philosophy: The New Scepticism*, Aldershot and Burlington, VT: Ashgate, 2000, p. 2.
18. Gayatri Chakravorty Spivak, 'Translator's Preface' to Jacques Derrida, *Of Grammatology* [1967], trans. Gayatri Chakravorty Spivak, Baltimore, MD, and London: Johns Hopkins University Press, 1976, p. xvii.
19. Ibid., p. 60.
20. John D. Barrow, *Impossibility: The Limits of Science and the Science of Limits*, London: Vintage, 1999, p. 249.
21. See Jean-François Lyotard, *Lessons on the Analytic of the Sublime* [1991], trans. Elizabeth Rottenberg, Stanford, CA: Stanford University Press, 1994. Immanuel Kant was another thinker to be much exercised by this phenomenon (see particularly his *Critique of Judgment* [1790], trans. James Creed Meredith, Oxford: Clarendon Press, 1952).
22. Jean-François Lyotard and Jean-Loup Thébaud, *Just Gaming* [1979], trans. Wlad Godzich, Manchester: Manchester University Press, 1985, p. 28.

23. Friedrich Nietzsche, *The Will to Power* [1901], trans. Walter Kaufman and R. J. Hollingdale, London: Weidenfeld and Nicolson, 1968, p. 267.
24. David Hume, *Enquiries Concerning Human Understanding and Concerning the Principles of Morals* [1748, 1751], 3rd edition, ed. L. A. Selby-Bigge, revised P. H. Nidditch, Oxford: Clarendon Press, 1975, p. 161.
25. The J. P. Morgan banker Bill Demchak (quoted in Gillian Tett, *Fool's Gold: How Unrestrained Greed Corrupted a Dream, Shattered Global Markets and Unleashed a Catastrophe*, London: Little, Brown, 2009, p. 58).
26. Al-Ghazali, *The Incoherence of the Philosophers* [1091–5], trans. Michael E. Marmara, Provo, UT: Brigham Young University Publishing, 1997.
27. Scepticism can also be found within other major world religions, such as Hinduism and Buddhism. The Madhyamika School in the latter encourages a suspension of judgement with regard to metaphysical questions that is very similar in form to Pyrrhonism (see Frederick J. Streng, *Emptiness: A Study in Religious Meaning*, Nashville, NY: Abingdon Press, 1967).
28. Whiteley, 'Epistemological strategies', p. 26.
29. For an analysis of recent trends in this direction, see Stuart Sim, *Fundamentalist World: The New Dark Age of Dogma*, Cambridge: Icon Press, 2004.
30. For a critique of IMF/World Bank policy in the last few decades, see Joseph Stiglitz, *Globalization and its Discontents*, London: Penguin, 2002, and *Making Globalization Work*, London: Allen Lane, 2006.
31. Jean-François Lyotard, *Political Writings*, trans. Bill Readings and Kevin Paul Geiman, London: UCL Press, 1993, p. 28.
32. See particularly the first book in the trilogy, *Titus Groan* [1946], Harmondsworth: Penguin, 1968.
33. Whiteley, 'Epistemological strategies', p. 26.
34. Derrida, *Of Grammatology*, p. 5.

7 The Market Paradigm: What Went Wrong?

1. For a classic study of the bubble phenomenon, see Charles B. Kindleberger, *Manias, Panics, and Crashes: A History of Financial Crises*, London and Basingstoke: Macmillan, 1978.
2. William D. Cohan, *House of Cards: How Wall Street's Gamblers Broke Capitalism*, London: Allen Lane, 2009.
3. See, for example, John Naish, *Enough: Breaking Free from the World of Excess*, London: Hodder and Stoughton, 2008, and Neal Lawson, *All Consuming: How Shopping Got Us Into this Mess and How We Can Find Our Way Out*, London: Penguin, 2009.
4. Douglas Rushkoff, *Life Inc.: How the World Became a Corporation and How to Take It Back*, London: Bodley Head, 2009, p. 70.
5. Sébastien Michenaud and Bruno Solnik, 'Applying regret theory to investment choices: currency hedging decisions', *Journal of International Money and Finance*, 27:5 (2008), pp. 677–94.

6. Ibid.
7. Tom Wolfe, *The Bonfire of the Vanities*, London: Picador and Jonathan Cape, 1988.
8. Kent H. Baker and John R. Nofsinger, 'Psychological biases of investors', *Financial Review Services*, 11 (2002), pp. 97–116.
9. John M. Coates and Joseph Herbert, 'Endogenous steroids and financial risk taking on a London trading floor', *Proceedings of the National Academy of Sciences*, 105 (2008), pp. 6167–72.
10. See Richard Bronk, *The Romantic Economist: Imagination in Economics*, Cambridge: Cambridge University Press, 2009.
11. See, for example, Paul Krugman, *The Return of Depression Economics and the Crisis of 2008*, London: Penguin, 2008; Graham Turner, *The Credit Crunch: Housing Bubbles, Globalisation and Worldwide Economic Crisis*, London: Pluto Press, 2008; Gillian Tett, *Fool's Gold: How Unrestrained Greed Corrupted a Dream, Shattered Global Markets and Unleashed a Catastrophe*, London: Little, Brown, 2009; Philip Augar, *Chasing Alpha: How Reckless Growth and Unchecked Ambition Ruined the City's Golden Decade*, London: Bodley Head, 2009; Vince Cable, *The Storm: The World Economic Crisis and What It Means*, London: Atlantic, 2009; George Soros, *The Crash of 2008 and What it Means: The New Paradigm for Financial Markets*, New York: PublicAffairs, 2009; Larry Elliott and Dan Atkinson, *The Gods that Failed: How Blind Faith in Markets Has Cost Us Our Future*, London: Bodley Head, 2009; Paul Mason, *Meltdown: The End of the Age of Greed*, London and New York: Verso, 2009; Kenneth and William Hopper, *The Puritan Gift: Reclaiming the American Dream Amidst Global Financial Chaos*, New York: I. B. Tauris, 2009. For an analysis of the overall response to the crisis, see Chapter 5 of Stuart Sim, *The End of Modernity: What the Financial and Environmental Crisis is Really Telling Us*, Edinburgh: Edinburgh University Press, 2010.
12. Quoted in Mason, *Meltdown*, p. 13.
13. Irving L. Janis, *Victims of Groupthink*, Boston, MA: Houghton Mifflin, 1972.
14. William Schiano and Joseph W. Weiss, 'Y2K all over again: how groupthink permeates IS and compromises security', *Business Horizons*, 49 (2006), pp. 115–25.
15. Abraham Carmeli, 'Social capital, psychological safety and learning behaviours from failure in organizations', *Long Range Planning*, 40 (2007), pp. 30–44.
16. Janis, *Victims of Groupthink*.
17. Ibid.
18. Ibid., p. 8.
19. Ibid., p. 9.
20. Ibid.
21. Jocelyn Pixley, 'Finance, organizations, decisions and emotions', *British Journal of Sociology*, 53:1 (2002), pp. 41–65.
22. Kenneth. J. Gergen, 'The social constructionist movement in modern psychology', *American Psychologist*, 40:3 (1985), pp. 266–75.

23. Kenneth J. Gergen, *Toward Transformation in Social Knowledge*, 2nd edition, London: SAGE, 1994, p. 96.
24. Kenneth J. Gergen, *Realities and Relationships: Soundings in Social Construction*, Cambridge, MA: Harvard University Press, 1997.
25. Peter L. Berger and Thomas Luckmann, *The Social Construction of Reality: A Treatise in the Sociology of Knowledge*, London: Penguin, 1991.
26. Kenneth J. Gergen, *An Invitation to Social Construction*, London: SAGE, 1999, p. 176.
27. Niall FitzGerald, Foreword to Avivah Wittenberg-Cox and Alison Maitland, *Why Women Mean Business*, Chichester: John Wiley, 2009.
28. Wittenberg-Cox and Maitland, *Why Women Mean Business*.
29. Michael Ferrary, 'Global financial crisis: are women the antidote?', CERAM Business School, October 2008.
30. For an argument about the beneficial effect of a more equal gender balance on the development of corporate strategy, see Angelique du Toit, *Corporate Strategy: A Feminist Perspective*, London and New York: Routledge, 2006.
31. Paul Krugman, *The Return of Depression Economics*, New York: W. W. Norton, 1999.
32. Krugman, *The Return of Depression Economics and the Crisis of 2008*, p. 5.
33. On the new financial products, see Janet M. Tavakoli, *Credit Derivatives and Synthetic Structures: A Guide to Instruments and Applications*, 2nd edition, New York: John Wiley, 2001.
34. Alex Brummer, *The Crunch: The Scandal of Northern Rock and the Escalating Credit Crisis*, London: Random House Business Books, 2008, p. 35.
35. See the discussion of this particular case in ibid.
36. The bank's announcement on 9 August 2007 that it was withdrawing from three funds with substantial investments in the American subprime mortgage market, effectively signalled the collapse of that market. Others soon came to the same conclusion and acted accordingly.
37. Tett, *Fool's Gold*, p. 286.
38. Augar, *Chasing Alpha*, p. ix.

8 A New Dawn: Applying Critical Theory to Coaching

1. See Diana Furchtgott-Roth, 'No quotas for women on corporate boards', <http://blogs.reuters.com/great-debate/2009/08/21/no-quotas-for-women-on-corporate-boards/> (accessed 5 May 2010).
2. Robert Kitson, 'Johnson drops Armitage and waits on Borthwick before French test', *The Guardian*, Sport section, 17 March 2010, p. 9. The topic was the English rugby union team's over-regimented style in the 2009–10 season Six Nations competition.
3. Jean-François Lyotard, *The Postmodern Condition: A Report on Knowledge* [1979], trans. Geoff Bennington and Brian Massumi, Manchester: Manchester University Press, 1984, p. 27.

4. David Boje, *Storytelling Organizations*, London: SAGE, 2008, p. 1.
5. Lyotard, *Postmodern Condition*, pp. xxiv, 60.
6. Slavoj Žižek, *On Belief*, London and New York: Routledge, p. 15.
7. Žižek regards the fetish as 'a kind of *inverse* of the symptom', with the latter being 'the exception which disturbs the surface of the false appearance', whereas the former 'is the embodiment of the Lie which enables us to sustain the unbearable truth' (*On Belief*, p. 13); but clearly there is the possibility of considerable interplay and overlap between the two states.

9 Coaching and the Whistleblowing Dilemma

1. Wim Vandekerckhove, *Whistleblowing and Organizational Social Responsibility: A Global Assessment*, Aldershot and Burlington, VT: Ashgate, 2006, p. 8.
2. For a detailed analysis of the sensitive relationship between CSR and whistleblowing, see ibid.
3. There is also a National Whistleblowers Center in the USA that provides guidance and legal information for those caught up in whistleblowing controversies.
4. Jesica R. Mesmer-Magnus and Chockalingam Viswesvaran, 'Whistleblowing in organizations: an examination of correlates of whistleblowing intentions, actions and retaliations', *Journal of Business Ethics*, 62 (2005), pp. 277–97 (p. 280).
5. Lars Lindblom, 'Dissolving the moral dilemma of whistleblowing', *Journal of Business Ethics*, 76 (2007), pp. 413–26 (p. 413).
6. Gillian Tett, *Fool's Gold: How Unrestrained Greed Corrupted a Dream, Shattered Global Markets and Unleashed a Catastrophe*, London: Little, Brown, 2009, p. ix.
7. See Steven Kaplan, Kurt Pany, Janet Samuels, and Jian Zhang, 'An examination of the association between gender and reporting intentions for fraudulent financial reporting', *Journal of Business Ethics*, 87 (2009), pp. 15–30.
8. Ibid.
9. Daniel Goleman, 'Developing a completely transparent and emotionally supportive system', *In View, the Journal from the NHS Institute*, 23 (2009), pp. 4–9.
10. Daniel Goleman, *Vital Lies, Simple Truths: The Psychology of Self-Deception*, London: Bloomsbury, 1997, p. 13.
11. Joyce Rothschild, 'Freedom of speech denied, dignity assaulted: what the whistleblowers experience in the US', *Current Sociology*, 56:6 (2008), pp. 884–903 (p. 889).
12. Eva E. Tsahuridu and Wim Vandekerckhove, 'Organizational whistleblowing policies: making employees responsible or liable?', *Journal of Business Ethics*, 82 (2008), pp. 107–18.
13. Rothschild, 'Freedom of speech', p. 898.

14. Harold Hassink, Meinderd de Vries and Laury Bollen, 'A content analysis of whistleblowing policies of leading European companies', *Journal of Business Ethics*, 75 (2007), pp. 25–44 (p. 25).
15. Mesmer-Magnus and Viswesvaran, 'Whistleblowing in organizations'.
16. Lindblom, 'Dissolving the moral dilemma'.
17. Jukka Varelius, 'Is whistle-blowing compatible with employee loyalty?', *Journal of Business Ethics*, 85 (2009), pp. 263–75 (p. 263).

10 Conclusion: Radical Coaching and Business as Usual

1. Karl-Erik Wärneryd, 'The economic psychology of the stock market', in Alan Lewis, ed., *The Cambridge Handbook of Psychology and Economic Behaviour*, Cambridge: Cambridge University Press, 2008, pp. 39–63 (p. 49).
2. John Naish, *Enough: Breaking Free from the World of Excess*, London: Hodder and Stoughton, 2009, p. 2. This issue is also addressed in Stuart Sim, *The End of Modernity: What the Financial and Environmental Crisis is Really Telling Us*, Edinburgh: Edinburgh University Press, 2010, which calls for the development of a 'politics of enough' (p. 22).
3. See Irving L. Janis, *Groupthink: Psychological Studies of Policy Decisions and Fiascoes*, 2nd edition, Boston, MA: Houghton Mifflin, 1982.
4. See, for example, John Bratton, Peter Sawchuk, Carolyn Forshaw, Militza Callinan, and Martin Corbett, *Work and Organizational Behaviour*, 2nd edition, London: Palgrave Macmillan, 2010.
5. House of Commons Treasury Committee Report, 'Women in the city', 3 April 2010, <www.parliament.uk> (accessed 5 May 2010).
6. Janis, *Groupthink*, p. 175.
7. BBC News, 'Q & A: Do bankers really need the bonuses?', 26 February 2010, <http://news.bbc.co.uk/1/hi/business/8540020.stm> (accessed 5 May 2010).
8. Lisa Matthewman, Amanda Rose, and Angela Hetherington, *Work Psychology*, Oxford: Oxford University Press, 2009, p. 363.
9. Ibid., p. 423.
10. BBC News, 'Foreign students not "cash cows", says British Council', 26 March 2010, <http://news.bbc.co.uk/1/hi/education/8584819.stm> (accessed 5 May 2010).
11. The full text is printed in *The Guardian*, Education Section, 10 April 2007: 'We must develop a new three Rs: rules, responsibility and respect' (accessed at <www.guardian.co.uk/education/2007/apr/10/schools.uk5> (accessed 1 May 2010).

Bibliography

Adorno, Theodor W. and Horkheimer, Max, *Dialectic of Enlightenment* [1944], trans. John Cumming, London and New York: Verso, 1979.

Al-Ghazali, *The Incoherence of the Philosophers* [1091–5], trans. Michael E. Marmara, Provo, UT: Brigham Young University Publishing, 1997.

Allcorn, Seth, 'Psychoanalytically informed executive coaching', in Dianne R. Stober and Anthony M. Grant, eds, *Evidence Based Coaching Handbook: Putting Best Practices to Work for Your Clients*, Hoboken, NJ: John Wiley, 2006, pp. 129–49.

Aristotle, *De Anima (On the Soul)*, trans. Hugh-Lawson Tancred, London: Penguin, 2004.

Askeland, Maj Karin, 'A reflexive inquiry into the ideologies and theoretical assumptions of coaching', *Coaching: An International Journal of Theory, Research and Practice*, 2:1 (2009), pp. 65–75.

Auerbach, Jeffrey E., 'Cognitive coaching', in Dianne R. Stober and Anthony M. Grant, eds, *Evidence Based Coaching Handbook: Putting Best Practices to Work for Your Clients*, Hoboken, NJ: John Wiley, 2006, pp. 103–28.

Augar, Philip, *Chasing Alpha: How Reckless Growth and Unchecked Ambition Ruined the City's Golden Decade*, London: Bodley Head, 2009.

Bachkirova, Tatiana, 'Role of coaching psychology in defining boundaries between counseling and coaching', in Stephen Palmer and Alison Whybrow, eds, *Handbook of Coaching Psychology: A Guide for Practitioners*, Hove: Routledge, 2007, pp. 351–66.

——— 'The cognitive-developmental approach to coaching', in Elaine Cox, Tatiana Bachkirova, and David Clutterbuck, eds, *The Complete Handbook of Coaching*, London: SAGE, 2010, pp. 132–45.

——— and Elaine Cox, 'A cognitive-developmental approach to coaching', in Stephen Palmer and Alison Whybrow, eds, *Handbook of Coaching Psychology: A Guide for Practitioners*, Hove: Routledge, 2007, pp. 325–50.

——— and Kauffman, Carol, 'Editorial', *Coaching: An International Journal of Theory, Research and Practice*, 2:2 (2009), pp. 96–105.

Back, Les, *The Art of Listening*, Oxford and New York: Berg, 2007.

Baker, Kent H. and Nofsinger, John R., 'Psychological biases of investors', *Financial Review Services*, 11 (2002), pp. 97–116.

Barrow, John D., *Impossibility: The Limits of Science and the Science of Limits*, London: Vintage, 1999.

Barthes, Roland, *Image Music, Text*, ed. and trans. Stephen Heath, London: Fontana, 1977.

BBC News, 'Q & A: Do bankers really need the bonuses?', 26 February 2010, <http://news.bbc.co.uk/1/hi/business/8540020.stm> (accessed 5 May 2010).

——— 'Foreign students not "cash cows", says British Council', 26 March 2010, <http://news.bbc.co.uk/1/hi/education/8584819.stm> (accessed 5 May 2010).

Beauvoir, Simone de, *The Second Sex* [1949], trans. and ed. H. M. Pashley, Harmondsworth: Penguin, 1972.

Berger, Jennifer Garvey, 'Adult development theory and executive coaching practice', in Dianne R. Stober and Anthony M. Grant, eds, *Evidence Based Coaching Handbook: Putting Best Practices to Work for Your Clients*, Hoboken, NJ: John Wiley, 2006, pp. 77–102.

Berger, Peter L. and Luckmann, Thomas, *The Social Construction of Reality: A Treatise in the Sociology of Knowledge*, London: Penguin, 1991.

Bluckert, Peter, 'Critical factors in executive coaching – the coaching relationship', *Industrial and Commercial Training*, 37:7 (2005), pp. 336–40.

Bohm, David and Nichol, Lee, eds, *On Dialogue*, London: Routledge, 1996.

Boje, David, *Storytelling Organisations*, London: SAGE, 2008.

Bratton, John, Sawchuk, Peter, Forshaw, Carolyn, Callinan, Militza, and Corbett, Martin, *Work and Organizational Behaviour*, 2nd edition, London: Palgrave Macmillan, 2010.

Brockbank, Anne, 'Is the coaching fit for purpose?: a typology of coaching and learning approaches', *Coaching: An International Journal of Theory, Research and Practice*, 1:2 (2008), pp. 132–44.

——— and McGill, Ian, *Facilitating Reflective Learning in Higher Education*, Buckingham: SAGE and Open University Press, 2006.

Bronk, Richard, *The Romantic Economist: Imagination in Economics*, Cambridge: Cambridge University Press, 2009.

Brummer, Alex, *The Crunch: The Scandal of Northern Rock and the Escalating Credit Crisis*, London: Random House Business Books, 2008.

Brunning, Halina, ed., *Executive Coaching: Systems-Psychodynamic Perspective*, London: H. Karnac, 2006.

Bryce, Robert, *Pipe Dreams: Ego, Greed, and the Death of Enron*, New York: PublicAffairs, 2002.

Burr, Vivien, *An Introduction to Social Constructionism*, London: Routledge, 1995.

Burrell, Gibson and Morgan, Gareth, *Sociological Paradigms and Organizational Analysis*, London: Ashgate, 1979.

Cable, Vince, *The Storm: The World Economic Crisis and What It Means*, London: Atlantic, 2009.

Carlberg, Gunnar, 'Laughter opens the door: turning points in child psychotherapy', *Journal of Child Psychotherapy*, 23:3 (1997), pp. 331–49.

Carmeli, Abraham, 'Social capital, psychological safety and learning behaviours from failure in organisations', *Long Range Planning*, 40 (2007), pp. 30–44.

Cavanagh, Michael, 'Coaching from a systemic perspective: a complex adaptive conversation', in Dianne R. Stober and Anthony M. Grant, eds, *Evidence Based Coaching Handbook: Putting Best Practices to Work for Your Clients*, Hoboken, NJ: John Wiley, 2006, pp. 313–54.

Chapman, Tony, Best, Bill, and Van Casteren, Paul, *Executive Coaching: Exploding the Myths*, Basingstoke: Palgrave Macmillan, 2003.

Chartered Institute of Personnel Development, 'Coaching at the BBC', <http://www.cipd.co.uk/helpingpeoplelearn/_bbcchg.htm> (accessed 5 May 2010).

——— <http://www.cipd.co.uk/helpingpeoplelearn/_cchng.htm> (accessed 5 May 2010).

Clutterbuck, David, 'Coaching reflection: the liberated coach', *Coaching: An International Journal of Theory, Research and Practice*, 3:1 (2010), pp. 73–81.

——— and Lane, Gill, *The Situational Mentor: An International Review of Competences and Capabilities in Mentoring*, Aldershot: Gower, 2004.

——— and Megginson, David, *Making Coaching Work: Creating a Coaching Culture*, London: Chartered Institute of Personnel and Development, 2005.

Coates, John M. and Herbert, Joseph, 'Endogenous steroids and financial risk taking on a London trading floor', *Proceedings of the National Academy of Sciences*, 105 (2008), pp. 6167–72.

Cohan, William, *House of Cards: How Wall Street's Gamblers Broke Capitalism*, London: Allen Lane, 2009.

Cope, Mick, *The Seven Cs of Coaching: The Definitive Guide to Collaborative Coaching*, Harlow: Pearson Education, 2004.

Coveney, Peter and Highfield, Roger, *Frontiers of Complexity: The Search for Order in a Chaotic World*, London: Faber and Faber, 1995.

Coward, Rosalind, *Sacred Cows: Is Feminism Relevant to the New Millennium?*, London: HarperCollins, 1999.

Cox, Elaine, 'An adult learning approach to coaching', in Dianne R. Stober and Anthony M. Grant, eds, *Evidence Based Coaching Handbook: Putting Best Practices to Work for Your Clients*, Hoboken, NJ: John Wiley, 2006, pp. 193–218.

——— Bachkirova, Tatiana, and Clutterbuck, David, eds, *The Complete Handbook of Coaching*, London: SAGE, 2010.

Csikszentmihalyi, Mihaly, *Flow*, London: Rider, 2002.

Day, Christopher and Leitch, Ruth, 'Teachers' and teacher educators' lives: the role of emotion', *Teacher and Teaching Education*, 17 (2001), pp. 403–15.

Day, David, 'Leadership development: a review in context', *The Leadership Quarterly*, 11:4 (2000), pp. 581–613.

De Haan, Erik and Burger, Yvonne, *Coaching with Colleagues: An Action Guide for One-to-One Learning*, Basingstoke: Palgrave Macmillan, 2005.

De Vries, Manfred F. R. Kets, 'Leaders who self-destruct: the causes and cures', *Organizational Dynamics*, 17 (1989), pp. 5–17.

——— Korotov, Konstantin, and Florent-Treacy, Elizabeth, *Coach and Couch: The Psychology of Making Better Leaders*, Basingstoke: Palgrave Macmillan, 2007.

Deering, Anne and Murphy, Anne, *The Difference Engine: Achieving Powerful and Sustainable Partnering*, Aldershot: Gower, 1998.

Deleuze, Gilles and Felix Guattari, *Anti-Oedipus: Capitalism and Schizophrenia* [1972], trans. Robert Hurley, Mark Seem, and Helen R. Lane, London: Athlone Press, 1983.

——— *A Thousand Plateaus: Capitalism and Schizophrenia* [1980], trans. Brian Massumi, London: Athlone Press, 1988.

Derrida, Jacques, *Of Grammatology* [1967], trans. Gayatri Chakravorty Spivak, Baltimore, MD and London: Johns Hopkins University Press, 1974.

——— *Margins of Philosophy* [1972], trans. Alan Bass, Chicago, IL and Hemel Hempstead: Harvester Wheatsheaf, 1982.

Descartes, René, *Meditations on First Philosophy*, in *Philosophical Writings*, trans. and ed. Elizabeth Anscombe and Peter Thomas Geach, London: Thomas Nelson, 1970.

Dobson, Keith S., ed., *Handbook of Cognitive-Behavioural Therapies*, 2nd edition. New York: Guildford Press, 2001.

——— and Dozois, David J., 'Historical and philosophical bases of the cognitive-behavioural therapies', in Keith S. Dobson, ed., *Handbook of Cognitive-Behavioural Therapies*, 2nd edition, New York: Guildford Press, 2001, pp. 3–39.

Downey, Miles, *Effective Coaching: Lessons from the Coach's Coach*, 2nd edition, New York: Texere, 2003.

Du Toit, Angélique, *Corporate Strategy: A Feminist Perspective*, London and New York: Routledge, 2006.

——— 'Making sense through coaching', *The Journal of Management Development*, 26:3 (2007), pp. 282–91.

Ehrenreich, Barbara, *Smile or Die: How Positive Thinking Fooled America and the World*, London: Granta, 2010.

Elliott, Larry and Atkinson, Dan, *The Gods that Failed: How Blind Faith in Markets Has Cost Us Our Future*, London: Bodley Head, 2009.

Engels, Frederick, *Ludwig Feuerbach and the End of Classical German Philosophy*, Peking: Foreign Languages Press, 1976.

Ferrary, Michael, 'Global financial crisis: are women the antidote?', CERAM Business School, October 2008.

Fillery-Travis, Annette and Lane, David, 'Research: does coaching work?', in Stephen Palmer and Alison Whybrow, eds, *Handbook of Coaching Psychology: A Guide for Practitioners*, Hove: Routledge, 2007, pp. 57–70.

Fink, Bruce, *A Clinical Introduction to Lacanian Psychoanalysis: Theory and Technique*, Cambridge, MA: Harvard University Press, 1997.

Foucault, Michel, *Madness and Civilization: A History of Insanity in the Age of Reason* [1964], trans. Richard Howard, London: Tavistock, 1971.

——— *The Birth of the Clinic: An Archaeology of Medical Perception* [1963], trans. A. M. Sheridan-Smith, New York, Vintage, 1973.

——— *Discipline and Punish: The Birth of the Prison* [1975], trans. Alan Sheridan, New York: Pantheon, 1977.

——— *Power/Knowledge: Selected Interviews and Other Writings 1972–1977*, ed. Colin Gordon, Brighton: Harvester, 1980.

——— *The History of Sexuality*, I–III: *The History of Sexuality: An Introduction* [1976], trans. Robert Hurley, Harmondsworth: Penguin, 1979; *The Use of Pleasure* [1984], trans. Robert Hurley, London: Penguin, 1987; *The Care of the Self* [1984], trans. Robert Hurley, London: Penguin, 1988.

Furchtgott-Roth, Diana, 'No quotas for women on corporate boards', <http://blogs.reuters.com/great-debate/2009/08/21/no-quotas-for-women-on-corporate-boards/> (accessed 5 May 2010).

Gallwey, Timothy, *The Inner Game of Tennis: The Classic Guide to the Mental Side of Peak Performance*, New York: Random House, 1974.

Garvey, Bob, Stokes, Paul, and Megginson, David, *Coaching and Mentoring: Theory and Practice*, London: SAGE, 2009.

Gergen, Kenneth J., 'The social constructionist movement in modern psychology', *American Psychologist*, 40:3 (1985), pp. 266–75.

——— *The Saturated Self: Dilemmas of Identity in Contemporary Life*, New York: Basic Books, 1991.

——— *Toward Transformation in Social Knowledge*, 2nd edition, London: SAGE, 1994.

——— *Realities and Relationships: Soundings in Social Construction*, Cambridge, MA: Harvard University Press, 1997.

——— *An Invitation to Social Construction*, London: SAGE, 1999.

——— *Social Construction in Context*, London: SAGE, 2001.

——— and Gergen, Mary. M., 'Social construction and research as action', in Peter Reason and Hilary Bradbury, eds, *The SAGE Handbook of Action Research: Participative Inquiry and Practice*, 2nd edition, London: SAGE, 2008, pp. 159–71.

Gershon, Sir Peter, 'Releasing resources to the front line: Independent Review of Public Sector Efficiency', July 2004, <www.hm-treasury.gov.uk> (accessed 1 May 2010).

Gibb, Stephen, *Human Resource Development: Process, Practices and Perspectives*, 2nd edition, Basingstoke: Palgrave Macmillan, 2008.

——— and Hill, Peter, 'From trail-blazing individualism to a social construction community: modeling knowledge construction in coaching', *The International Journal of Mentoring & Coaching*, IV:2 (2006), pp. 58–77.

Giglio, Leo and Urban, Julie, M., 'Coaching a leader: leveraging change at the top', *Journal of Management Development*, 17:2 (1998), pp. 93–105.

Goleman, Daniel, *Vital Lies, Simple Truths: The Psychology of Self-Deception*, London: Bloomsbury, 1997.

——— 'Developing a completely transparent and emotionally supportive system', *In View, the Journal from the NHS Institute*, 23 (2010), pp. 4–9.

Grant, Anthony M., 'Past, present and future: the evolution of professional coaching and coaching psychology', in Stephen Palmer and Alison Whybrow, eds, *Handbook of Coaching Psychology: A Guide for Practitioners*, Hove: Routledge, 2007, pp. 23–39.

——— and Palmer, Stephen, 'Coaching psychology workshop', Annual Conference of the Division of Counselling Psychology, British Psychological Society, Torquay, UK, 18 May 2002.

Gray, David E., 'Executive coaching: towards a dynamic alliance of psychotherapy and transformational learning processes', *Management Learning*, 37:4 (2006), pp. 475–97.

Hart, Vicki, Blattner, John, and Leipsic, Staci, 'Coaching versus therapy', *Consulting Psychology Journal: Practice and Research*, 53:4 (2001), pp. 229–37.

Hartmann, Heidi, 'The unhappy marriage of marxism and feminism: towards a more progressive union', in Lydia Sargent, ed., *The Unhappy Marriage of Marxism and Feminism: A Debate on Class and Patriarchy*, London: Pluto Press, 1981, pp. 1–42.

Hassink, Harold, de Vries, Meinderd, and Bollen, Laury, 'A content analysis of whistleblowing policies of leading European companies', *Journal of Business Ethics*, 75 (2007), pp. 25–44.

Hegel, Georg Wilhelm Friedrich, *The Phenomenology of Spirit* [1807], trans. A. V. Miller, Oxford: Oxford University Press, 1977.

d'Holbach, Baron, *Christianity Unveiled: Being an Examination of the Principles and Effects of the Christian Religion* [1761], trans. William Martin Johnson in *The Deist, or Moral Philosopher*, vol. II, London: R. Carlile, 1819.

——— *The System of Nature*, I [1770], trans. H. D. Robinson and Alastair Jackson, Manchester: Clinamen Press, 1999.

Hopper, Kenneth and William, *The Puritan Gift: Reclaiming the American Dream Amidst Global Financial Chaos*, New York: I. B. Tauris, 2009.

House of Commons Treasury Committee Report, 'Women in the city', 3 April 2010, <www.parliament.uk> (accessed 5 May 2010).

Hume, David, *A Treatise of Human Nature* [1739], ed. D. G. C. Macnabb, Glasgow: Fontana/Collins, 1962.

——— *Enquiries Concerning Human Understanding and Concerning the Principles of Morals* [1748, 1751], 3rd edition, ed. L. A. Selby-Bigge, revised P. H. Nidditch, Oxford: Clarendon Press, 1975.

——— *Dialogues and Natural History of Religion* [1779, 1757], ed. J. C. A. Gaskin, Oxford: Oxford University Press, 1993.

Illeris, Knud, 'A model for learning in working life', *The Journal of Workplace Learning*, 16:8 (2004), pp. 431–41.

Irigaray, Luce, *This Sex Which Is Not One* [1977], trans. Catherine Porter, with Carolyn Burke, Ithaca, NY: Cornell University Press, 1985.

Janis, Irving, L., *Victims of Groupthink*, Boston, MA: Houghton Mifflin, 1972.

——— *Groupthink: Psychological Studies of Policy Decisions and Fiascoes*, 2nd edition, Boston, MA: Houghton Mifflin, 1982.

Jencks, Charles, *The Language of Post-Modern Architecture*, 6th edition, London: Academy Editions, 1991.

Johnson, Alan, 'We must develop a new three Rs: rules, responsibility and respect', <www.guardian.co.uk/education/2007/apr/10/schools.uk5> (accessed 1 May 2010).

Jones, Graham and Spooner, Kirsty, 'Coaching high achievers', *Consulting Psychology Journal: Practice and Research*, 58:1 (2006), pp. 40–50.

Joseph, Stephen and Bryant-Jefferies, Richard, 'Person-centred coaching psychology', in Stephen Palmer and Alison Whybrow, eds, *Handbook of Coaching Psychology: A Guide for Practitioners*, Hove: Routledge, 2007, pp. 211–28.

Joy-Matthews, Jennifer, Megginson, David, and Surtees, Mark, *Human Resource Development*, 3rd edition, London: Kogan Page, 2004.

Jung, Carl G., *Symbols of Transformation*, vol. 6 of *The Collected Works*, eds Gerhard Adler, Michael Fordham, and Sir Herbert Read, trans. R. F. C. Hull, London: Routledge and Kegan Paul, 1956.

Kampa-Kokesch, Sheila and Anderson, Mary, Z., 'Executive coaching: a comprehensive review of the literature', *Consulting Psychology Journal: Practice and Research*, 53:4 (2001), pp. 205–28.

Kant, Immanuel, *Critique of Pure Reason* [1781], trans. Norman Kemp Smith, 2nd edition, London and Basingstoke: Palgrave Macmillan, 1933.

——— *Critique of Judgment* [1790], trans. James Creed Meredith, Oxford: Clarendon Press, 1952.

Kaplan, Steven, Pany, Kurt, Samuels, Janet, and Zhang, Jian, 'An examination of the association between gender and reporting intentions for fraudulent financial reporting', *Journal of Business Ethics*, 87 (2009), pp. 15–30.

Kaufman, Carol, 'Positive psychology: the science at the heart of coaching', in Dianne R. Stober and Anthony M. Grant, eds, *Evidence Based Coaching Handbook: Putting Best Practices to Work for Your Clients*, Hoboken, NJ: John Wiley, 2006, pp. 219–54.

——— 'The evolution of coaching: an interview with Sir John Whitmore', *Coaching: An International Journal of Theory, Research and Practice*, 1:1 (2008), pp. 11–15.

Kemp, Travis J., 'Searching for the elusive model of coaching: could the "holy grail" be right in front of us?', *International Psychology Review*, 3:3 (2008), pp. 219–26.

Kindleberger, Charles B., *Manias, Panics, and Crashes: A History of Financial Crises*, London and Basingstoke: Palgrave Macmillan, 1978.

Kitson, Robert, 'Johnson drops Armitage and waits on Borthwick before French test', *The Guardian*, Sports section, 17 March 2010, p. 9.

Knowles, Malcolm S., *The Modern Practice of Adult Education: From Pedagogy to Andragogy*, Englewood Cliffs, NJ: Prentice Hall, 1980.

Krugman, Paul, *The Return of Depression Economics*, New York: W. W. Norton, 1999.

——— *The Return of Depression Economics and the Crisis of 2008*, London: Penguin, 2008.

Kuhn, Thomas, *The Structure of Scientific Revolutions*, 2nd edition, Chicago, IL and London: University of Chicago Press, 1970.

Laclau, Ernesto and Chantal Mouffe, *Hegemony and Socialist Strategy: Towards a Radical Democratic Politics*, London: Verso, 1985.

Lawson, Neal, *All Consuming: How Shopping Got Us Into this Mess and How We Can Find a Way Out*, London: Penguin, 2009.

Lee, Graham, 'The psychodynamic approach to coaching', in Elaine Cox, Tatiana Bachkirova, and David Clutterbuck, eds, *The Complete Handbook to Coaching*, London: SAGE, 2010, pp. 23–36.

Lenhardt, Vincent, *Coaching for Meaning*, Basingstoke: Palgrave Macmillan, 2004.

Leonard-Cross, Elouise, 'Developmental coaching: business benefit – fact or fad? An evaluative study to explore the impact of coaching in the workplace', *International Coaching Psychology Review*, 5:1 (2010), pp. 36–47.

Lewis, Alan, ed., *The Cambridge Handbook of Psychology and Economic Behaviour*, Cambridge: Cambridge University Press, 2008.

Lindblom, Lars, 'Dissolving the moral dilemma of whistleblowing', *Journal of Business Ethics*, 76 (2007), pp. 413–26.

Linley, P. Alex and Harrington, Susan, 'Integrating positive psychology and coaching psychology: shared assumptions and aspirations?', in Stephen Palmer and Alison Whybrow, eds, *Handbook of Coaching Psychology: A Guide for Practitioners*, Hove: Routledge, 2007, pp. 40–56.

Lo, Andrew W., Repin, Dmitry V., and Steenbarger, Brett N., 'Fear and greed in financial markets: a clinical study of day-traders', *Cognitive Neuroscientific Foundations of Economic Behaviour*, 95:2 (2005), pp. 352–59.

Lukács, Georg, *History and Class Consciousness: Studies in Marxist Dialectics* [1923], trans. Rodney Livingstone, London: Merlin Press, 1971.

Lyotard, Jean-François, *The Postmodern Condition: A Report on Knowledge* [1979], trans. Geoff Bennington and Brian Massumi, Manchester: Manchester University Press, 1984.

——— *The Differend: Phrases in Dispute* [1983], trans. Georges Van Den Abbeele, Manchester: Manchester University Press, 1988.

——— *Political Writings*, trans. Bill Readings and Kevin Paul Geiman, London: UCL Press, 1993.

——— *Lessons on the Analytic of the Sublime* [1991], trans. Elizabeth Rottenberg, Stanford, CA: Stanford University Press, 1994.

——— and Jean-Loup Thébaud, *Just Gaming* [1979], trans. Wlad Godzich, Manchester: Manchester University Press, 1985.

McVeigh, Tracy, 'The party's over for Iceland, the island that tried to buy the world', *The Observer*, 5 October 2008, <http://www.guardian.co.uk/world/2008/oct/05/iceland.creditcrunch> (accessed 1 August 2009).

Marcuse, Herbert, *One-Dimensional Man: Studies in the Ideology of an Advanced Capitalist Society*, London: Routledge and Kegan Paul, 1964.

Marx, Karl, *Theses on Feuerbach*, XI, in Frederick Engels, *Ludwig Feuerbach and the End of Classical German Philosophy*, Peking: Foreign Languages Press, 1976, pp. 61–5.

——— *The Communist Manifesto* [1848], ed. Frederic L. Bender, New York and London: W. W. Norton, 1988.

Maslow, Abraham, *Motivation and Personality*, 2nd edition, New York: Harper and Row, 1970.

Mason, Paul, *Meltdown: The End of the Age of Greed*, London and New York: Verso, 2009.

Matthewman, Lisa, Rose, Amanda, and Hetherington, Angela, *Work Psychology*, Oxford: Oxford University Press, 2009.

Mesmer-Magnus, Jesica, R. and Viswesvaran, Chockalingam, 'Whistleblowing in organisations: an examination of correlates of whistleblowing intentions, actions and retaliations', *Journal of Business Ethics*, 62 (2005), pp. 277–97.

Mezirow, Jack, 'A critical theory of adult learning and education', *Adult Education Quarterly*, 32 (1981), pp. 3–24.

——— *Transformative Dimensions of Adult Learning*, San Francisco, CA: Jossey-Bass, 1991.

Michenaud, Sébastien and Solnik, Bruno, 'Applying regret theory to investment choices: currency hedging decisions', *Journal of International Money and Finance*, 27:5 (2008), pp. 677–94.

Naish, John, *Enough: Breaking Free from the World of Excess*, London: Hodder and Stoughton, 2009.

Neale, Stephen, Spencer-Arnell, Lisa, and Wilson, Liz, *Emotional Intelligence Coaching: Improving Performance for Leaders, Coaches and the Individual*, London: Kogan Page, 2009.

Nietzsche, Friedrich, *The Will to Power* [1901], trans. Walter Kaufman and R. J. Hollingdale, London: Weidenfeld and Nicolson, 1968.

Ogbor, John O., 'Critical theory and the hegemony of corporate culture', *Journal of Organizational Change*, 14:6 (2001), pp. 590–608.

O'Neill, Mary B., *Executive Coaching with Backbone and Heart: A Systems Approach to Engaging Leaders with their Challenges*, San Francisco, CA: Jossey-Bass, 2000.

O'Shaughnessy, Steve, 'Executive coaching: the route to business stardom', *Industrial and Commercial Training*, 33:6 (2001), pp. 194–7.

Palmer, Stephen and Szymanska, Kasia, 'Cognitive behavioural coaching: an integrative approach', in Stephen Palmer and Alison Whybrow, eds, *Handbook of Coaching Psychology: A Guide for Practitioners*, Hove: Routledge, 2007, pp. 86–117.

——— and McDowall, Almuth, eds, *The Coaching Relationship: Putting People First*, London: Routledge, 2009.

——— and Whybrow, Alison, eds, *Handbook of Coaching Psychology: A Guide for Practitioners*, Hove: Routledge, 2007.

Passmore, Jonathan, 'Behavioural coaching', in Stephen Palmer and Alison Whybrow, eds, *Handbook of Coaching Psychology: A Guide for Practitioners*, Hove: Routledge, 2007, pp. 73–85.

——— 'Coaching ethics: making ethical decisions – novices and experts', *The Coaching Psychologist*, 5:1 (2009), pp. 6–10.

Peake, Mervyn, *Titus Groan* [1946], Harmondsworth: Penguin, 1968.

Peltier, Bruce, *The Psychology of Executive Coaching: Theory and Application*, 2nd edition, London: Routledge, 2010.

Peterson, David. B., 'People are complex and the world is messy: a behavior-based approach to executive coaching', in Dianne R. Stober and Anthony M. Grant, eds, *Evidence Based Coaching Handbook: Putting Best Practices to Work for Your Clients*, Hoboken, NJ: John Wiley, 2006, pp. 51–76.

Pixley, Jocelyn, 'Finance organizations, decisions and emotions', *British Journal of Sociology*, 53:1 (2002), pp. 41–65.

Popkin, Richard H., *The History of Scepticism from Erasmus to Spinoza*, Berkeley, CA, Los Angeles, CA and London: University of California Press, 1979.

Price, John, 'The coaching/therapy boundary in organizational coaching', *Coaching: An International Journal of Theory, Research and Practice*, 2:1 (2009), pp. 65–75.

Quick, James. C. and Macik-Frey, Marilyn, 'Behind the mask: coaching through deep interpersonal communication', *Consulting Psychology Journal: Practice and Research*, 56:2 (2004), pp. 67–74.

Reason, Peter and Bradbury, Hilary, eds, *The SAGE Handbook of Action Research: Participative Inquiry and Practice*, 2nd edition, London: SAGE, 2008.

Richard, James T., 'Ideas on fostering creative problem solving in executive coaching', *Consulting Psychology Journal: Practice and Research*, 55:4 (2003), pp. 249–56.

Roberts, Vega Zagier and Jarrett, Michael, 'What is the difference and what makes the difference? A comparative study of psychodynamic and non-psychodynamic approaches to executive coaching', in Halina Brunning, ed., *Executive Coaching: Systems-Psychodynamic Perspective*, London: H. Karnac, 2006, pp. 3–40.

Rogers, Carl R., *On Becoming a Person*, London: Constable, 1967.

——— *A Way of Being*, New York: Mariner Books, 1980.

Rothschild, Joyce, 'Freedom of speech denied, dignity assaulted: what the whistleblowers experience in the US', *Current Sociology*, 56:6 (2008), pp. 884–903.

Rowan, John, 'The transpersonal approach to coaching', in Elaine Cox, Tatiana Bachkirova and David Clutterbuck eds, *The Complete Handbook of Coaching*, London: SAGE, 2010, pp. 146–57.

Rushkoff, Douglas, *Life Inc.: How the World Became a Corporation and How to Take It Back*, London: Bodley Head, 2009.

Said, Edward, *Orientalism: Western Conceptions of the Orient*, 2nd edition, Harmondsworth: Penguin, 1995.

Sargent, Lydia, ed., *The Unhappy Marriage of Marxism and Feminism: A Debate on Class and Patriarchy*, London: Pluto Press, 1981.

Saussure, Ferdinand de, *Course in General Linguistics*, ed. Charles Bally, Albert Sechehaye, and Albert Reidlinger, trans. Wade Baskin, London: Peter Owen, 1960.

Schiano, William and Weiss, Joseph, W., 'Y2K all over again: how groupthink permeates IS and compromises security', *Business Horizons*, 49 (2006), pp. 115–25.

Senge, Peter, *The Fifth Discipline: The Art and Practice of the Learning Organization*, London: Routledge, 1990.

Sextus Empiricus, *Outlines of Scepticism*, trans. Julia Annas and Jonathan Barnes, Cambridge: Cambridge University Press, 1994.

Silsbee, David, *Presence-Based Coaching: Cultivating Self-Generative Leaders Through Mind, Body and Heart*, San Francisco, CA: Jossey-Bass, 2008.

Sim, Stuart, *Contemporary Continental Philosophy: The New Scepticism*, Aldershot and Burlington, VT: Ashgate, 2000.

——— *Fundamentalist World: The New Dark Age of Dogma*, Cambridge: Icon Press, 2004.

——— *The End of Modernity: What the Financial and Environmental Crisis is Really Telling Us*, Edinburgh: Edinburgh University Press, 2010.

Soros, George, *The Crash of 2008 and What It Means: The New Paradigm for Financial Markets*, New York: PublicAffairs, 2009.

Spinelli, Ernesto, 'Coaching and therapy: similarities and divergences', *International Psychology Review*, 3:3 (2008), pp. 219–26.

——— 'Existential coaching', in Elaine Cox, Tatiana Bachkirova and David Clutterbuck, eds, *The Complete Handbook of Coaching*, London: SAGE, 2010, pp. 94–106.

——— and Horner, Caroline, 'An existential approach to coaching psychology', in Stephen Palmer and Alison Whybrow, eds, *Handbook of Coaching Psychology: A Guide for Practitioners*, Hove: Routledge, 2007, pp. 118–132.

Stelter, Reinhard, 'Coaching: a process of personal and social meaning making', *International Coaching Psychology Review*, 2:2 (2007), pp. 191–201.

Stern, Daniel N., *The Present Moment in Psychotherapy and Everyday Life*, New York: W. W. Norton, 2004.

Stewart, Lorna J., O'Riordan, Siobhain, and Palmer, Stephen, 'Before we know how we've done, we need to know what we're doing: operationalising coaching to provide a foundation for coaching evaluation', *The Coaching Psychologist*, 4:3 (2008), pp. 127–33.

Stiglitz, Joseph, *Globalization and its Discontents*, London: Penguin, 2002.

——— *Making Globalization Work*, London: Allen Lane, 2006.

Stober, Dianne. R., 'Coaching from a humanistic perspective', in Dianne R. Stober and Anthony M. Grant, eds, *Evidence Based Coaching Handbook: Putting Best Practices to Work for Your Clients*, Hoboken, NJ: John Wiley, 2006, pp. 17–50.

——— 'Making it stick: coaching as a tool for organizational change', *Coaching: An International Journal of Theory, Research and Practice*, 1:1 (2008), pp. 71–80.

——— and Grant, Anthony M., eds, *Evidence Based Coaching Handbook: Putting Best Practices to Work for Your Clients*, Hoboken, NJ: John Wiley, 2006.

Streng, Frederick J., *Emptiness: A Study in Religious Meaning*, Nashville, NY: Abingdon Press, 1967.

Tavakoli, Janet M., *Credit Derivatives and Synthetic Structures: A Guide to Instruments and Applications*, 2nd edition, New York: John Wiley, 2001.

Tett, Gillian, *Fool's Gold: How Unrestrained Greed Corrupted a Dream, Shattered Global Markets and Unleashed a Catastrophe*, London: Little, Brown, 2009.

Thach, Elizabeth C., 'The impact of executive coaching and 360 feedback on leadership effectiveness', *Leadership & Organization Development Journal*, 23:4 (2002), pp. 205–14.

Tourish, Dennis and Robson, Paul, 'Sensemaking and distortion of critical upward communication in organizations', *Journal of Management Studies*, 43:4 (2006), pp. 711–30.

Tsahuridu, Eva E. and Vandekerckhove, Wim, 'Organisational whistleblowing policies: making employees responsible or liable?', *Journal of Business Ethics*, 82 (2008), pp. 107–18.

Turner, Graham, *The Credit Crunch: Housing Bubbles, Globalisation and Worldwide Economic Crisis*, London: Pluto Press, 2008.

Vandekerckhove, Wim, *Whistleblowing and Organizational Social Responsibility: A Global Assessment*, Aldershot and Burlington, VT: Ashgate, 2006.

Varelius, Jukka, 'Is whistle-blowing compatible with employee loyalty?', *Journal of Business Ethics*, 85 (2009), pp. 263–75.

Wärneryd, Karl-Erik, 'The economic psychology of the stock market', in Alan Lewis, ed., *The Cambridge Handbook of Psychology and Economic Behaviour*, Cambridge: Cambridge University Press, 2008, pp. 39–63.

Wasylyshyn, Karol M., 'Executive coaching: an outcome study', *Consulting Psychology Journal: Practice and Research*, 55:2 (2003), pp. 94–106.

Weick, Karl E., *The Social Psychology of Organizing*, New York: McGraw-Hill, 1979.

Welman, Peter and Bachkirova, Tatiana, 'The issue of power in the coaching relationship', in Stephen Palmer and Almuth McDowall, eds, *The Coaching Relationship: Putting People First*, London: Routledge, 2009, pp. 139–58.

Whiteley, C. H., 'Epistemological strategies', *Mind*, 78 (1969), pp. 25–34.

Whitmore, John, *Coaching for Performance: Growing People, Performance and Purpose*, 2nd edition, London: Nicholas Brealey, 1996.

Whitworth, Laura, Kimsey-House, Henry, and Sandahl, Phil, *Co-Active Coaching: New Skills for Coaching People Toward Success in Work and Life*, Palo Alto, CA: Davies-Black, 1998.

Whybrow, Alison, 'Coaching psychology: coming of age?', *International Psychology Review*, 3:3 (2008), pp. 219–26.

——— and Henderson, Vic, 'Concepts to support the integration and sustainability of coaching initiatives within organisations', in Stephen Palmer and Alison Whybrow, eds, *Handbook of Coaching Psychology: A Guide for Practitioners*, Hove: Routledge, 2007, pp. 407–30.

Wilson, Carol, *Best Practice in Performance Coaching: A Handbook for Leaders, Coaching, HR Professionals and Organizations*, London: Kogan Page, 2007.

Witherspoon, Robert and White, Randall P., 'Executive coaching: what's in it for you?', *Training and Development Journal*, 50 (1996), pp. 14–15.

——— *Four Essential Ways that Coaching Can Help Executives*, Greensboro, NC: CCL Press, 1997.

Wittenberg-Cox, Avivah and Maitland, Alison, *Why Women Mean Business*, Chichester: John Wiley, 2009.

Wolfe, Tom, *The Bonfire of the Vanities*, London: Picador and Jonathan Cape, 1988.

Žižek, Slavoj, *The Sublime Object of Ideology*, London and New York: Verso, 1989.

——— *On Belief*, London and New York: Routledge, 2001.

——— *Enjoy Your Symptom! Jacques Lacan in Hollywood and Out*, 2nd edition, London and New York: Routledge, 2008.

Index

Note: The letter 'n' followed by the locators refer to notes in the text.